fancyapint?

IN LONDON

The comprehensive guide to
drinking in the capital

JOHN BLAKE

Published by John Blake Publishing Ltd,
3 Bramber Court, 2 Bramber Road,
London W14 9PB, England

www.blake.co.uk

First published in hardback in 2006

ISBN-13: 978 1 84454 287 1
ISBN-10: 1 84454 287 4

British Library Cataloguing-in-Publication Data:

A catalogue record for this book is available from the British Library.

Design by www.envydesign.co.uk

Printed in Spain by Bookprint SL

1 3 5 7 9 10 8 6 4 2

Papers used by John Blake Publishing are natural, recyclable products made
from wood grown in sustainable forests. The manufacturing processes conform
to the environmental regulations of the country of origin.

A-Z of London Underground Stations

A few tube stations are very close together so we have combined them in one map. The index below will guide you to the appropriate section. Where necessary, pointers have been placed throughout the book to direct you to the correct map.

Please note the maps are not to scale.

A-Z OF LONDON UNDERGROUND STATIONS

Contents

CONTENTS

Acknowledgements

Fancyapint.com and this book would not be possible without the participation of the people listed below. They have all contributed in one way or another to the success of Fancyapint.com and helped bring our idea to life. We couldn't have done it without their help.

Harriet Brown, Mark Coaten, Stacey Collins, James Cone, Michael Crossland, Bill Dornan, Robert Dunnett, Jade Fothergill, Dee Fancett, Pat Fanning, John Faithfull, Debra Fetzer, Catriona Finlayson, Neil Foston, Valerie Gonet, Ken Grint, Phoebe Harkins, Dominic Heaney, Terry Hermon, Adam Hickford, Chris Hill, Louise Jordan, David Little, Ben Locker, Simon Luker, Gerry Lynch, Jennie Lynch, Laura McAulay, Ross MacFarlane, Doug McCarthy, Jim McKenzie, Andy McNally, Dan Moore, Ciaran Norris, Stephen O'Dea, Arthur Rabatin, Sean Robinson, Ellie Seaward, Fiona Stevens, Steve Watson, Dan Wilson.

We would also like to thank our loyal Fancyapint.com visitors who have, through their use of the site and insightful feedback, helped make it the the success it is today.

Cheers

Gordon Butler and Dean Fetzer

Fancyapint? ... it's about going to the pub

There are many different reasons for going to the pub – great beer, a nice location, good food or lively clientele. It's not about just one thing: it's to do with a combination of many. Fancyapint? and our website, www.fancyapint.com, are about how we feel all the different aspects of the pub experience work together. From this, we think you'll get an honest insight and an impartial guide to having a drink in London.

In this guide, as on the site, you'll find our entirely subjective opinions and observations about the pubs we've been to. If you're like us, you'll love the same pubs, and, if you're not, you won't – but that's life. The only points there shouldn't be any dispute about are the factual items: the pub's name, its location etc. The rest is up for (sometimes heated) debate.

This book is a selection of the best and a few of the worst pubs on our website. We've created this selection to help visitors and people who live in London find somewhere decent for a drink, in just about anywhere in central London and a couple of outlying parts. We may have missed out your favourite – we've missed out some of our own – and, much as we'd like to, there just isn't space in a book to include all our reviews from Fancyapint.com. If you can't find what you want in our book, you can try our text-message service: text 'PINT' to 83248 and the network will look up where you are and send you details of the three nearest pubs to you at a cost of £1. You can also visit mobile.fancyapint.com, if your phone is Internet-capable, and get a text-only version of Fancyapint.com.

We've organised the pubs by tube station, because this is often the easiest way to find your way around London. There are also listings by location and in alphabetical order. We have also created some Top Ten lists that will help if you know what you want but just can't decide where to go.

When it comes down to it, at Fancyapint? we only really care about two things: that you should enjoy our guide and you have a great time down the pub.

Cheers – the Fancyapint? team

About pubs

'As soon as I enter the door of a tavern, I experience an oblivion of care, and a freedom from solicitude; when I am seated, I find the master courteous and the servants obsequious to my call, anxious to know and ready to supply my wants; wine there exhilarates my spirits and prompts me to free conversation, and an interchange of discourse with those whom I must love; I dogmatise and am contradicted; and in this conflict of opinions and sentiments I find delight.'

Dr Samuel Johnson

An almost uniquely British institution, the pub has been at the heart of our communities for centuries. The pub has had a long and often chequered history, but it remains an important part of our society – even in multicultural, multimedia, stay-at-home, jet-off-to-foreign-parts, twenty-first-century Britain. The pub is still the focus of many people's social lives; it is a microcosmic mirror of its community and of the country as a whole. Changes in pub culture reflect changes in larger society – such as the increase in wine consumption, the marked improvement in food standards and the larger numbers of women in pubs. The pub's image is changing but its importance hasn't diminished.

But, even though they've been around for a long time, pubs have not always been in the form they are now. They're the bastard offspring of at least four parents, combining elements of alehouses and taverns with coaching inns and coffee houses as well as beer shops. Over the centuries, as the significance of ale and wine (and other forms of alcohol) has changed in our society, the essence of these forerunners has been distilled and mutated until we have a distinct presence in our neighbourhoods known as the 'public house'. But one thing is clear: pubs have had an important place in society for a long time – read Pepys or Johnson, Dickens or Orwell and you won't have to read much before you find a mention of a tavern or two – they were important both socially and personally.

ABOUT PUBS

Over the years, the pub has developed its own rituals, foibles and etiquette, which to people from other cultures seem quaint and impenetrable – we know, because we get the emails to prove it. We do odd things in pubs: we line up at bars to order drinks, instead of having them brought to us; we don't tip the bar staff when we buy a drink; we buy a round of drinks for eight of our mates and expect eight in return, knowing damn well we can't possibly manage them; and the list goes on. However, there's no logic to it, it's just how things are. To truly get to know pubs, you have to visit them, and that's what this book is about.

At Fancyapint? we're great fans of the pub – all pubs – from sixteenth-century half-timbered alehouses to sleek, plasma-screened bars; if you can get a pint in it and spend some time with good friends, we're in.

We hope you'll understand that this book (and Fancyapint.com) is a celebration of pubs. We want you to enjoy the pub at its best and avoid its worst – we've already experienced that for you. And, if we do seem overly critical, it's only because we care about them – if your best friend can't tell you you're a hopeless case, who can?

About Fancyapint?

Fancyapint? is a collaborative effort. We have a team of more than thirty reviewers – all volunteers, aged 22–50+, female and male, straight and gay, smokers and nonsmokers, from all walks of life. A disparate, and often dissipated, bunch, what they do have in common is a love of pubs.

Every pub listed on the site has been visited by a Fancyapint? reviewer, and the review he or she writes has to answer one simple question: 'What's it like?' The aim is to capture what we feel about a pub in 150 words or so and, while we might mention ales and food, we don't go into these in depth – there are plenty of other guides for that. It's a bit like asking a knowledgeable friend about it: you want a quick answer, not a life story, so that you can make your mind up about where you want to go. And that's why we have our pint rating system too – with a few words, a rating and a picture, you should be able to decide pretty quickly where you're going next for a drink.

Of course, we don't get it right every time: pubs change (sometimes in a single day); sometimes there's an atypical bad or good experience that we base our review on; we sometimes make mistakes – we're only human; or there's simply a difference of opinion. So a word of caution: if you're planning something big at a pub, check the details with the pub first – we'd hate you to turn up and find you're drinking in someone's living room because the pub's been converted into flats.

A little history

Fancyapint? started life as a personal database written in HyperCard on an Apple Mac in the 1980s. Distributed on a tiny local network and on floppy disk, it provided the answer to that vital after-work question: 'Where are we going tonight?' Even at that early stage, all the necessary ingredients, including our 'pint' rating system, were in place; so, when the Web came along in the 1990s, it was an obvious next step.

Fancyapint.com, in its current form, launched in early 1999 and since then it has grown, now listing more than 2,200 London pubs (with plans to cover the rest of the country soon) and getting more than 2,500,000 people visiting in a year.

We've always wanted to do a book of the site. Sure, we have mobile and PDA versions of Fancyapint.com, but even with 3G mobiles you don't always have access to the Web and it can be slow. But a book is portable, its batteries don't go flat and you can still read it when you've dropped it in a pint of beer (try doing that with your PDA!).

So here you have it, the first Fancyapint? book – the first, we hope, of many more to come.

FAQs – the Fancyapint? guide to drinking in London

Here are the answers to questions we frequently get asked by visitors to London.

Drinking age in the United Kingdom

You can buy an alcoholic drink in the UK if you're over the age of 18. A few words of advice: if you look young, you may be asked for identification – your passport should do the trick. Some pubs run identity-card schemes, but if you're a visitor you probably won't have one of these cards.

What may be somewhat confusing to visitors is the fact that some pubs, clubs and bars operate their own minimum age limit, a limit that's above the minimum legal age. This can be 21, 23 or 25 and is entirely down to the discretion of the management. If they refuse to allow you in, don't argue: it won't get you anywhere other than chucked out into the street. There are plenty of other places to go. Admittance to any establishment is at the discretion of the management – if they don't want you in the place, there's no legal obligation for them to let you in.

UNDERAGE DRINKING

It is illegal for anyone under the age of 18 to buy an alcoholic drink or for anyone knowingly to purchase a drink for someone underage. It is also against the law for anyone running licensed premises (or their employees) to sell a drink to someone underage. There is an exception: it is not an offence to buy a drink for a sixteen- or seventeen-year-old in conjunction with a table meal in a restaurant as long as the meal is not in the bar area. Similarly, a sixteen- or seventeen-year-old can purchase a drink in a restaurant with a table meal under these restrictions.

Some pubs allow families in for meals and some don't. Some even have areas where children can play, but they still require parents to supervise their offspring. Children under fourteen years of age are allowed into pubs that hold a children's certificate. They must be accompanied by an adult and are restricted to those areas that have been certified suitable for young children. Pubs holding such a certificate must serve meals and nonalcoholic drinks, normally until 9 p.m.

The Visit Britain website has more information at www.visitbritain.com.

Opening and closing times

Pub opening and closing times are down to the licence that applies to the establishment, although most pubs stick to a pretty standard schedule. See below for late-night drinking.

'Normal' times are as follows for England and Wales. Scotland is slightly different, it has had more liberal opening times for some time and as a consequence there's less of a pattern. We expect the same will happen in England and Wales over time.

	Opening	Closing
Monday to Saturday	11 a.m.	11 p.m.
Sunday	12 noon	10.30 p.m.

Pubs usually call 'last orders' ten minutes before closing time and this is often indicated by ringing a bell. It's merely a warning and you can continue to drink until closing time. When time is called – by ringing the bell again or calling 'Time, please, ladies and gents' – that's it: drink sales are closed; you can't buy booze to take home at this point either. What follows next is 'drinking-up time', when the pub will allow you up to twenty minutes to finish your drink. Some pubs do this more aggressively than others. But, if you find a more relaxed one, they will often let you finish up at your own pace. 'Lock-ins' (drinking beyond the times allowed by the pub's licence) are illegal, even with the new laws, but they do happen in some instances. If you find yourself locked in a pub after last orders and still getting a drink you may count yourself lucky, but be warned: you could get into trouble with the law.

LATE-NIGHT DRINKING

The law changed in 2005 to allow pubs to apply for a licence to serve outside 'normal' hours, theoretically at any time in a 24-hour period. This means pubs can now open at the hours they would like to rather than the rather restrictive 11 a.m. to 11 p.m. they had to previously (except where licence extensions had been permitted). However, not every pub's application has been successful and, even when they are successful, it is often difficult to find out which pubs do have late opening hours. And in any case sometimes pubs will close when the landlord feels like it.

As the pub trade is still getting to grips with the new laws, we are finding that pubs tend to cluster late-night opening at the end of the week, primarily Thursday, Friday and Saturday nights. This often means they're open just a few extra hours, say to 1 or 2 a.m. on those nights, or even just until midnight in a lot of pubs.

There are alternative places to go for a late-night drink, but they are more likely to be clubs and bars than pubs, and there are a few things to consider before trying to get into one:

- Most of these establishments have gentlemen on the door for the express purpose of keeping pissed, aggressive or unwanted punters from entering. If you are too drunk, you won't get in.
- Some places charge an entry fee around closing time. Most clubs charge to get in, for instance, but many will often let you in for free if you arrive earlier.
- Clubs and bars tend to have music, often making it difficult to have a conversation – if that's what you wanted to do. Some are obviously better than others for this sort of thing, but the venues can be variable.

Public transport should also be taken into consideration when you're drinking late, since the tube and normal bus services start closing down around 11.30 to midnight. There may still be the odd tube after midnight (usually from central London outwards), but it's a good idea to check the last-train listings before you leave the station. Night buses, while fairly dependable, can also be crowded (often so packed you can't get on) and full of people in the same state as you! There are plenty of black cabs around, but, if you travel any distance, owing to recent changes in the fare structure, you might need a second mortgage to pay the fare.

The Visit Britain website has more information at www.visitbritain.com.

A few pointers on pub etiquette

Pubs are usually pretty relaxed and informal places, so there are not too many rules, but visitors do sometimes get caught out, so here are a few pointers.

ORDERING DRINKS

Generally, you order your drink from the bar and take it to where your friends are sitting or standing. You often order food from the bar, too, although food will usually be brought to you after you've ordered. Ask the person behind the bar about ordering food. One common exception is when you're sitting down and eating – you may be able to ask the waiter or waitress for more drink while you eat.

When you go to the bar to order a drink and there's a group of you, don't all go together, since there won't be room. One or two of you should go and order the drinks and bring them back.

Don't order drinks one by one, the person behind the bar can usually handle more than one at a time. And an important word of advice: when you order a round of drinks that includes Guinness, order the Guinness first!

If there are lots of other people standing at the bar drinking and not waiting to order a drink, ask someone to let you get to the bar in order to get a drink – don't push in. When you've got your drinks, leave the bar. Don't stay where you are, because it will annoy the people who let you in. If people are queuing to order drinks, wait your turn. A good way to start a fight in a pub is to try to push to the head of a queue two minutes before closing time. If the bar staff have seen you waiting, they'll serve you.

There are a growing number of pubs in London that are offering Continental table service: you don't have to go to the bar because someone comes and takes your order! While not traditional pub behaviour, it is convenient, and we find that the atmosphere in these pubs is often more convivial than in pubs that still make you join a scrum at the bar.

PAYING FOR DRINKS

You usually pay for the drink when you order. If you're using a debit/credit card, then you can probably run a tab. Often there's a minimum order amount of £5 or £10 – not difficult to achieve in London – but you'll often have to leave your card behind the bar for security. Some places add a surcharge to your drinks bill to cover bank charges.

With technology the way it is, some even offer cashback if you use your card! Others have cash machines in the pub, but these usually charge a fee for withdrawing your money! These are both dangerous developments, because they often lead to staying in the pub, headaches, memory loss and empty bank accounts. Be careful.

TIPPING

In pubs, you rarely tip at the bar, even when the bar staff give you your change on a platter – this is a cheap ploy to extract more money from customers, who are usually already paying exorbitant prices for the drink.

However, if you feel someone in the pub has provided exceptional service you can offer to buy him or her a drink. Sometimes, he or she will actually take the drink (and drink it with you), but more often than not will take money equivalent to the price of a drink – usually a half. This is acceptable.

A few pubs provide table service for drinks, especially if they do food, and, where you get this, it's OK to tip for good service (around 10–12.5 per cent).

DRINKING OUT OF DOORS

It's actually illegal to drink on the street in most places, unless an area outside the pub is part of, or owned by, the pub. Local authorities are very sensitive about this, so, if you are asked to stay inside a particular area by the staff or even to move indoors, please do so. If you don't, the pub could possibly lose its licence.

TO SMOKE OR NOT TO SMOKE

With legislation on its way to make all pubs, clubs, bars and restaurants smoke-free zones, the tide has definitely turned against having a pint and a fag. While they are still in the minority, we are finding that more and more pubs have a designated nonsmoking area, and there are some that have instituted total bans, even though the legislation isn't coming into effect until 2007 at the earliest.

Some pubs now publish a smoking policy, which usually states that they use air purifiers to clean up the atmosphere. Many don't allow smoking at the bar, as a measure to protect the health of their staff.

However, most pubs still let you smoke just about anywhere.

Don't worry if this all sounds bewildering. If you're not sure about something, just ask someone who works in the pub. As long as you respect the other people around you, you'll get on fine.

Guide to the pint ratings

Every pub reviewed has a Fancyapint? 'pint' rating. It's intended to show at a glance what we feel about a pub, here's what they mean:

A five pint rated pub is worth a special effort to visit. It will be in a good location, architecturally interesting, offers a good range of well-kept beers and food of a high standard in a pleasant atmosphere. This combination of unique features and high standards makes this something we award very occasionally.

Whilst the four pint rating may be awarded more often than the five, it's still a special pub that merits this. It is usually awarded for having a combination of some – but not all – of the features listed above. A four pint pub is worth a detour.

Three pints are awarded to decent pubs that offer reasonable beer and food, have a pleasant atmosphere and are easy enough to get to. Whilst you might not go too far out of your way to get to one, if you're in the vicinity of a three pint pub, don't miss it.

Two pint pubs may not have any outstanding features but are competent in most of the key areas. They have sometimes let us down in a small way – often not their fault – but nevertheless we feel they could be better. Two pint pubs are usually good, honest boozers often frequented by regulars and, depending on the occasion, usually do the job.

One pint pubs cover the basics, but there are things that let them down. It could for example be: poor beer or selection of beers, poor service or just frequented by a crowd of regulars that resent the presence of outsiders on their patch. We usually end up going to these pubs if we're really thirsty and there's no nearby alternative.

In our opinion, zero pint-rated pubs should be avoided until significant improvements are made.

We like or dislike pubs for all kinds of subjective reasons and we often want different things from pubs at different times. Maybe a quiet pint in cozy surroundings or a full-on games pub with every machine imaginable, or fantastic food, whatever. It should be clear from our reviews why we give a pub a particular rating.

We also know pubs change and ratings can go up or down, so be aware that any rating is based on our experiences to date. If you feel a pub's rating has changed let us know by email to editor@fancyapint.com.

Guide to the feature symbols

GOOD BEER/REAL ALE
This icon signifies that the pub has very good real ales, unusual beers, regular guest ales or Cask Marque status. As Fancyapint? is not a good-beer guide, we don't normally go into a lot of detail.

TV
The pub has at least one TV showing Sky TV, Freeview, Setanta etc. The review will describe this in more detail if it's a major attraction for the pub (e.g. a large projector screen, showing major sporting events).

FUNCTION ROOM
Shows the pub has a function room, part of the pub can be reserved for private parties or the whole pub can be hired (quite often at weekends).

ALFRESCO DRINKING
The pub has space for outdoor drinking. This can be anything from an enclosed beer garden to a couple of tables on the street. We try to distinguish between these pubs, so, if you're looking for somewhere to have a

barbecue, for instance, you should be able to find one. The review usually carries more details. Don't forget that in the UK it's usually illegal to drink in the street and, at the slightest hint of sun, any pubs with outdoor space will get mobbed – so get there early.

POOL TABLE
The pub has at least one pool table (we say if there are more than one). We don't mention the cost, as it's something that can change.

WATERSIDE
The pub is by water, or has waterside views. Usually, in London, it will be by the Thames, but there are also nice pubs by canals, lakes and ponds. Not all pubs with waterside views have outdoor seating (hence the distinction). Check the review for more info.

MUSIC
The pub features music – often live – and, if it's a specific kind of music, then we'll say. We don't list events: you need to call the pub for that information,

although the review usually gives more information if there's something of interest.

PLAY AREA/CHILD POLICY

These pubs either have an area set aside for children – it's not something you get very often in central London, more often it's in the suburbs – or let children into specific areas of the pub at certain times of the day.

QUIZ NIGHT

The pub hosts a quiz night or nights – if it's a regular weekly occurrence, we usually say. Some pubs hold quizzes less frequently, sometimes monthly. Pubs can host quizzes for fun and some offer prizes such as drink or cash. You may have to pay to enter some quizzes – phone the pub to check.

RESTAURANT

Most pubs do some kind of food, so we don't mention that fact here. This is to indicate pubs that have separate restaurants or eating areas, distinct from the drinking areas. We indicate any speciality food the pub offers here, e.g. Thai, French, Czech.

ACCOMMODATION

A few pubs in London have rooms. You should call the pub for prices, more information and availability.

THEATRE/COMEDY

A few pubs have theatres attached; others have comedy evenings and cabaret in function rooms, or even in the main bar. Quite often, these pubs are where some very well-known comedians honed their material over the years, so a visit to a comedy night now might well be to see future stars. We don't list pubs near, or next door to, theatres, only pubs that actually host these kinds of event.

TRADITIONAL PUB GAMES

Some pubs still have traditional games available for you to play – e.g. darts, bar billiards, shove ha'penny, skittles, table footy and pinball. Fruit machines and video games (even Space Invaders, Asteroids and Defender) don't count.

DISABLED FACILITIES

Shows pubs with disabled facilities. Where we have more detail – e.g. access ramps – we will say. However, it usually means there's at least disabled access and a disabled toilet on the premises.

GUIDE TO THE FEATURE SYMBOLS

COUNTRY THEME

This indicates that a pub is themed on a country – e.g. Irish, Canadian, Scottish, Dutch. You may find people from these countries congregating here, or it may mean you can consume produce from the country in question here. The appropriate flag for the country will be displayed in the features of the review.

OPEN LATE

Now the licensing laws allow more flexible opening, we will list, where we can, the pubs that are open after 11 p.m. This information can change very quickly, so, if your night out depends on a pub being open (at any time), check first with the pub.

ATM

Signifies pubs with an ATM on the premises. Be warned: there's usually a charge for using these machines – usually about £1.50. Many pubs will give you cashback with a debit card (if you buy more than a minimum amount of drink). We don't list pubs that happen to be near to ATMs.

WIFI

Some of you can't bear to be away from the Net for very long, so we've listed the pubs that offer WiFi access. Some charge for this, others don't – you'll need to check with the bar staff what you have to do to get logged on.

SMOKING POLICY

Some pubs now have a smoking policy – from a complete smoking ban through no-smoking areas to allowing people to smoke anywhere in the pub. Where a pub has a stated policy, we'll publish it.

GAY/GAY-FRIENDLY

These pubs are either gay pubs or welcome gays. We don't go into any kind of detail about what kind of gay pubs they might be or any special events – there are plenty of other places for that kind of information.

DOGS WELCOME

Many pubs don't let our canine friends accompany us for a pint, but there are some that do. These you will find marked with a doggy icon.

Top Ten pubs

To help you, if you're looking for something in particular, we've created a few lists of our favourite ten pubs for a range of topics (with the exception of the Top Ten attractions, where we've listed our closest favourite pub to an attraction). Some lists could easily go on for much longer, but, for the sake of brevity and clarity, we've limited the choices to ten. All the pubs here are listed in alphabetical order.

FANCYAPINT? TOP TEN

Our Top Ten pubs in the book – these you must see.

- Churchill Arms (Notting Hill Gate)
- Colton Arms (Barons Court)
- The Grapes (Westferry)
- Jerusalem Tavern (Farringdon)
- King's Arms (Waterloo)
- Lamb (Holborn)
- Nag's Head (Knightsbridge)
- The Royal Oak (Borough)
- Windsor Castle (Edgware Road)
- Ye Olde White Bear (Hampstead)

TOP TEN THAMES-SIDE PUBS

- Angel (Bermondsey)
- Captain Kidd (Shadwell/Wapping)
- Dove (Ravenscourt Park)
- Founders Arms (Blackfriars)
- The Narrow Street (Limehouse DLR)
- Mayflower (Rotherhithe)
- Old Thameside Inn (London Bridge)
- Prospect of Whitby (Shadwell/Wapping)
- Trafalgar (Cutty Sark DLR)
- White Cross (Richmond)

TOP TEN PUBS FOR ALFRESCO DRINKING

- 1802 (West India Quay DLR)
- The Albion (Highbury & Islington)
- The Banker (Cannon Street)
- Clifton (Kilburn Park)
- Duke of Edinburgh (Brixton)
- The Hope (Balham)
- Prince's Head (Richmond)
- Richard I (Greenwich DLR)
- Torriano (Kentish Town)
- Windsor Castle (Notting Hill Gate)

TOP TEN PUBS FOR FOOD

- The Atlas (West Brompton), modern
- The Camel (Bethnal Green), fabulous pies
- Cock Tavern (Farringdon), meat, loads of it
- Coopers Arms (Sloane Square), modern and unpretentious
- Czechoslovak National House (West Hampstead), Czech
- Newman Arms (Goodge Street), excellent pies
- Old China Hand (Angel), dim sum
- The O'Conor Don (Bond Street), traditional Irish
- The Grapes (Westferry), fine fish
- Princess of Wales (Chalk Farm), Sunday roast

TOP TEN PUBS FOR WATCHING SPORT

- Alexandra (Clapham Common)
- Carpenters Arms (Marble Arch)
- The Cockpit (Blackfriars)
- Elgin (Ladbroke Grove)
- F3K (Barons Court)
- The Gun (Liverpool Street)
- Pakenham Arms (Russell Square)
- One Tun (Goodge Street)
- O'Neill's (Shepherds Bush)
- Rob Roy (Edgware Road) – Scotland matches

TOP TEN PUBS

🍺 TOP TEN INTERESTING PUBS

- Blackfriar (Blackfriars)
- Cittie of York (Holborn)
- The George Inn (Borough)
- Holly Bush (Hampstead)
- Nag's Head (Knightsbridge)
- Princess Louise (Holborn)
- Seven Stars (Chancery Lane)
- The Warrington Hotel (Maida Vale)
- Ye Olde Cheshire Cheese (Fleet Street)
- Ye Olde Mitre Tavern (Holborn)

🍺 TOP TEN PUBS NEAR VISITOR ATTRACTIONS

- Buckingham Palace, The Mall – Buckingham Arms (St James's Park)
- Houses of Parliament, Parliament Sq. – St Stephen's Tavern (Westminster)
- London Eye, South Bank – King's Arms (Southwark)
- London Zoo, Regents Park – Windsor Castle (Marylebone)
- Old Royal Observatory, Greenwich – Plume of Feathers (Cutty Sark) Sir John Soane Museum, Lincolns Inns Fields, Holborn – Seven Stars (Chancery Lane)
- Tate Modern, Bankside – Founders Arms (Blackfriars)
- Tower of London, Tower Hill – Bridge House (Tower Hill)
- Wallace Collection, West End – Golden Eagle (Bond Street)
- Westminster Abbey, Parliament Sq. – Two Chairmen (St James's Park)

TOP TEN PUBS FOR BEER
- Bridge House (Tower Bridge)
- Clachan (Oxford Circus)
- Carpenters Arms (Marble Arch)
- Jerusalem Tavern (Farringdon)
- Market Porter (London Bridge)
- Old Dr Butler's Head (Moorgate)
- Priory Arms (Stockwell)
- Radnor Arms (Kensington Olympia)
- The Royal Oak (Borough)
- Wenlock Arms (Old Street)

TOP TEN JUKEBOXES
- Boogaloo (Highgate)
- Bradley's Spanish Bar (Tottenham Court Road)
- Good Ship (Kilburn)
- Half Moon (Putney Bridge)
- The Legion (Old Street)
- McGlynn's (King's Cross)
- New Rose (Angel)
- Power's Bar (Kilburn)
- The Social (Oxford Circus)
- T-Bird (Arsenal)

TOP TEN PUBS FOR LIVE MUSIC
- Brook Green Hotel (Goldhawk Road), Brook's Blues Bar
- Enterprise (Chalk Farm), another pub with a long history of great bands
- Filthy McNasty's Whiskey Café (Angel), live music, DJs and poetry
- Golden Eagle (Bond Street), singalong around the joanna
- Hope & Anchor (Highbury & Islington), hosted some of the greats
- Old Blue Last (Old Street), grubby and loud – just how we like it
- Palm Tree (Mile End), traditional East End music nights
- Princess of Wales (Chalk Farm), jazz
- Red Lion & Sun (Highgate), singalong, Irish music and jazz
- Spitz (Shoreditch), stuff you don't get to hear in many other places

🍺 TOP TEN PUBS FOR QUIZZES
- Approach Tavern (Bethnal Green)
- Boogaloo (HIghgate), music and film
- Lord Nelson (Island Gardens)
- Old Eagle (Camden Town)
- One Tun (Goodge Street)
- The Pineapple (Kentish Town)
- Snooty Fox (Highbury & Islington)
- Ten Bells (Shoreditch), music
- Town of Ramsgate (Shadwell/Wapping)
- Ye Olde White Bear (Hampstead)

🍺 TOP TEN PUBS FOR GAMES
- Alexandra (Clapham Common), pinball
- Café Kick (Farringdon), table footy
- Coborn Arms (Mile End), darts
- Ferry House (Island Gardens) darts – London Fives
- Glasshouse Stores (Piccadilly Circus), bar billiards
- Harrison (King's Cross), chess
- Lord Clyde (Borough), darts
- Owl & Pussycat (Shoreditch), bar billiards
- Queen's Head (Limehouse DLR), darts – including London Fives
- Radnor Arms (Kensington Olympia), darts

🍺 TOP TEN PUBS FOR POOL
- The Banker (Cannon Street)
- Duchy Arms (Kennington)
- F3K (Barons Court)
- Hope & Anchor (Highbury & Islington)
- The Horseshoe (Farringdon)
- Good Mixer (Camden Town)
- King's Arms (Chancery Lane)
- King Harold (Leyton)
- The Landor (Clapham North)
- Water Poet (Whitechapel)

Fancyapint Award Winners 2005

The nineteenth of October is Fancyapint.com's anniversary – and it's also the day we make our awards for our top London pubs of the year. These awards are to showcase London's best pubs and to thank the people who have worked so hard over the year to provide an enjoyable drinking environment for everyone and, in doing so, making the pub-going experience an outstanding one.

In 2005 we selected thirteen London pubs for special recognition, making awards in two categories: the Reviewers' awards and the Visitors' awards.

The Reviewers' awards are based on the Fancyapint? review team's experiences and, with more than 2,200 pubs reviewed in the guide and thousands of pub visits made in the year, that's a lot of experience.

In addition to our best-London-pub awards, there are three special awards for best newcomer, best renovation and, perhaps the most difficult one to achieve, the most improved.

Our Visitors' awards are based on the pubs Fancyapint.com's users, well over a million of them, visited in 2005 – these pubs are 'the people's choice'.

Reviewers' award – best London pub

The Lamb (overall winner)
Monkey Chews
Robin Hood & Little John
The Market Porter
Windsor Castle

Reviewers' award – best newcomer

Defectors Weld

Reviewers' award – best pub renovation

Pig's Ear

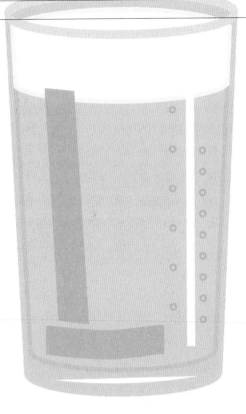

Reviewers' award – most improved pub

Island Queen

Visitors' award – best London pub

Scarsdale Arms (overall winner)

The Ship & Shovell

Queen's Arms

Carpenters Arms

Nag's Head

Pubs listed North, South, East and West

CITY

Anchor Tap
The Apple Tree
Artillery Arms
The Banker
Bar Aquarium
The Bell
Bishops Finger
The Blackfriar
Blue Anchor
Bricklayer's Arms
Brown Bear
The Bull
Bunch of Grapes
Café Kick
Calthorpe Arms
Cantaloupe Bar and
   Restaurant
Cartoonist
City Pride
Clock House
Cock and Woolpack
Cock Tavern
The Cockpit
Commercial Tavern
Counting House
The Crosse Keys
Crown & Sugarloaf
Dickens Inn
Dirty Dick's
Doggett's Coat & Badge
The Dovetail Bar
Duke (of York)

East India Arms
Exmouth Arms
Filthy McNasty's
   Whiskey Café
Fox & Anchor
The Globe
The Globe
The Golden Heart
The Gun
Gunmakers
Hamilton Hall
Hand & Shears
Harlequin
The Hatchet
Hoop & Grapes
The Hope
Horniman at Hays
The Horseshoe
Jamaica Wine House
Jerusalem Tavern
King's Arms
King's Head
Lamb Tavern
The Legion
Liberty Bounds
The Light
The Market Porter
The Minories
New Moon
Old Bank of England
The Old Blue Last
Old China Hand

The Old Doctor
   Butler's Head
Old King's Head
Old Red Lion Theatre
   Club
Old Thameside Inn
Pakenham Arms
Paternoster
Peasant
Queen's Head
Railway Tavern
Red Lion
Rising Sun
T.S.P. (The Samuel
   Pepys)
Sekforde Arms
Shakespeare's
   Head
The Ship
The Ship
Slaughtered Lamb
Spitz
St Brides Tavern
St Paul's Tavern
Still & Star
Sutton Arms
The Swan Tavern
The Telegraph
Ten Bells
Three Kings
Tipperary
Viaduct Tavern

PUBS LISTED NORTH, SOUTH, EAST AND WEST

The Walrus & the
    Carpenter
The Water Poet
The Well

White Hart
White Hart
Williamson's Tavern

Ye Olde Cheshire
    Cheese
Ye Olde Cock Tavern
Ye Olde Mitre Tavern

WEST END

Adam & Eve
Admiral Duncan
Ain't Nothin' But Blues
    Bar
The Albany
The Albert
The Angel
Argyll Arms
Audley
Bar Polski
Barley Mow
Bear & Staff
The Beehive
Bierodrome
Black Lion
Bloomsbury Tavern
Blue Posts
Blue Posts
The Bountiful Cow
Bradley's Spanish Bar
The Brewmaster
The Bridge House
The Britannia
Buckingham Arms
Bunch of Grapes
Cambridge
The Cardinal
Carlisle Arms
Carpenters Arms
Cask & Glass

The Cellars Bar at the
    Landmark
The Champion
The Chandos
Chequers Tavern
Cheshire Cheese
Chester Arms
Churchill Arms
Cittie of Yorke
The Clachan
Coach & Horses
Coach & Horses
Coach & Horses
Coal Hole
Cock & Lion
The Cock Tavern
The Colonies
Colton Arms
The Constitution
The Cove
De Hems
Devereux
Dog & Duck
Dolphin Tavern
Dover Castle
Drayton Arms
Duke of Kendal
Duke of Wellington
The Duke of
    Wellington

Duke of York
Edgar Wallace
Elephant & Castle
The Endurance
The Enterprise
F3K (Famous 3 Kings)
The Feathers
Fox & Hounds
Freemasons Arms
The French House
Friend at Hand
The Gallery
The George
The Glassblower
Glasshouse Stores
The Globe
Goat Tavern
Golden Eagle
Golden Lion
Gordon's Wine Bar
Grafton Arms
Green Man & French
    Horn
Grenadier
Grouse & Claret
Guinea
The Hansom Cab
Harcourt Arms
Harp
The Harrison

PUBS LISTED NORTH, SOUTH, EAST AND WEST

Hereford Arms
Hobgoblin
Hog in the Pound
Hoop & Toy
The Hope
Horse & Groom
Horse & Groom
The Intrepid Fox
Iron Duke
The Jeremy Bentham
John Snow
The Jugged Hare
Kensington Arms
King & Queen
The King's Arms
King's Arms
King's Head
King's Head
King's Head
Knights Templar
The Lamb
Lamb & Flag
Lord John Russell
Lowlander
Maple Leaf
Marquess of Anglesey
Marquis of Granby
Marquis of Granby
The Masons Arms
The Masons Arms
The Mitre
Moon Under Water
Morpeth Arms
Museum Tavern
Nag's Head
Nell Gwynne Tavern

Newman Arms
O'Conor Don
Old Coffee House
Old Crown
Old Nick
Old Red Lion
One Tun
Opera Tavern
Plough
Plumbers Arms
Polar Bear
Pontefract Castle
Porterhouse
Prince Edward
Prince of Wales
    Feathers
Prince Regent
Princess Louise
Punch & Judy
Punch Bowl
Queen's Arms
The Queen's Head
    & Artichoke
Queen's Larder
Red Lion
Red Lion
The Red Lion
The Red Lion
The Red Lion
    (Crown Passage)
The Red Lion
    (Duke of York St)
Retro Bar
Rising Sun
Rob Roy
Royal Exchange
The Royal Oak

Rugby Tavern
Running Footman
Salisbury
Salvador & Amanda
Scarsdale Arms
The Seven Stars
Seven Stars
Shakespeare's Head
The Shaston Arms
Shepherds Tavern
Sherlock Holmes
The Ship
The Ship & Shovell
Ship Tavern
The Social
The Speaker
The Spice of Life
St Stephen's Tavern
Stanhope Arms
Star & Garter
The Star Tavern
The Swan
The Talbot
Tattersall Castle
Tea Clipper
Three Greyhounds
Tom Cribb
The Tottenham
The Toucan
Tudor Rose
Turks Head
Two Chairmen
The Tyburn
Uxbridge Arms
The Victoria
Victoria & Albert

PUBS LISTED NORTH, SOUTH, EAST AND WEST

Volunteer	Wilton Arms	Windsor Castle
Waxy O'Connors	Windsor Castle	Ye Grapes
Wheatsheaf	Windsor Castle	Yorkshire Grey

NORTHEAST

1802	The Essex Arms	New Rose
The Albion	Faltering Fullback	North Pole
Alwyne Castle	The Ferry House	The Oakdale
Approach Tavern	The Florist	The Old Ale Emporium
Bank of Friendship	George & Dragon	The Old Dairy
Birkbeck	George & Vulture	Old Globe
Black Bull	The Grapes	The Old Rose
The Blind Beggar	The Greenwich	The Orwell
Booty's Riverside Bar	Pensioner	The Owl & The
Bow Bells	The Griffin	Pussycat
Builders Arms	Half Moon	Palm Tree
Camden Head	The Hare	Pride of Spitalfields
The Camel	Hemingford Arms	Prince Arthur
Canal 125	Hen & Chickens	Prospect of Whitby
Canonbury Tavern	Henry Addington	Queen's Head
Captain Kidd	Hope & Anchor	Railway Tavern
Charlie Wright's	Hubbub	The Railway Tavern
International Bar	Island Queen	The Resolute
City Pride	Jorene Celeste	The Salisbury Hotel
Clockwork	King Charles I	The Snooty Fox
Coborn Arms	King Edward VII	Swimmer at the
The Compton Arms	King Harold	Grafton Arms
The Crown	Lincoln Lounge	T-Bird
Davy's	Little Driver	Town of Ramsgate
The Dove	Lord Nelson	The Twelve Pins
Dream Bags Jaguar	Marquess Tavern	The Watermans Arms
Shoes	McGlynn's	Wenlock Arms
Driver	The Morgan Arms	William IV
The Eagle	Mucky Pup	Ye Olde Black Bull
Elk in the Woods	The Narrow Street	The York
Embassy Bar	The Narrowboat	

PUBS LISTED NORTH, SOUTH, EAST AND WEST

NORTHWEST

The Adelaide
The Albert
The Archway Tavern
Auntie Annie's Porter
 House
Big Red
The Black Lion
Blackbird
The Boogaloo
Boston Arms
Bull & Gate
Bull & Last
The Castle
The Clifton
The Constitution
The Corrib Rest
The Cow
Czechoslovak National
 House
Dartmouth Arms
The Defectors Weld
Devonshire Arms
The Dublin Castle
Duchess of Kent
Duke of Hamilton
Earl of Lonsdale
Edinboro Castle
El Comandante
The Elgin
The Enterprise
The Flask
The Flask
The Goldhawk

Good Mixer
The Good Ship
Ground Floor Bar
Hand & Flower Hotel
Head of Steam
Holly Bush
Hope & Anchor
The Kilburn
Ladbroke Arms
Lock Tavern
The Lord Nelson
Masons Arms
McLaughlins
The Mitre
Monkey Chews
Mother Red Cap
Nambucca
New Inn
The Newmarket Ale
 House
North London Tavern
The Old Black Lion
Old Eagle
O'Neill's
The Ordnance
Paradise by Way of
 Kensal Green
Pineapple
Portobello Gold
Power's Bar
Prince Albert
Prince Arthur
Prince of Wales

Prince of Wales
Princess of Wales
The Quays
Queen's Arms
Queens No. 1
Quinn's
Radnor Arms
Red Lion & Sun
Roebuck
Salusbury Pub &
 Dining Room
Shepherd & Flock
The Sir Richard Steele
Somers Town Coffee
 House
The Spread Eagle
St John's Tavern
Sun In Splendour
The Torriano
The Victoria
The Warrington Hotel
Warwick Arms
Warwick Castle
The Washington
The Westbourne
The White Horse
The Winchester Hotel
Woodbine
World's End
The Wrestlers
Ye Olde Swiss Cottage
Ye Olde White Bear

PUBS LISTED NORTH, SOUTH, EAST AND WEST

SOUTHEAST

Admiral Hardy
Albert Arms
Ancient Foresters
Angel
Ashburnham Arms
Blacksmith's Arms
The Bridge House
The Coach & Horses
Cutty Sark Tavern
Dog & Bell
Founders Arms
The Gate Clock
George Inn
Goldsmiths Tavern
The Greenwich Union
The Half Moon
Hobgoblin
Hole in the Wall
King's Arms

King's Arms
Lord Clyde
Lord Hood
Marquis of Granby
The Mayflower
Miller of Mansfield
Moby Dick
Pilot Inn
Plume of Feathers
Prince Albert
Prince of Wales
Prince Regent
Queen Victoria
Richard I
The Ring
Rock the Boat
Roebuck
Rose & Crown
The Royal George

The Royal Oak
The Ship
The Ship
The Ship York
Southwark Tavern
Spanish Galleon
Stage Door
Town House
Trafalgar Tavern
The Victoria
Walrus Social
Waterloo Bar and
    Kitchen
The Wellington at
    Waterloo
White Hart
The Yacht

SOUTHWEST

Admiral Codrington
The Alexandra
Andover Arms
Anglesea Arms
The Anglesea Arms
The Atlas
The Bedford
Bell & Crown
Black Lion
Blue Anchor
Bread & Roses
The Britannia
Brook Green Hotel

Builders Arms
The Bull's Head
The Chancellors
Chelsea Potter
The City Barge
The Clarence
Coach & Horses
Coach & Horses Hotel
Coopers Arms
The Cricketers
Cross Keys
Dog House
The Dove

Duchy Arms
The Duke of
    Devonshire
The Duke of
    Edinburgh
Duke of York
The Eagle Ale House
Effra
The Eight Bells
Elm Park Tavern
Fentiman Arms
Finch's
Fox & Pheasant

PUBS LISTED NORTH, SOUTH, EAST AND WEST

Frog & Forget-Me-Not
George IV
The Greyhound
Hanover Arms
Hobgoblin
The Hope
The Ifield
Jolly Gardeners
The Jolly Maltster
Kelly's Bar
The Landor
Latymers
Manor Arms
The Morrison
Nightingale
The Old Fire Station
The Old Pack Horse
Old Red Lion
The Old Ship

Old Ship Inn
Orange Tree
Pickwick's Wine Bar
The Pig's Ear
The Prince
Prince of Wales
Prince of Wales
Prince's Head
Priory Arms
The Queen's Head
Queen's Head
The Railway
The Railway
The Raven
The Red Cow
Rose & Crown
The Salisbury
Salutation
The Ship

The Sporting Page
Star & Garter
The Sun
Sun Inn
The Surprise
The Surprise
Tim Bobbin
Trafalgar
Trinity Arms
Waterman's Arms
White Cross
The White Horse
White Swan
Windmill on the
   Common
Ye Olde Spotted Horse
Zetland Arms

Stations listed North, South, East and West

NORTHWEST

Archway
Belsize Park
Camden Town
Chalk Farm
Euston
Goldhawk Road
Hampstead
Highgate
Holland Park

Kensal Green
Kensington (Olympia)
Kentish Town
Kilburn
Kilburn Park
Ladbroke Grove
Maida Vale
Mornington Crescent
Notting Hill Gate

Queen's Park
St John's Wood
Shepherd's Bush
Swiss Cottage
Tufnell Park
Warwick Avenue
West Hampstead
Westbourne Park

SOUTHEAST

Bermondsey
Borough
Canada Water
Cutty Sark (DLR)
Elephant & Castle
Greenwich (DLR)

Kennington
London Bridge
New Cross
New Cross Gate
North Greenwich
Oval

Rotherhithe
Southwark
Surrey Quays
Waterloo

SOUTHWEST

Balham
Barons Court
Brixton
Chiswick Park
Clapham Common
Clapham North
Clapham South
Earl's Court
Fulham Broadway
Gloucester Road
Gunnersbury
Hammersmith

High Street
Kensington
Hyde Park Corner
Kew Gardens
Knightsbridge
Lambeth North
Parsons Green
Pimlico
Putney Bridge
Ravenscourt Park
Richmond
St James's Park

Sloane Square
South Kensington
Stamford Brook
Stockwell
Turnham Green
Vauxhall
Victoria
West Brompton
West Kensington
Westminster

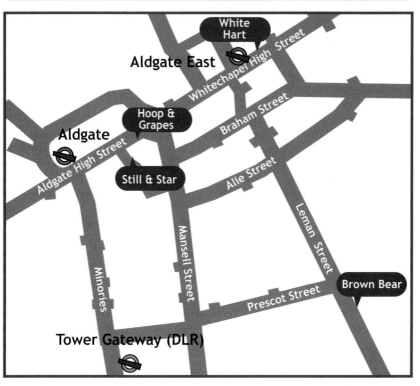

White Hart

Aldgate East

Whitechapel High Street

Braham Street

Hoop & Grapes

Aldgate

Aldgate High Street

Still & Star

Alie Street

Leman Street

Mansell Street

Minories

Brown Bear

Prescot Street

Tower Gateway (DLR)

Brown Bear

RATING:

139 Leman Street
E1 8EY
020 7481 3792

Whereas most of the land immediately east of the Square Mile has been turned over and redeveloped, Aldgate still has a few unaltered patches (if you look hard enough you'll even find some old warehouses that haven't become flats). In keeping with this, the Brown Bear is an unpretentious pub seemingly untouched by modern pub trends. Of note on our visit were a good range of real ales (nothing out of the ordinary, but decently kept), a dartboard and a very easygoing atmosphere. It feels as if it hasn't changed in years – an increasingly rare thing in a part of town where stasis is a rarity.

FEATURES:

1

Hoop & Grapes

RATING:

47 Aldgate High Street
EC3N 1AL
020 7265 5171

This place was rescued from near dereliction in the eighties and turned into a posh pub. It is one of a very tiny number of timber-framed buildings (it claims to be the only one) left in the City – thanks to careless bakers and the Luftwaffe. The building's quaintness is probably the most appealing aspect of what is now a really a pretty ordinary pub – it's now not as upmarket as it initially set out to be. There are real ales, pub grub etc. on offer, but, truth be told, we prefer some of the seamier and more characterful pubs, not so very far away. Oh, and it's not open on the weekends.

FEATURES: HANDY FOR: Whitechapel Gallery

Still & Star

RATING:

1 Little Somerset Street
E1 8AH
020 7702 2899

Tiny, rather quaint pub, which becomes a haven for a mixed bunch of punters after clocking off. It would be unremarkable in other parts of town, but in this location becomes something more rare and precious as the years go by. It's a solid, traditional old boozer – the sort of place that folk take for granted until it closes, and then they start complaining. We've already lost too many of them, so give this one a look if you're passing, before it's too late. Open at the usual City hours.

FEATURES:

White Hart

89 Whitechapel High Street

E1 7RA

020 7247 1546

This pub has had its ups and downs over the years, but is still going strong. Even though the pub was opened up a little (with the removal of a partition wall some time ago), the unwritten rule of City types in the back and local drunks in the front seems still to be observed. (We usually end up in the front part: there are often fewer people there.) The service is OK; the beer on offer is pretty decent, although your wine-drinking companions will prefer to be elsewhere when the place is lively. It's a relief from the bravado of many of the nearby City pubs, the grimness of some of the local hostelries and the pomposity of Shoreditch. It's open at the weekends, too – just keep an eye out for the odd Ripper tour or two.

FEATURES:

HANDY FOR: Whitechapel Gallery

ALL SAINTS (DLR)

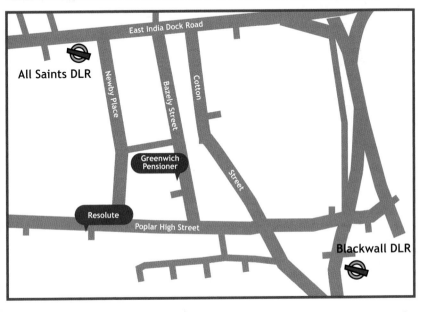

All Saints DLR

East India Dock Road

Newby Place

Bazely Street

Cotton

Greenwich Pensioner

Street

Resolute

Poplar High Street

Blackwall DLR

The Greenwich Pensioner

RATING:

2 Bazely Street
E14 0ES
020 7987 4414

Poplar is an area that rarely gets attention. It's surrounded on three sides by main trunk roads that whisk commuters to and from the City, Canary Wharf, over the river and points north and east. The area is a mix of early nineteenth century, with 20th century council housing plugging gaps created by the Luftwaffe, bordered by the very new Canary Wharf. It's not an area that people generally would seek out, but here you'll find the Greenwich Pensioner. If you're expecting a traditional local you're in for a surprise – stepping through the door takes you from a dreary East End street to an interior worthy of *Wallpaper*. The pub tries very hard to create, and largely succeeds, a contemporary bar/restaurant atmosphere of the sort that's popped up in Clerkenwell, Shoreditch, Hoxton over the past few years. If you're here for the ale you're going to be disappointed – but if you're into modern cuisine, wines, sprits and cocktails, then you'll be happy. It's pretty relaxed, everyone seems to know each other and the (table) service is knowledgeable, prompt, polite, friendly and justifiably proud of the standards. So, if you do live in one of the new developments nearby, you now have a handy place for decent eating and drinking and the money you've saved on taxi fares will buy an extra cocktail or two.

FEATURES:

The Resolute

RATING:

210 Poplar High St
E14 0BB
020 7987 1429

It's nice to know that not all pubs in Poplar have slipped into local no-go zones. A well-kept house with friendly staff and bantering punters; we caught it just as Saturday night was kicking off and the lively atmosphere made us want to stay. There's decent ale on the hand pumps, including the not-so-easy-to-find (nowadays) Tetley's. There'll probably be sport on at least one of the TVs, which sometimes show a different sport on each of them, but that doesn't detract from the air of conviviality. One question, though: we can understand an East End pub having darts trophies in its cabinet, but how did it get the one for golf round here?

FEATURES:

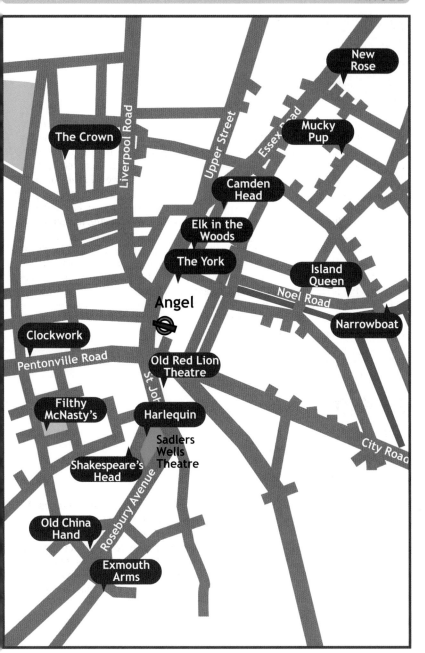

Camden Head

RATING:

2 Camden Walk
N1 8DY
020 7359 0851

This is a big, ornate pub that's been thoroughly reliable for as long as we can remember. The drink and food are pretty standard, and it can get pretty crowded quite often (especially weekends). Its biggest claim to fame is the Comedy Club, which ran on Monday nights, where many, now familiar, faces would try new material out on an enthusiastic audience. Those were the days. Then, every pub got in on the act, hosting comedy nights for Eddie Izzard wannabes. We guess they started using the simple hypothesis that 'all comics are drunks and, if their audiences like them, they must be drunks too = big drinkers = massive profits'. So for us the pub comedy thing died. The Camden Head was way ahead of them. The club's still there, but we haven't plucked up the courage to visit one for a long time, so unfortunately we can't comment on the current quality of the comedy.

FEATURES:

Clockwork

RATING:

66–68 Pentonville Road
N1 9HS
020 7837 5387

Painted in a striking red and black with transfers on the windows announcing all the hip things inside, the exterior of Clockwork looks knowingly cool. Unusually, though, this bar lives up to its own hype. The variety of customers helped, with New Age types, goths, Hoxtonites and office workers all creating a genuinely friendly atmosphere. Even the staff had a rare sense of humour. For a Friday night it was pleasantly full – rather than annoyingly packed – and there was (pricey) pizza on offer. Although there were no real ales, it didn't look as if people were coming here for ale and the huge vodka choice nicely compensated. Sadly, on the negative side, pinball wasn't the only 'old-skool' facility – as the grubby toilets illustrated – but it's a minor complaint. On top of all this, there's also a club upstairs, which might be rather tempting if you're still having a good time by 11 p.m. Overall, Clockwork is a strong three-pinter.

FEATURES:

The Crown

RATING:

116 Cloudesley Road
N1 0EB
020 7837 7107

One of Fuller's more upmarket efforts and clearly aiming at the N1 demographic, this is a grand Victorian pub in a very picturesque part of Barnsbury. Apart from the blander back dining-style room, much of the ornate decoration remains, with plenty of etched glass and dark wood panels in evidence. If you're lucky enough to grab the seats in front of it, you can even enjoy the real fire in the winter evenings. Add to this a great selection of beers (including Honey Dew on tap), plus a pretty extensive wine list, and it gets hard to fault the place. The service is good and the well-made food is deservedly popular. Even with the perfectly acceptable Islington Tap and Albion both a few minutes away, it's still easily the best of the lot and – unlike some other pubs in the area – isn't remotely pretentious. Recommended.

FEATURES:

Elk in the Woods

RATING:

37 Camden Passage
N1 8EA
020 7226 3535

Well, we'd say it's more of a restaurant/bar than bar/restaurant, although there were no objections to our sitting down for just a few drinks. There's nothing special in the beer department – San Miguel, Guinness etc. – but a range of Scandinavian liquors began to pique our interest. In the end, the menu got the better of us and we had some pretty reasonable, interesting grub, such as meatballs with a glass of liqueur to pour over them/down your throat (as you saw fit). We went on to try a cocktail or two, but even they had a Scandinavian twist. It's a relaxed place and the service is helpful and friendly and there's not a hint of plywood or flat-packs anywhere. We didn't find the Elk (apart from a few little antlers), but we guessed that the reclaimed floorboards cladding the walls were the eponymous woods. We can't wait for the owners to open up an Edinburgh branch, then they can call it – wait for it – Moose in the Hoose.

Exmouth Arms

23 Exmouth Market

EC1R 4QR

020 7837 5622

Here's a pub that has completely failed to get with the programme. There's nowhere to plug in your iPod for a start and you have to leave your skateboard outside. The people playing darts in the back appeared not to be doing so ironically. There was no absinthe behind the bar, either. It's stubbornly persisting as a high-street boozer. Disgraceful. And a blessed relief. It's not too busy, there are no frills and no gimmicks, except for very good ale (Harvey's Sussex for one – the only pub north of the river where we've ever seen it – and that is nectar). The service is prompt and friendly and most of the punters look as if they've been there all day and don't see any compelling reason why they should go home, either. Nor could we. The obligatory Scotsman is there making sure the bar doesn't fall over. We didn't bother with the food – the ale is nutritious enough. A refuge for those who just can't keep up with modern life (which Damon Albarn always told us was rubbish, anyway).

FEATURES:

Filthy McNasty's

68 Amwell Street

EC1R 1UU

020 7837 6067

Any pub that has pulled a pint for Nick Cave can't be doing much wrong. A short stagger to Angel tube, Filthy McNasty's is a bit of a hidden gem in the cesspit of Islington theme and chain bars. Offering a cracking range of whiskeys, as well as the ubiquitous Guinness and Caffrey's, McNasty's offers welcome relief from the cold winter evenings with a homely red interior (well, homely if you reside in a bordello), comfy chairs and slouchy sofas you'll want to nod off on; and in summer it's got plenty of outside tables for you to enjoy your pint. A range of Thai food is available during the week, and roasts on Sundays keep you well fed. A lively events programme offers gigs, DJ nights and book launches, readings and even the odd poetry slamdown. Definitely something different, and definitely not to be confused with the nearby Filthy O'Neill's.

FEATURES:

Harlequin

RATING:

27 Arlington Way
EC1R 1UY

This pub, being next to Sadler's Wells, used to be the haunt of the techies and orchestra members from the theatre. It even had a phone from the backstage area. Sadly, with the demolition of the old theatre, that seems to have gone. Still, it's friendly enough and far enough off Islington's main drags to be very civilised. Worth going out of your way for and ideal if you're off to see a show at Sadler's Wells.

FEATURES: **HANDY FOR:** Sadler's Wells Theatre

Island Queen

RATING:

87 Noel Road
N1 8HD
020 7704 7631

Once again, after a long period in the wilderness, the Island Queen is a pub we at Fancyapint? can heartily recommend. The owners of this fabulous old place have taken the time, care and patience to reverse the decline of recent years and make it a pub to be proud of. The beer line-up is excellent: Pride, Landlord and Deuchars on the hand pumps, with Kolsch, Fruli, Leffe, Hoegaarden, Staropramen and de Konninck all on draft. The wine list is pretty decent and the food is worth visiting for – we especially like the fish-and-chip Friday thing (although can we have proper chips, not 'hand-cut wedges', please?). The pool table has gone, to be replaced with much needed extra seating and there's a loungey bit in the opposite corner. The much-loved papier-mâché political caricatures of old may be long gone, but the spirit of the old Island Queen is back with us again. Cheers!

FEATURES: *Reviewers' award – most improved pub 2005*

Mucky Pup

RATING:

39 Queen's Head Street

N1 8NQ

020 7226 2572

Given the tired chain pubs and bars of Upper Street, it's nice to know there are decent alternatives hidden away on the nearby streets. This one's a lovely surprise and also one of the best modern takes on the pub experience we've seen for a while. Whereas others go wholesale on the food front or contrive an ironic take on old-fashioned pubs, this one keeps things simple. The friendly service is rare for London, but particularly so for this part of town. A pool table and a dartboard in the backroom are welcome sights. It's not the biggest pub you'll ever see, but that just adds to the genial atmosphere. Shame this one couldn't be cloned and dumped on Upper Street. However, perhaps being concealed behind Essex Road plays in the pub's favour. It's certainly the sort of pub you want to keep just for you and your mates. The only niggle is the food. The recently introduced concept of cooking your own food at your table on a hot plate, although interesting, won't endear vegetarians or those who prefer to keep the cooking smells in the kitchen.

FEATURES:

The Narrowboat

RATING:

119 St Peter's Street

N1 8PZ

020 7288 0572

Since our last review, this pub has been refitted and relaunched. Cue stripped floorboards and leather sofas and large windows giving an airy feel to the place (as well as offering views straight from an estate agent's brochure of the canal-side flats). On tap are up to four real ales (pick of the bunch for us being the Adnams) and emerging from the kitchen is a plentiful supply of modern pub grub. Two plasma screens at the front and back of the pub mean that football is never far away, though on the evidence of our last visit not too many punters involve themselves with the efforts of the Premiership's finest. A solid effort in a pub-crawlable stretch of N1.

FEATURES:

New Rose

RATING:

84–86 Essex Road
N1 8LU
020 7226 1082

This former old man's local is another addition to the I-spy book of trendy Essex Road bars and now sports the name of our favourite Damned tune. The primary-coloured façade is now more subtle and inside, the atmosphere moody, with a dark wooden bar and a plethora of uplighters and tea lights. There's lots of exposed brickwork, but the look is elegant and upmarket, rather than industrial. The toilet signs however, titled 'George' and 'Mildred', are a joke likely lost on anyone under 25. A few locals from its previous incarnation hang on, but as the place gets ever more popular, it seems their appetency to drink here is diminishing. We do like their unusual methods to encourage customer participation on a Friday night: a competition involving drawing a matchstick-man comic strip and the chance to nominate albums to appear on the (already good) jukebox. Who knows? Perhaps we might see our choice of albums appearing here soon.

FEATURES:

Old China Hand

RATING:

16 Tysoe Street
EC1R 4RQ
020 7278 7630

Once it was the great O'Hanlon's, then it was the average Mulligan's. Now, this one's the Old China Hand. 'No ordinary London pub', it proclaims outside, and for once the advertising has a point. The USP of this one is real ale and dim sum – a combination few pubs promise, so perhaps this one sees a gap in the market. The food is simple but effective and the regular guest beers, which usually include something from the O'Hanlon's range, are top-notch. There were also two fridges filled with scores of different bottled beers from around the world to sample. Alas, the interior isn't to everyone's taste, with wooden furnishings out of *Lord of the Rings* (or at least Waxy O'Connors): strange stumpy stools and tables. But throw into the mix a jazz night during the week and you have somewhere attempting to stand out from the other pubs of the area. For that, at least, you've got to give this one some credit.

FEATURES:

Old Red Lion Theatre Club

RATING:

418 St John Street
EC1V 4NJ
020 7837 7816

The ideal spot to sink your life savings in producing and premiering the play wot you wrote – then drowning your sorrows on the proceeds of the handful of tickets you actually manage to sell. The little theatre upstairs probably seats no more than fifty, but is a lively, vibrant venue. Some great stuff and some mind-blowing rubbish gets put on there. The whole place has a theatrical, arty air but it is also a first-class local boozer. So you'll find bottle-nosed middle managers from the big offices across the road necking it down at one end of the bar while girly-boy actor wannabes giggle down the other – all interspersed with locals of all types enjoying the draft 6X, Abbot, Leffe and Staropramen. The décor could come from a set designer's template – that heavy, old, dull red, embossed wallpaper for the walls and essence-of-nicotine paint for the ceiling, comfortable benches running round, a scattering of tables and chairs and plenty of space for those who prefer to stand and bray at one another. One puzzle. The gents' walls are a mass of scrawled graffiti celebrating lower-league football clubs – and yet this place is least likely to attract the knuckle-dragging element of our beautiful game. Perhaps it's a neo-ironic artistic statement. One day they'll probably gentrify this place – and the world will be poorer for it.

FEATURES:

Shakespeare's Head

RATING:

1 Arlington Way
EC1R 1XA
020 7837 2581

Going by the exterior, it's easy to write this one off as a grim estate pub, but actually crossing the threshold reveals not a fight over the pool table but a friendly boozer, decorated with signed photos of numerous thespians. The traditional pub grub on offer may not be too tempting to the dancers of Sadler's Wells Theatre over the road, but it caught our eye. There are decent beers, great service, a sleepy pub cat, friendly punters (sometimes too friendly) and a lovely beer garden out the back. It's a singular little place that stands out from your average modern-day pub.

FEATURES:

The York

RATING:

82 Islington High Street
N1 8EQ
020 7713 1835

One of the few proper pubs left on Islington's main drag. It's now a Nicholson's and does everything to the standards we've come to expect from them. The beer is pretty decent – Pride, Bombardier and guests on the hand pumps – and it's promptly and pleasantly served. It's a big pub, so there's usually plenty of room, although it does get crowded, at the times you'd expect, towards the end of the week. However, unlike most of the clientele it seems, we don't feel the outside seating is particularly enticing (unless you're really into NO_x, particulates and avant-garde poetry as practised by some of the local street residents), but thank goodness not everywhere around here has gone trendy.

FEATURES: **HANDY FOR:** Business Design Centre

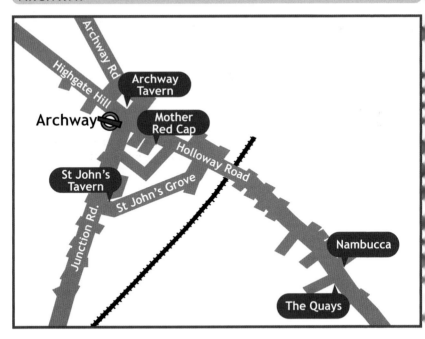

The Archway Tavern

RATING:

Archway Close, Archway Road
N19 3TD
020 7272 2840

The first thing that hits you as you come out of Archway tube station (apart from the monolithic Archway Tower) is the roundabout with the huge Archway Tavern stuck in the middle of it. However, once inside, we noticed what can only be described as an anti-TARDIS effect. For, despite its large footprint, what we discovered inside seemed to be a rather small pub for sports fans. Six screens, showing two football matches and one rugby match, seemed to be keeping people entertained; after all, there was certainly no fear of not having a good view. But, despite this and friendly service, we felt that, overall, it's a rather unremarkable, even drab pub. Once we left, the reason for the lack of space inside became apparent: the back half of the pub is a music venue and nightclub, the latter promising everything from 'Ibiza Dance Anthems' and chart music to R&B and indie.

FEATURES:

Mother Red Cap

665 Holloway Road
N19 5SE
020 7263 7082

Curtains drawn, door shut. From the outside it's easy to assume the worst: lump this one in with Holloway's hardcore Irish boozers and walk past. Fear not, though. Step inside and you'll be hit by a glorious pub interior: wall mirrors, intricate tile work, fitted banquettes – the full Victorian monty. The stark exterior probably puts a few off but when we last looked in there was still a fairly wide representation of N19 filling this one up. What with a pool table, darts, enough screens for the sport (oh, and a decent drop of Guinness), it's easy to see why. Throw in friendly and efficient staff and you have one of the best pubs in the area.

FEATURES:

Nambucca

596 Holloway Road
N7 6LB
020 7272 7366

For an establishment proclaiming itself 'the best pub in North London', Nambucca looks fairly unremarkable inside and out. It is, though, not the décor that attracts the punters but the variety and quality of music on offer. There are regular events by record labels and webzines covering anything from electro to rock to hip-hop, while every fortnight you can settle down with a whisky to enjoy the country to Americana night 'Heartworn Fridays'. Nambucca is also the home of 'Sensible Sundays', with DJs and even an open mike and decks for anyone who believes he or she can improve the entertainment provided. If you'd rather listen to others show off their talent or watch Kung Fu films on the TVs, then just grab a seat and a five-quid roast. There is a late licence until midnight, but don't try to get here too early: it isn't open until 6 p.m., except on Sunday.

FEATURES:

The Quays

RATING:

471 Holloway Road
N7 6LE
020 7272 3634

The exterior of The Quays is certainly interesting. Views through the windows are blocked by shelves of old bottles, while uplighters illuminate the blue walls in a tacky alternating spectrum of colour. The interior was also unusual, with three distinct areas, including a front bar adorned with etched mirrors and ornate woodwork and a back section featuring a huge 10-foot screen. Coupled with two plasma screens it verged on 'sports bar' territory. On our Monday visit, however, it was fairly quiet and we enjoyed some genuinely excellent food in peace, aided by friendly staff. Conversely, on weekend nights, a young crowd descends and it gets pretty lively, as it does when big matches are shown. Ultimately, this is a pub that appeals to different people at different times for different reasons – so time your visit well.

FEATURES:

St John's Tavern

RATING:

91 Junction Road
N19 5QU
020 7272 1587

St John's Tavern is a trendy, modern and spacious gastropub and offers something different from the boozers around Archway tube. There are three real ales on tap and a good selection of wines and Continental lagers. The food is very good, the staff are friendly and there is an easygoing atmosphere. Save up enough cash and it's a great place to while away a day. It can get very busy, so booking is recommended if you want to eat. One of the better gastropubs around.

FEATURES:

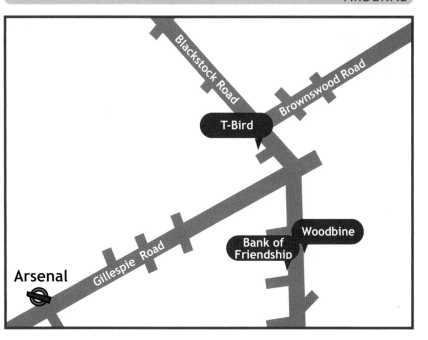

Bank of Friendship

RATING:

224 Blackstock Road
N4 3NG
020 7288 9891

It's always a pleasure to have a drink at this venerable boozer. There are no quiz machines or one-armed bandits to spoil enjoyment of fine draught Guinness, so those who prefer conversation to noise will be at home here. The place has a relaxed and friendly atmosphere, despite its proximity to Arsenal's ground. Unlike the nearby Arsenal Tavern or Gunners pubs, the Bank is not generally frequented by beery football fans, although it gets extremely busy on match days. The coal fires are really cosy on winter days, and a nice rear terrace opens during the summer months. When you come here, just make sure Arsenal aren't playing at home.

FEATURES:

T-Bird

RATING:

132 Blackstock Road
N4 2DX
020 7503 6202

Aside from the horrible pubs that rely on proximity to Highbury Stadium for custom, in Finsbury Park you're going to find only Irish pubs and this: a bar. It immediately loses points for not having any bitter on tap, and only intermittently bottles of the stuff, and its location isn't in the hub of things, but that's where the grumbling stops. The first thing immediately to strike you on entering is the unusual décor, which is regularly changing and kitschily ramshackle, but avoids being pretentious. Comfortably worn sofas with an assortment of armchairs and straight-backed chairs, allowing slouching and conversation in the pleasantly dim atmosphere. There is a rather good, if malfunction-prone, jukebox, focusing on the indie end of the spectrum, but the music's not too loud for chatting and there are occasional acoustic music nights too. All in all, not a bad place. Bear in mind this is Finsbury Park and it makes a very welcome change and useful place to know in the area.

FEATURES:

Woodbine

RATING:

215 Blackstock Road
N5 2LL
020 7354 1061

Fresh from a refit, the new-look Woodbine, with its chandeliers, mirrors and swish wallpaper, offers a rather different drinking experience from the nearby Gunners haunts. Perhaps the new owners think that, with Arsenal moving grounds, this patch might not see so many fans stopping off on a Saturday afternoon. Certainly catch it when there's not a match on down the road and you may (as we did) stop off for longer than you expect. It's a Leffe/Staropramen kind of place with a decent jukebox, should you feel the need to part with your change. A screen at the back keeps you informed of sporting developments, but this one feels the sort of place you could easily pass the time in without recourse to the ever-present Sky Sports News. Its look and feel may seem par for the course in London nowadays, but add to it the T-Bird and the Bank of Friendship and you'll find that Blackstock Road's got itself a pleasant little pub crawl.

FEATURES:

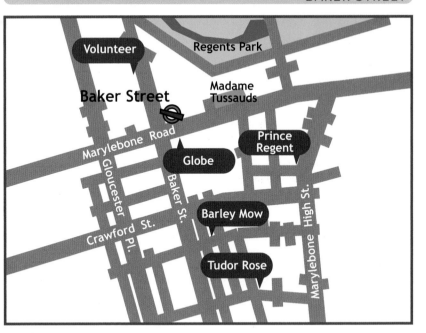

Barley Mow

8 Dorset Street
W1U 6QW
020 7935 7318

RATING:

The Barley Mow has an extremely attractive exterior decorated with hanging baskets and gas lanterns. Stepping inside, you are greeted by a handsome bar with two snugs, or wooden cubicles, on the left. The pub was built in 1791, and claims to be the oldest pub in Marylebone – and we've no reason to dispute that. These days, its small space means that it will get packed at the usual times – you're likely to appreciate the surroundings more if you can visit at a quiet time. To quench your thirst, there's Pride and Courage Best, which are well kept. Note that it's closed on Sundays.

The Globe

RATING:

43 Marylebone Road
NW1 5JY
020 7935 6368

How prescient of someone to build this pub in 1735. And how patient to wait a century and a half for Baker Street tube to be constructed underneath creating the meeting point for Wembley goers just two stops up the line. Once the stadium is complete, look forward to this place switching in a moment from commuters' beer stop to heavy-metal heaven or Reds 'r' Us, depending on the schedule. But the place copes. Dickens, William Pitt the younger and Conan Doyle are claimed as past regulars. Decent, honest, plain tables and chairs, oldish floorboards and panelling and well-kept beers make for a pleasant oasis. The upstairs bar is nonsmoking; there are tables outside for those who want copious carbon monoxide and traffic noise with their get-you-home slurp. It's easy to mock (no, it's not really: we work at it), but The Globe has been getting it more or less right for most of two centuries, shows no signs of getting it wrong and deserves praise as a simple thing done well.

FEATURES:

Prince Regent

RATING:

71 Marylebone High Street
W1U 5JN
020 7467 3811

The last refit has put a fair bit of the Victorian charm back in, albeit with a completely new twist. Another pub in the Mitchells and Butlers stable in London to be remodelled, this one's interior now matches up fairy lights, frilly brollies and chandeliers with soft furnishings and dark wood walls. As with other M&B pubs, it heavily promotes Continental beers, though there are some good traditional English ales on tap too. The pub food is decent too – there's plenty of it and there's something for all appetites, but it doesn't dominate, as it does in so many pubs nowadays. The overall effect of this one is of an elegant and swish drinking den, with the Opium Lounge taking this notion even further. Add live music and it shows that you can modernise a pub yet avoid turning it into a bare-boarded gastropub or overdesigned style bar. We're impressed and, with its newfound popularity with the locals, it seems the M&B formula is a winner.

FEATURES:

Tudor Rose

RATING:

44 Blandford Street
W1U 7HS
020 7935 5963

After a few identity changes in recent years, this place has settled down. It's not a bad place at all, with Courage Best and Directors on the hand pumps and proper pub grub served downstairs (upstairs there's a restaurant), including such delights as Spam fritters. Being in a Marylebone backwater, this place hardly ever gets crowded, although there's a weekday lunchtime trade, so, if you need a place for a quiet pint in the area, this one will do nicely. The service is prompt and friendly and the prices are par for the area. While you wouldn't make a special effort to seek this place out, if you're in the locale, do drop in. Oh, except on a Sunday – it's closed.

FEATURES:

Volunteer

RATING:

247 Baker Street
NW1 6XE
020 7486 4090

Since it's just a few doors down from 221b, you'd expect the Volunteer to be a pub in honour of Conan Doyle's detective. It's not (you have to go to Charing Cross for that). A few years back we had it pigeonholed as 'a seemingly nondescript pub' and, though it still has an unassuming exterior, the inside has been altered to something rather more extravagant. All leather settles and beaded curtains, this pub is one of the growing number owned by the Mitchells and Butlers group that opt for a loungey décor and a drink selection heavy on the Belgian beers. The changes suggest a growing market for the high-powered brews of the Low Countries. But the more we visit places like the Volunteer, with their ever so slightly contrived feel (M&B also own the All Bar One, O'Neill's and Scream chains), the more we're sensing some clever branding and marketing at work. We've not got a problem with quality food and drink: it's just the thought of a massive warehouse filled with beaded curtains and leather pouffes (à la the O'Neill's sheds ready to dispatch potato sacks and road signs to bars from Buenos Aires to Beijing) giving us the fear. If you can put such thoughts out of your mind, you'll have a fine time at this one.

FEATURES:

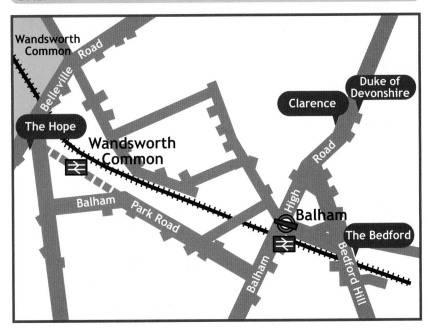

The Bedford

77 Bedford Hill
SW12 9HD
020 8682 8940

RATING:

If we were rating this place just on range of entertainment on offer, it would definitely be a five-pinter. With everything from line dancing to stand-up comedy on offer, it's certainly a world away from boozers that think entertaining the punters means installing a jukebox. It's a little disappointing, then, that, as a place to drink, the Bedford is solid rather than spectacular. Granted, you do get a fair range of ales (stretching to Marston's Pedigree), but the atmosphere can often be no better than that of some of the other bars in the area. Aim for this one's smaller side bar for optimum results.

FEATURES:

The Clarence

RATING:

90–92 Balham High Road
SW12 9AG
020 8772 1155

Second relaunch in two years for this ex-Puzzle Pub Co pub, so here's hoping this one lasts longer than the ill-fated Balham Arms. It's been taken on by the people behind The Bishop (on Lordship Lane) and The Castle (in Camberwell), though they've dropped the chess theme in favour of canines (Clarence, it seems, is the owner's four-legged friend). So, is this one now the dog's cojones? Well, on first impressions it didn't seem too different from its predecessor, its loungey layout much in keeping with the high gentrification of SW12 (even the estate agent's across the road is decked out like a style bar). Hard to quibble too with its drink offerings: beers and wines from all over the world will keep all but the most picky of punters from complaining. What strikes us as odd, though, is the layout of the TV: there seemed to be only one screen (fair enough) but it was tucked away in the alcove at the back, almost as a preserve for those lucky enough to nab the seats around it. What developed then was a queue of punters around that space pushing in and trying to eye the screen. All most odd, and not in keeping with the laid-back air this one is trying to pull off. Quibbles aside, this one's quickly picked up a regular clientele, and for its range of drinks alone deserves a three pint rating (not many pubs in London offer up Budvar Dark on tap, for example). We were just a bit bemused that a pub named after a dog, comes across as rather too stylish to have a pub dog.

FEATURES:

The Duke of Devonshire

RATING:

39 Balham High Road
SW12 9AA
020 8673 1363

This one does its best to cater to as many of Balham's locals as possible. Old geezers sup away contentedly during the week, while at the weekends both the late licence and the Sunday roasts help to fill the place up. And what with the huge main bar, a sizable backroom and a beer garden, there's usually space for everyone. In case that isn't enough, the gin-palace-style interior (all etched mirrors and high ceilings) puts most Wetherspoon refits in the shade. Its classic status is slightly marred by a recent refit that's turned the back bar rather more towards a dining room than perhaps was needed. It's still one of your better bets for a drink on Balham High Road, though we don't think it's quite as good as it used to be. Definitely worth a look, though.

FEATURES:

The Hope

RATING:

1 Bellevue Road
SW17 7EG
020 8672 8717

An absolutely cracking makeover since our last visit a couple of years ago now combines comfort, style and class with superb beers and great, good-value food – guinea fowl in red wine or cod loin with pesto and parmesan, for example, are each less than nine quid. The corner site provides a triple aspect on to Wandsworth Common and the big windows and high ceilings contribute to a light airy feel. Furnishing is an eclectic mix of squashy and arty sofas, traditional wood and just-this-side-of practical modern stuff, mixed with features such as traditional butchers' chopping tables. It's bigger than it looks with that airy lounge and a few steps up to the bar area, and then a couple of smaller areas just off that. Beers change regularly and have included Pride, Black Sheep, Harvey's, Ringwood and Deuchars, and there's a decent wine list. Pricing reflects the aspirational nature of the area – it is virtually next door to the Michelin-starred Chez Bruce.

FEATURES:

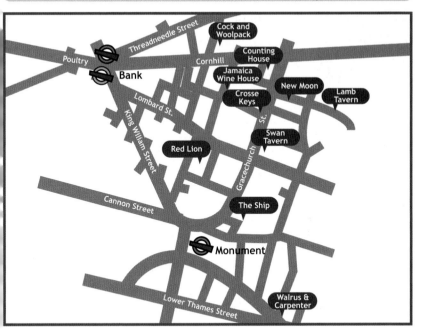

Cock and Woolpack

RATING: ▮▮▮

6 Finch Lane

EC3V 3NA

020 7626 4799

This unobtrusive pub is something of a City institution and, thanks to its location, is generally frequented only by those lucky few in the know or when felicity smiles upon the unwary commuter in search of a shortcut (given its size, this is not such a bad thing). When Mr Wetherspoon came up with the concept of a pub where one could go, sit in plush surroundings, drink a nice pint of ale and converse without being interrupted by loud jukeboxes, I've no doubt that the Cock and Woolpack was the sort of pub he had in mind. The difference, however, between the cavernous JD establishments and this rather pleasing Shepherd Neame snug is that the conversation actually generates an atmosphere, rather than being lost in the commodious ceilings of the former. A good pub for a quick pint on the way home (if you can find it).

FEATURES:

Counting House

RATING:

50 Cornhill
EC3V 3PD
020 7283 7123

NatWest really has got it the wrong way round: the Counting House demonstrates just how much better suited a city cathedral is for drinking and dining than, in its previous guise, yet another bank. If you step inside this cavernous, soaring basilica and a 'wow' doesn't form on your lips, then you truly deserve a life as a bank clerk. From the colossal island bar to the huge glass-domed roof at stratospheric levels, beautiful wood, brass and marble fittings abound – wherever the eye settles, it is magnificent. The pub absorbs regiments without excessive crush (even at Friday lunchtime) at stools and tables, in a collection of smaller rooms at the back, in the many dining tables running round the mezzanine. Fuller's classic beer range is of course available, but the smart, friendly and plentiful staff also have the pick of a dizzying range of other taps running up and down the bar counter. Food matches the overall standard too. Not only the eponymous pies – excellent though they are – but other classic dishes are supported by the adventurous traditional fare such as corned-beef hash and Welsh rarebit with a poached egg. We could stay here all day – er, we nearly did!

FEATURES:

The Crosse Keys

RATING:

9 Gracechurch Street
EC3V 0DR
020 7623 4824

Another gigantic Wetherspoon conversion, this one was a monumental banking hall. And while it doesn't have the aesthetic charm of some nearby competitors, this place impresses with its Stalinist proportions. There's the usual Wetherspoon range of drink and food on offer at the usual unbeatable Wetherspoon prices, which probably explains the advanced state of inebriation of the clientele when we arrived late one evening – apparently, we're just not used to cheap drink in the City. With Wetherspoon's excellent (some might say challenging) range of beers, it's a pretty reasonable pub for the area.

FEATURES:

Jamaica Wine House

St Michaels Alley, Cornhill
EC3V 9DS
020 7929 6972

Located in the myriad courtyards and alleyways off Cornhill, this venerable City watering hole is now under the ownership of the people who brought you Tup pubs. But fear not: over 300 years of atmosphere haven't been traded in for stripped pine and Jamiroquai CDs. That said, there is a bit of a 'Tup' air to the downstairs bar, with treated wood and high stools replacing the leather sofas and clubby atmosphere. The main bar retains an old-fashioned feel, with enough nooks and crannies to satisfy the most furtive of drinkers. It's a popular pub and can fill up quickly, usually for the duration. Quaint touches include a self-service, coin-operated humidor, but this setting surely deserves a real butler for this. A five-pint setting, then, but still only a three-pint pub.

FEATURES:

Lamb Tavern

RATING:

10–12 Leadenhall Market
EC3V 1LR
020 7626 2454

This splendid Young's pub has a very fine Victorian interior, with marvellous tile work and all the fixtures and fittings you'd expect of a pub in such dazzling surroundings. The pub's location, the beer and its visual appeal, we guess, make it staggeringly popular, just after work and at lunchtimes, thronged with the suits from the surrounding City institutions. So at these times it's tricky to see the décor, let alone admire it, and trying to sample the pub's produce can be quite taxing. However, a visit outside the busy times is well worth the effort, to enjoy the pub and its unique surroundings accompanied by Young's excellent beer.

FEATURES:

New Moon

RATING:

88 Gracechurch Street
EC3V 0DN
020 7626 3625

This is a very popular pub, thanks to its location – in the heart of the City and inside the grand old Leadenhall Market. You can stand outside in the covered market when it's not too cold, and that's what many people choose to do. But, even with the very long bar and plenty of staff, this pub's popularity still means getting served on a Friday just after work can be a bit of an ordeal. The New Moon serves a decent range of beer that's pretty well looked after and everyday pub grub at lunchtimes.

FEATURES:

Red Lion

RATING:

8 Lombard Court
EC3V 9BJ
020 7929 2552

Another hidden gem in the City. The wrought-iron above the door hints at some of the details within. While not all is original (what pub is, these days?), there are quite a few nice features about this pub to reassure us that it's not a new build. Most of the action takes place in the Main Bar, downstairs, with its nooks and crannies for parties or quiet conversations, and karaoke on Thursday nights at 7, if you're interested. Gets busy at commuting times and Thursday's a sell-out, though it tends to be empty of City folk at weekends. Hot food at lunchtimes, Pride, Adnams, Green King's IPA and a decent wine list make this a good all-rounder. It's also quiet in the afternoons, in case you need someplace for that chat or rendezvous. Worth a look.

FEATURES:

The Ship

RATING:

11 Talbot Court
EC3V 0BP
020 7929 3903

You could pass Talbot Court – an essay in concrete that looks like a loading bay – a hundred times and never notice the Ship tucked on an inside corner just a hundred yards down, where the slab work gives way to a traditional London yard. It's a gem. Rebuilt in the seventeenth century after the original ale house was incinerated in the Great Fire, it's smallish, simple and comfortable, offering decent Pride and Bombardier and a wide food menu. The spiral wooden staircase leads up to the narrow-ish upper bar, where – perhaps a trick of the eye – the limited space seems to have been enhanced by installing slightly undersized tables and chairs and a tiny serving area in the corner. Perhaps it is the location, but we are told you can nearly always get a seat upstairs. Not the most happening of pubs but a splendid place for local workers to catch up on the gossip or for a relaxing one if you are passing. Closed weekends – but open until 11 p.m. during the week.

FEATURES:

Visitors' Award Winner

The Swan Tavern

RATING:

77–80 Gracechurch Street
EC3V 0AS
020 7283 7712

A solid Fuller's pub, this is the sort of miniature pub that would fit a few times over into a Wetherspoon bank conversion. Give it a look if you fancy a change from large-scale City bars. Sure, the narrow bar becomes pretty impossible to navigate if more than a few suits start to hold court. If so, head upstairs to the confines of a slightly larger bar, the presence of which seemed to have passed by the punters we saw outside in the inclement weather with their pints.

The Walrus & the Carpenter

RATING:

45 Monument Street
EC3R 8BU
020 7626 3362

A decent pub, split into two ground-floor rooms and a downstairs wine bar. It's a little pokey so can get crowded very quickly just after work in the evenings. The beer is decently kept Young's and there's a refreshingly unpretentious lunchtime menu. The Lewis Carroll theme has not been exploited – it's just an ordinary City boozer, but, as there aren't many of those in this part of the City, that's no bad thing. A word of warning: if you're meeting someone here, make sure they know which of the rooms you're going to be in (or both of you carry mobiles).

FEATURES:

BARBICAN

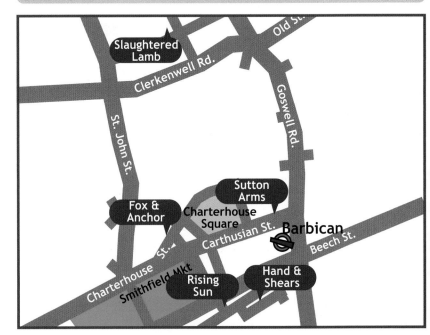

Fox & Anchor

RATING:

115 Charterhouse Street
EC1M 6AA
020 7253 5075

If the name Nicholson's appears on a pub, then you know it is going to be one to look at as well as consume food and drink in. But the Fox & Anchor is a bit special. Walk in, shut your eyes and you may think you hear the shrill whine of an air-raid siren. The place is straight out of the 1940s. You can imagine young Johnny, apprentice butcher and a private in the East Surrey, having his first proper pint before his train leaves for Southampton. Quite an unusual interior. The back areas are small rooms or snugs, which can be closed for privacy and hired for private functions – it's worth a look for these alone. Smithfield is getting trendier by the day and Charterhouse Street has plenty of wine bars, if needs must. But the street forks strangely at the Barbican end – off into a dark cul-de-sac, and the Fox is right down the bottom of it. Like other traditional market boozers it can shut early on weekdays (6 p.m. commonly) and opens early for a hearty breakfast. The beer is fine (especially if you use it to wash down a freshly cooked full English breakfast) and Nicholson's usually do a good pint of Guinness. This is a fantastic pub, well worth going out of your way for.

FEATURES:

Hand & Shears

RATING:

1 Middle Street, Cloth Fair
EC1A 7JA
020 7600 0257

This is a great little pub, with separate bar areas still divided up into public, private and saloon bars. It hasn't changed in years, and we guess it's only a matter of time before some well-meaning developer mucks it up. It's got a great atmosphere, but it can get a bit crowded – possibly the secret of its avoidance of the renovator's hammer. It hasn't been neglected, though, and it feels just as an English pub should. With Courage Best and Directors on the taps and regular guest beers, it's a real drinker's pub that happens to get a bit busy on Friday nights.

FEATURES: HANDY FOR: Museum of London

Rising Sun

38 Cloth Fair
EC1A 7JQ
020 7726 6671

An old, traditional-style (but quite attractive) pub, this Smith's hostelry seems to attract an interesting mix of regulars. Tuesday is quiz night but it was still pretty quiet. A comfortable place with darts and fruit machines up at one end. Well-priced, well-kept Sam Smith's beer. A good pub if you happen by, and it's one of the few places open at weekends in Smithfield.

FEATURES:

Slaughtered Lamb

RATING:

34–35 Great Sutton Street
EC1V 0DX
020 7253 1516

This remodelling of an old gallery space – so an ideal pub for an area with so many loft-converted flats – has a slouchy style similar to many pubs in the capital, a mixture of squishy sofas and well-worn wooden furniture. There's the slight feeling that this pub ought to exist in ironic quotation marks: it's the sort of pub where the dartboard is artily displayed in a cabinet, rather than actually available for play. As for its name, the pub doesn't go silent when one enters, like its namesake in *American Werewolf in London*, though the too-cool-for-school attitude of the bar staff was just as chilly. That said, this one grew on us during our visit. For a start, the (rather rare) Sleeman Honey Brown Lager slipped down a treat and the varied music mix (the Stones to Pink Floyd via trance and dub) suggested a great MP3 player stuck on random. Just as impressive was the menu: we were fully expecting to be flicking through our Gastronglish–English translation dictionaries, but the choices were simple and clear and also under a tenner. We'll be back to try the food and perhaps take a look at the regular music nights in the basement bar. Judging from our visit then, this one (just) edges a three.

FEATURES:

Sutton Arms

RATING:

6 Carthusian Street

EC1M 6EB

020 7253 0723

This handsome pub has been given the refurbishment it deserves and has been brought into the twenty-first century with a bit of style and attention to detail. On the beer pumps there are well-kept beers, including Belgian beer, and there's also a pretty imaginative and well-presented food menu. The décor is a bit eclectic with its plaster busts and so forth, but the place feels much more comfortable and in keeping with the building and its environs and for this we salute the new owners. The upstairs restaurant has now taken on the role of lounge/restaurant, hinting at a more leisurely approach to the excellent menu; but, judging from how busy it was last time we were in, it's not hurt business.

FEATURES:

BARONS COURT/WEST KENSINGTON

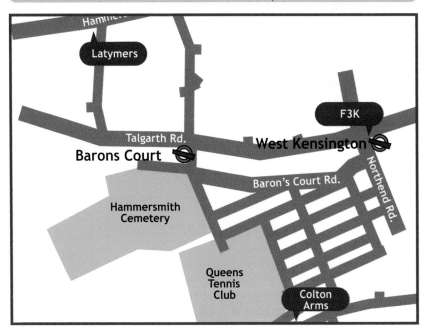

Hammer—

Latymers

F3K

Talgarth Rd.

West Kensington

Barons Court

Baron's Court Rd.

Northend Rd.

Hammersmith
Cemetery

Queens
Tennis
Club

Colton
Arms

Colton Arms

RATING:

187 Greyhound Road
W14 9SD
020 7385 6956

Secreted away in the suburban no-man's-land of Barons Court, this pub has the feel of a village local. A small affair with a main bar and two tiny back alcoves and a wee patio garden at the rear. The rural feel stems as much from its original oak furniture and handled pint glasses as from the courteous bar staff. Such behaviour could easily result in a faux and touristy atmosphere, but there's nothing contrived here. With excellently kept beers – and the sort of warm and homely atmosphere gastropubs strive for yet seldom attain – the pub enjoys a mixed clientele and surely your patronage as well (and, while we're at it, a preservation order wouldn't go amiss). A classic boozer.

FEATURES:

Reviewers' Award Winner 2004

F3K (Famous 3 Kings)

RATING:

171 North End Road
W14 9NL
020 7603 6071

Can't find a pub showing the match? Don't give up and go home until you've tried here. With about fifteen different screens and feeds from sports channels across the globe, it's a pretty fair bet they'll be showing your game of choice. In case that isn't enough to keep you occupied, two pool tables, a labyrinthine layout and a video jukebox are there to amuse you, too. It's like a pub based on the inside of a teenage boy's brain (especially with the rap videos on the jukebox). Although there are always some guest ales, it's hardly a place for the quiet contemplation of them. A full-on, hyperactive sort of place but also one of the best sports bars around. Oh, it also has a late licence.

FEATURES:

Latymers

RATING: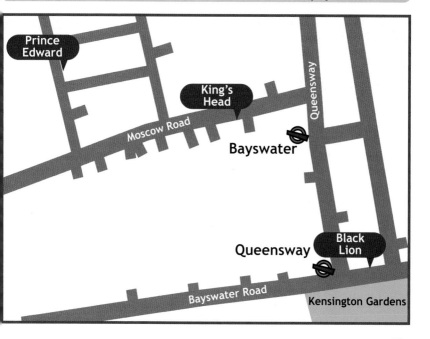

Hammersmith Road

W6 7JP

020 8748 3446

Though maybe not the first pub in London to have its own Thai restaurant, Latymers is certainly one of the best, for quality, service and value for money. The pub itself is late-eighties modern and a bit too shiny for our liking (it replaced the Red Cow, where the Jam and the Stranglers first played London, and was also the 'local' in *The Sweeney*), but the beer is always very well looked after and the service is excellent. It also has a nice relaxed atmosphere at weekends, being far enough away from Hammersmith station to avoid concertgoers, even with the footy on the tellies. But the food is the real draw – if you want to make your eyebrows sweat, make sure you order the homok talay to start.

FEATURES:

BAYSWATER/QUEENSWAY

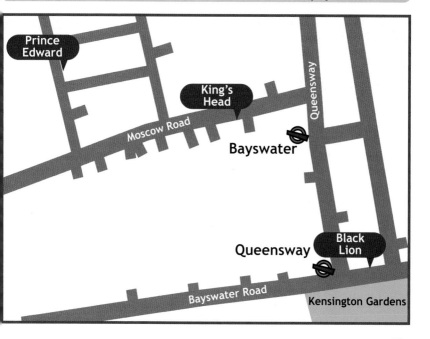

Black Lion

RATING:

123 Bayswater Road
W2 3JH
020 7229 0917

Apparently built in 1720, the Black Lion retains some attractive features today. Its ornate original brickwork and later Victorian ceiling and columns are lovely. However, the elegant surroundings are somewhat compromised by the pub of today. Sure, there's enough selection to keep you sufficiently fed and watered, but the big TV doesn't really add anything. You can well imagine that this was a charming pub in bygone centuries, but today it's marred by the heavy traffic on Bayswater.

FEATURES:

King's Head

RATING:

33 Moscow Road
W2 4AH
020 7229 4233

Quoting Flann O'Brien on a blackboard is a good start for any boozer, and this place didn't do much wrong after that. Bombardier and Greene King IPA were available on tap, and the pub had a local feel that was pleasant, added to by the landlady's friendly service. Worth a look if you're nearby.

FEATURES:

Prince Edward

73 Princes Square
W2 4NY
020 7727 2221

A decent, no-nonsense boozer with none of the pretensions of some of the places not so far away from here. It's a big, well-looked-after place, with good Hall & Woodhouse ales (e.g. Badger, Tanglefoot and Fursty Ferret) and fast and friendly service. The food is pretty pub-grub ordinary, but it can be a relief from some of the painful gastro twaddle on offer around and far more economical if all you need is a fuel stop. It's got a good local feel and also offers karaoke on Fridays. Not a bad place at all.

FEATURES:

BELSIZE PARK

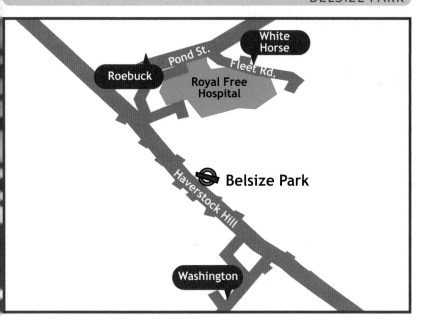

Roebuck

RATING:

15 Pond Street

NW3 2PN

020 7433 6871

Superficially, this is a bit mix-and-match. It apparently used to be a hotel; now it is a deceptively large bar/pub crossover. The post-ironic seventies and cod-African wallpaper in the main bar would make Austin Powers feel at home, almost, while gentle lighting, from a diverse and arty collection of lamps, and a low, gently pumping soundtrack add to the flavour. There's a good selection of areas to sit in the main bar, ranging from open tables to private nooks, while there is another, basement, bar, and a conservatory out the back. The range of good-quality beers is wide, both in bottles and on tap, ranging from Belgians and Czechs through to St Petersburg's Baltika number 3. There's a food menu, too, if a bit less extensive than you might expect in a place like this. All in all, a first-rate establishment. And there are antlers on the outside.

FEATURES:

The Washington

RATING:

50 Englands Lane

NW3 4UE

020 7722 8842

Into its third incarnation in five years, 'The Wash', as it now nicknames itself, has veered back from the precipice of gastrodom. It's been taken over by the Mitchells and Butlers group as part of their continually expanding, non-themed, upmarket chain of pubs. As such, emphasis is on a good choice of beer, wine and well-made food. In contrast with the bland exterior, the Victorian interior is splendid, with original etched glass, wood panelling and high ceilings all intact and an eclectic mix of tables and couches, all laid out with thought. On our Sunday-afternoon visit a pianist was playing some easy-listening jazzy music and the whole atmosphere was equally easy. Despite its being part of a clever M&B marketing plan to cater to a specific socioeconomic group, it would be churlish to do anything except recommend this place highly.

FEATURES:

The White Horse

RATING:

154 Fleet Road

NW3 2QX

020 7485 2112

This place held out for a long time against the trend of refurbishments sweeping over much of north London. A major renovation has done for the mankier aspects of this place, without destroying the finer architectural features of the building; if anything the makeover has been too comprehensive, making the pub too clean and polished. A feature of the pub's location – at a sharp road junction with large windows running the length of two sides around an island bar – means that much of the pub is too exposed for the comfort of some, bar two rooms at the back. On the plus side, there are real ales on the pumps and a decent selection of (principally New World) wines, and it's a friendly enough place. It's just a pity that it's become rather too generic for a pub by Hampstead Heath – let alone one opposite George Orwell's former flat and Joe Orton's favourite pick-up joint – should, by rights, be.

FEATURES:

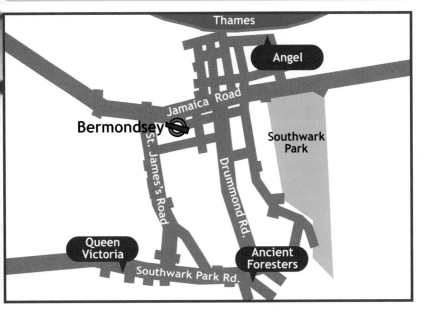

Ancient Foresters

RATING:

282 Southwark Park Road

SE16 2HB

020 7394 1633

Should you find yourselves in need of musical accompaniment in SE16, the Ancient Foresters seems the place to visit. The side room – with backdrop incorporating Sammy, Deano and Frank – brings the air of the Sands Hotel to Bermondsey and hosts a range of bands. Otherwise, this one's a fairly dependable pub – the sort of place where locals are always up for a bit of banter with the staff. Expect this one to fill up when Millwall are at home, but, as pubs (fairly) close to the New Den go, this one certainly makes the grade.

FEATURES:

Angel

RATING:

101 Bermondsey Wall East

SE16 4TY

020 7394 3214

After a period of closure, the Angel is serving once more. It's had a comprehensive refurbishment, which is thankfully sympathetic to the history of the place. Perhaps this pub is now ready to capitalise on its superb location. Whether you're sitting outside on the terrace or inside near a window, the Thames is impossible to ignore. Passing river traffic of various types and eras will catch your attention, as well as the very fine view towards Tower Bridge and beyond. There are a couple of pleasant (and fairly private) rooms near the bar downstairs and a handsome upstairs room with sofas, comfy chairs and historical pictures on the walls. A varied menu of main courses is available for less than a tenner, and the beer is Samuel Smith's usual range. After a dubious past, things are looking up for the Angel.

FEATURES:    HANDY FOR: Tower Bridge

Queen Victoria

RATING:

148 Southwark Park Road

SE16 3RP

020 7237 9904

A pub of such a vintage that the sign outside lists 'day trips' as one of the facilities on offer. We're not sure if their char-a-banc still heads off to Margate; it certainly didn't the day we were in, as the pub was packed. Venerable bar staff keep an eye on proceedings, as the punters watch the sport on TV or indulge in a bit of it themselves (pool table at the front, dartboard at the side). One for the locals perhaps, but judging from our visit newcomers won't have any problems (aside from finding a seat).

FEATURES:

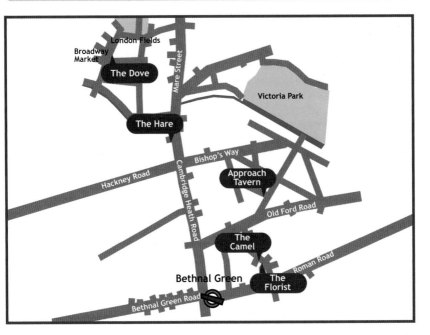

Approach Tavern

RATING:

47 Approach Road
E2 9LY
020 8980 2321

The Approach Tavern's had its up and downs over the years, but it has, in recent years, established itself as a firm favourite with the locals. The beer is pretty decent, with an excellent range of (mostly Fuller's) hand-pulled, plus a few Continentals on the other pumps – Czech beer being a speciality. Wine lovers are catered for too and there's not a bad menu if you're feeling peckish. The jukebox is pretty trendy, i.e. heavily retro – there are only so many times you can hear 'Hey Jude' of an evening – but, all in all, the Approach is a pretty decent package. There's a beer garden at the back and a terrace at the front, replete with awnings and patio heaters. The locals especially love to sit out front on a summer's evening shouting at their mates, which can be a bit irritating, but, if you avoid bank holiday weekends and summer evenings towards the end of the week, you won't be unhappy here.

FEATURES:

The Camel

RATING:

277 Globe Road
E2 0JD
020 8983 9888

If you like the nearby Florist, but find it getting a bit too crowded and noisy for you, then your best bet is to try here. Run by the same people, it's a smoke-free, family affair. The service is good, the food's good – really excellent pies – and there are a couple of ales from Adnams on the hand pumps. Understandably popular Sunday lunchtime.

FEATURES: HANDY FOR: Museum of Childhood

The Dove

RATING:

24 Broadway Market
E8 4QJ
020 7275 7617

Now well established, the Dove's Belgian theme is so well executed that it doesn't seem to be anything out of the ordinary any more. If you're in the mood for a seemingly endless range of excellent Belgian beers and some pretty decent food that's not twenty-first-century gastropub fare, then this is the place for you. The expansion of the premises a while ago means it rarely suffers the overcrowding it used to and with so many nooks and crannies to accommodate the clientele, it shouldn't take long to find a table. A reason to visit Hackney, the Dove is well worth the tramp up from Bethnal Green tube.

FEATURES:

The Florist

RATING:

255 Globe Road
E2 0JD
020 8981 1100

Numbering among its neighbours the London Buddhist Centre, a centre for Tibetan art and a longstanding vegetarian café, it's no surprise that this old boozer got made over a couple of years back. While not as painstakingly trendy as the bars a mile or so east, the Florist sticks to the standard bare floorboards and weathered leather furniture look. It's busier and noisier, in the evening, though, usually with someone having a go behind the DJ decks. Shame, then, that the choices behind the bar don't greatly inspire: it's the usual lager-y suspects. However, since the place makes a fuss about its cocktails, we perhaps should have opted for one of them. As for food, tapas are the order of the day here. As rejigged East End pubs go, not a bad one at all.

FEATURES: HANDY FOR: Museum of Childhood

fancyapint?

BETHNAL GREEN

The Hare

505 Cambridge Heath Rd
E2 9BU
020 7613 0519

RATING:

This pub's unprepossessing exterior hides an excellent local. A popular, friendly place. it serves decent beers – IPA on the hand pumps, for instance – and jolly good sarnies too. There's always a buzz of conversation going on and the sport on TV is not solely limited to the footy (although it will take precedence). In fact, more than one sort can sometimes be viewed on different tellies simultaneously, catering for a number of tastes. It's a thoroughly decent place, and we wish there were more like them.

FEATURES: **HANDY FOR:** Museum of Childhood

BLACKFRIARS

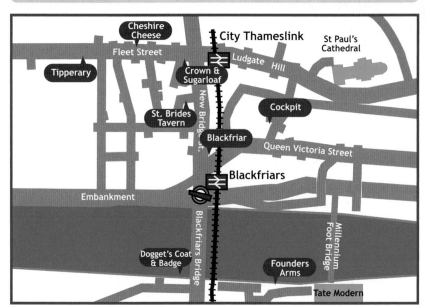

The Blackfriar

RATING:

174 Queen Victoria Street
EC4V 4EG
020 7236 5474

A cheat, but an honest cheat as the almost mediaeval appearance is an Arts & Crafts extravaganza on the site of an ancient priory. Inside, the eye delights at a thousand features and whether perching on a stool by the marbled bar or tucked into a semiprivate booth you feel it's a special place. Braying City suits make it a bit of an ordeal on weeknight evenings, although most of them are happy to cram shoulder-to-shoulder on the virtually table-and-chair-less pavement outside. Perhaps we'll be joining them as the Blackfriar has just anticipated legislation by becoming a smoke-free pub – 'full of character, not smoke' say the rather smug signs. Now that it's open on the weekends, you can visit it at a time when you can have a quiet pint and contemplate the wonderful interior. One to see.

FEATURES: HANDY FOR: St Paul's Cathedral, Tate Modern, Globe Theatre

The Cockpit

RATING:

7 Andrews Hill
EC4V 5BY
020 7248 7315

We usually avoid clichés like the plague (a cliché to us is like a red rag to a bull), but 'steeped in history' could have been minted for this hidden gem. Outside it says established 1787; inside, rebuilt in 1842 but had been Shakespeare's house in a 16th century incarnation. An odd-looking little place in a tangle of alleys. Count every bar stool and narrow bench and you'll never reach 30 seats, look up and ponder why the ceiling is 18 feet high, then open your eyes and listen for ghosts. The Cockpit is what it says it is – you're sitting where razor-spurred fighting cocks tore blood, feathers and very life from one another. Look up again and notice the narrow, balustraded galleries where the mob once roared. Appreciate the strutting, stuffed fighting bird over one door, carved models, prints and paintings wherever the eye roams. Feel London's sometimes unpalatable history wash over you. Nothing else really matters – it's a four-pinter from the moment you pass through the door. But for the record, it's quite homely. Working men mix with City workers and it can get busy at the usual times. Has hand-pulled beers, the food is pretty basic and the landlord is friendly and helpful.

FEATURES: HANDY FOR: St Paul's Cathedral

45

Crown & Sugarloaf

RATING:

26 Bride Lane

EC4Y 8DT

020 7353 3693

A little history first. The Punch Tavern on Fleet Street was originally called The Crown & Sugarloaf but was renamed in honour of the founders of *Punch* magazine, who met there. Back in the 1990s The Punch was relaunched but, because the co-owners fell out, the bar at the side was walled off. This Crown & Sugarloaf, then, is that walled-off bar – newly reopened in all its High Victorian grandeur. The Sam Smith's brewery – the Marmite of pub chains – are in charge here, so you're either going to love the fact that only their brews are available or you're not. Even if you're not a fan, it's worthwhile sticking your head around the door to marvel at the cut glass, mosaic floor and period furniture. This one started off in 2004 as a no-smoking pub, but the ban has since been lifted. Perhaps by allowing smoking again, it may entice more customers. It was certainly quiet on previous visits, lending a curiously aspic feel: the restoration was eye-catching, but it had the rather arid and lifeless feel of a museum exhibit rather than the buzz and energy of a living and breathing pub. Perhaps one day the original Crown & Sugarloaf will be reunited, but, given how the Punch Tavern is doing its best to transform itself into an 'informal gastropub' (translation: buffet), perhaps it's best to leave things alone for a while yet.

Doggett's Coat & Badge

RATING:

Blackfriars Bridge

SE1 9UD

020 7633 9081

This modern pub is spread over four floors, all of which are arranged to take advantage of the pub's position and the views of the river it commands. The service is friendly and the drink and food are pretty standard – decent, but not remarkable. If it's not crowded, it's pleasant to be in, but it does collect great hordes of tourists and office parties from time to time, because of its prime location.

FEATURES:

HANDY FOR: Tate Modern

Founders Arms

RATING:

52 Hopton Street
SE1 9JH
020 7928 1899

A modern Young's pub on the south side of the river very close to Blackfriars Bridge, it offers the usual Young's range of drinks and pretty decent food. Its location is what makes this place popular (and in summer it is very popular). It has a large terrace with seats and tables by the river, there are no major roads nearby (the heavy traffic on Blackfriars Bridge is shielded by the closer railway bridge) and there's a nice view of the dome of St Paul's rising above the squalid mass of buildings on the north bank, that is the Mermaid Theatre complex. The opening of the Tate Modern has increased the clientele substantially, especially with the Millennium Bridge connecting across to the City, so sometimes service can be a little slow. The addition of a proper coffee bar in the corner suggests they know who their main clientele are and where they're coming from. It's still less crowded, has much better beer and is better value for money than the Tate café ...

FEATURES: HANDY FOR: Tate Modern, Globe Theatre

St Brides Tavern

RATING:

1 Bridewell Place
EC4V 6AP
020 7353 1614

The Fleet Street area has quite a bevy of decent pubs that have not yet fully succumbed to the All Bar One invasion. There are places like the Olde Cheshire Cheese to siphon off the tourists, and trendier places such as Shaw's and the Evangelist for the young crowd. That leaves this little local secret for the aficionado. There's a tiny wood-panelled front bar that wouldn't look out of place in an Ealing Comedy. There are decently kept beers, and we've heard excellent things about the food. The place never gets too busy but caters well for its locals. Only one (slight) downside for us: the rather harsh lighting. Such a cosy little pub deserves something a bit softer.

Tipperary

RATING:

66 Fleet Street
EC4Y 1HT
020 7583 6470

A quaint, narrow, old (just had its 400th birthday) pub with a rather welcoming wood-panelled interior, impressive mirrors and a groovy, shamrock-design mosaic floor. In case you are interested in such things, there is a history of the pub on the wall outside. There's another room (with a bar upstairs) but the place is so narrow it's mostly standing room only. As you'd expect with a pub called the Tipperary, there's plenty of Guinness on tap, unpretentious food is served all day and a jolly time is to be had by all.

FEATURES:

Ye Olde Cheshire Cheese

RATING:

145 Fleet Street
EC4A 2BU
020 7353 6170

This pub is something of an institution on Fleet Street. As the sign outside the entrance ostentatiously states, it was rebuilt in 1667 (the year after the Great Fire, in case you don't recognise the date) and has tried, and mostly succeeded, to hang on to its distinguished heritage. Nooks and crannies abound; there are fireplaces; there's plenty of dark wood; and there's not a right angle in the place. Over the years, the clientele has had an equally distinguished and colourful past, but, now that the journalistic tradition that was Fleet Street has passed, this pub is really one for the tourists. The usual Sam Smith's offering is competently served and for some pub goers, this may be a drawback – not everybody likes Sam Smith's beers. Though, if you find yourself on Fleet Street, you should pop in and have a look.

FEATURES:

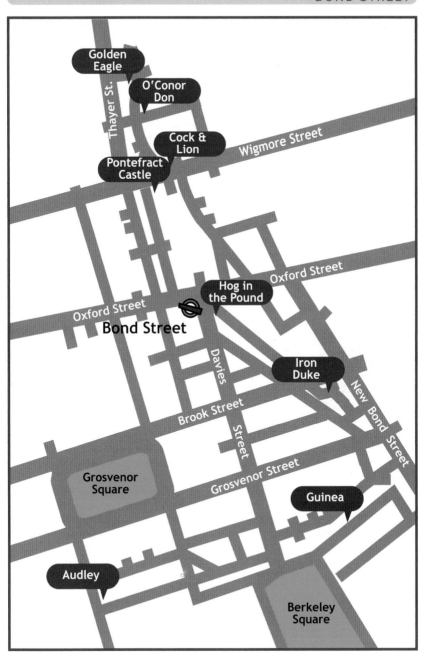

49

Audley

RATING:

41–43 Mount Street
W1K 2RP
020 7499 1843

Largish Mayfair pub that gives off the authentic Victorian feel that so many Wetherspoon refits are after. It's fairly grandiose with its chandeliers and leather banquettes and it aims clearly at the tourist target (note the sign outside for fish and chips). Given the swanky surroundings, we had this one down for a makeover. For the time being though, it's still a traditional pub.

FEATURES:

Cock & Lion

RATING:

62 Wigmore Street
W1U 2SB
020 7935 8727

Nestling parallel to Oxford Street, this pleasant little place offers refuge from the horrors of consumerism lurking just down the road, and a lovely pint to be getting on with. There are usually three beers on, with one of those a guest. The pub has regular sports coverage, though thankfully it never seems to be too packed. There can be outside seating when the rain stops too. The wide range of food on offer is proper pub food, and makes a nice change from the usual fish, chips and not a lot else. The prices aren't too frightening, although the kitchen or dumbwaiter struggles to cope at peak times. If pool is your thing, you'll be pleased to know that the upstairs sports room has a table. The staff know what they're doing, and how to pull a pint, but will leave you in peace, without stealing your still half-full glass away from the table as soon as you put it down, for the want of something better to do.

FEATURES: HANDY FOR: Wallace Collection

Golden Eagle

RATING:

59 Marylebone Lane
W1U 2NW
020 7935 3228

Excellent little pub – and we do mean little – that was spruced up not so long ago, retaining its original character and eliminating the dingy route to the toilets. The beer is excellent, a good range – e.g. St Austell's Tribute and Tinners – and well kept, which alone makes it worth a visit, and the wine list has recently been updated. It's not always open (especially at the weekend), but it is one to seek out, if only to see what a traditional English boozer used to be like. The place is usually brimming with people who enjoy a singsong around the upright piano, when the pianist's in (Tuesday, Thursday and Friday), but it can be undeservedly quiet when he's not. It's straight out of an Ealing comedy. I say!

FEATURES:

Guinea

RATING:

30 Bruton Place
W1J 6NR
020 7409 1728

Although the term 'pub & dining room' has recently been commandeered by reworked gastropubs, the time-honoured connotations of the term are fully evoked by this place. It's located just off Berkeley Square on Bruton Place – on a site where a pub has stood since the fifteenth century – and you'll find the Guinea Grill serving up award-winning pies and other traditional fare, and the separate Guinea Bar playing host to the local office staff. Due to the titchy size of the bar, this one can get tremendously busy during the week. However, on Saturday nights the bar is often deserted, so, if you're after a quiet night out in secluded surroundings, this could be the one for you.

FEATURES:

Hog in the Pound

RATING:

29 South Molton Street
W1K 5RF
020 7493 7720

This one should be familiar to any shopper on Oxford Street. Right by Bond Street Station and at the head of South Molton Street (favoured by clothes shoppers) it's a hard pub to miss. It's not much of a place, actually, carrying a pretty standard range of beers, including real ales on the hand pumps, and it pushes the food heavily – which is why many people come into this place. But it's nothing special and comes at a premium price – even if you use one of the discount cards scattered around the place. The service is OK and keeps up well with the relentless waves of footsore, hungry and thirsty people coming and going with their large carrier bags (and probably larger credit-card bills). Its location means it doesn't have to try too hard to pull in the punters and in the evenings, and it packs in crowds meeting up for a drink or two before moving on to clubs in the West End. On Friday nights it has a late (1 a.m.) licence and hosts karaoke.

FEATURES:

Iron Duke

RATING:

11 Avery Row
W1K 4AL
020 7629 1643

It's had a lick of paint and some new furniture to go with the name change. It's still a pretty small pub (no building work in this refurbishment), but the well-kept Fuller's beers, good traditional pub food and quick and friendly service haven't changed the drinking experience. The usual crowd of local workers still frequent it, the atmosphere is still the same and we're relieved that it's not been altered beyond recognition, as is so often the case after a refurbishment. It can still be a hard pub to find, hence the common sight of chaps on mobiles outside the pub barking out directions to their chums. Maybe not one to go out of your way for, but in a rather exclusive part of town it's nice to stumble across a relatively down-to-earth pub.

FEATURES:

O'Conor Don

RATING:

88 Marylebone Lane
W1U 2PZ
020 7935 9311

One of the few Irish places that are not Irish theme pubs, this is a hostelry that does an honest job of serving good food and drink with an Irish theme. The service is friendly, including table service in the bar downstairs. The food is great – especially in the upstairs dining room – and the Guinness (it goes without saying, really) is excellent. It gets crowded towards the end of the week, so either go earlier in the week or book to go in the restaurant. The bar food is pretty impressive too. We love it. (Not open weekends.)

FEATURES:

Pontefract Castle

RATING:

71 Wigmore Street
W1U 1QB
020 7486 4941

A large pub on several floors, it tends to get packed with office workers weekday evenings, shoppers during shop-opening times at weekends and then shop workers relaxing after the day's mayhem. The layout is designed to get as many people in as possible (especially the ground floor), so it's not really a place for a relaxing pint. Given the crowds, you are constantly moving out of the way to allow access to the bar, but it is a little more relaxed upstairs. However, it's quite a handy place to meet up in, since it's easy to find and there is food to sustain you if high-octane shopping has worn you down. The nonsmoking downstairs bar seems to show a side of Pontefract we never knew existed – a Spanish-style bar. It's available for hire and can be quiet when the rest of the pub is heaving.

FEATURES:

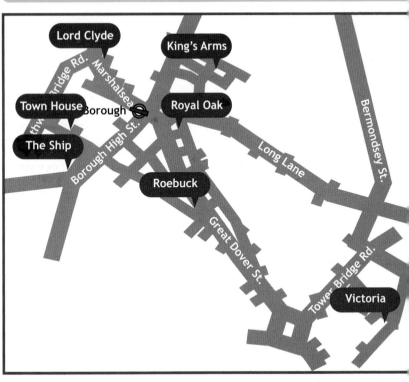

King's Arms

RATING:

65 Newcomen Street
SE1 1YT
020 7407 1132

A quiet, comfortable pub a short walk away from London Bridge and Borough stations, the King's Arms has Courage Best and Directors on tap, among others. The service is excellent and the clientele a good mixture of locals and people who work nearby. The big TV is there for big sporting occasions, but otherwise tucked well away. The old-fashioned decoration with large windows, pictures on the walls and sparing use of ornaments makes for a surprisingly stylish interior, and there is a fireplace for winter evenings. Food is typical pub grub and cheap with it (available 12–3 p.m.). Give it a try.

FEATURES:

Lord Clyde

RATING:

27 Clennam Street

SE1 1ER

020 7407 3397

The Lord Clyde is a gem of a pub tucked away on what must be one of the tiniest streets in London. It's a welcoming place with friendly staff, a good atmosphere and a fine selection of real ales. An inn has stood on this site for almost 300 years and the current building is wonderfully preserved as rebuilt in 1913, featuring glazed tiles, wood panelling, brass fittings and long leather seats. The pub has been run by the Fitzpatrick family since 1956, and the landlady offers a menu of home-cooked English fare. If you need a literary incentive to come here, you might want to know that the Lord Clyde is located close to the original site of the Tabard Inn, where Chaucer's pilgrims started out towards Canterbury. The young Dickens also lodged nearby so that he could visit his father in the debtors prison at Marshalsea. Unfortunately, it's now getting to be a victim of its own success, with many more people flocking to this excellent boozer. Consequently, it is now getting rather crowded and it sometimes takes an age to get served.

FEATURES:

Roebuck

RATING:

50 Great Dover Street

SE1 4YG

020 7357 7324

Regular visitors to the Fancyapint? site might undergo *déjà vu* while reading this review. Why? The Roebuck is another refurb in the predictable style consisting of leather sofas, exposed floorboards and unobtrusive dance music – hell, you know the routine by now. Gastro-ish main courses can be enjoyed for around £10 and imported lagers on tap await, along with a couple of ales. The Roebuck is definitely a smart, relaxing pub aimed at a certain audience who clearly love it. After all, Newington Borough is hardly Clapham (yet) and there aren't many places of this kind nearby. For us, however, it is slightly predictable, but the lively atmosphere means it still receives a solid three-pint rating.

FEATURES:

The Royal Oak

RATING:

44 Tabard Street
SE1 4JU
020 7357 7173

A wonderful Victorian pub in the heart of Borough, the Royal Oak is a winner in every department. It serves a selection of excellent ales (including mild, pale, best and Christmas ale and porter in winter) by Harvey's of Lewes, and also offers a very good menu; on our weekday visit, we enjoyed an excellent steak-and-ale pie with side vegetables for less than a fiver. The wine list is pretty decent too. The pub has the feel of a vibrant local rather than just an after-office drinker, with a good mix of people who are in no hurry to leave. On this evidence, why would they? And now it's open at the weekends, great!

FEATURES:

Reviewers' Award Winner 2004

The Ship

RATING:

68 Borough Road
SE1 1DX
020 7403 7059

Home to some of our favourite drinkeries, Borough has an unusually high concentration of top-class boozers. The Ship, located a short walk from Borough tube, has some of the features that make other nearby pubs so great: a relaxed but lively atmosphere, a truly varied crowd of punters who live and work nearby, a decent range of beers (a good selection of Fuller's finest) and a healthy disrespect for pretension. Don't be put off by the somewhat 'estatey' exterior of this place, inside it's a good old-fashioned boozer. The décor's a little on the faded side, but this all adds to the atmosphere. There's pretty much something for everyone here: a dartboard at the back, a quiet seating area at the top (with its own bar, although this wasn't in operation when we were last there) and the main bar, which, in addition to great beer, was serving up a pretty good selection of tunes (we didn't spot a jukebox anywhere). If there were international standards in 'decent' and 'solid', then this pub would be able to display its certification proudly.

FEATURES:

Town House

RATING:

125 Great Suffolk Street
SE1 1PQ
020 7407 1312

The Town House is friendlier than some other pubs we could mention nearby, even though it's also a locals' pub. It's got decent beer on tap and regular music nights, as well as pub food. On occasion we have also witnessed what can only be described as an over-sixties' knees-up/karaoke evening, with the place full to the rafters with singing and music. A definitive thriving backstreet local.

FEATURES:

The Victoria

RATING:

68–70 Pages Walk
SE1 4HL
020 7237 3248

Located on the same street as UK's leading supplier of heating and plumbing products, the Victoria is a cracking boozer. The beautifully preserved Truman's exterior gives way to an island bar with comfy leather banquettes. Things are governed over by your archetypal friendly landlord: all the regulars get a greeting that's almost as friendly as those he reserves for newcomers. As for drinks, we stuck to London Pride, but were nearly swayed by the fine selection of spirits topping the bar. We didn't have the chance to sample the food, but the simple lunchtime menu (sandwiches, salads etc.) looks worth chancing. All in all, a fine pub and one all but the most nervous of north Londoners should cross the Thames and visit.

FEATURES:

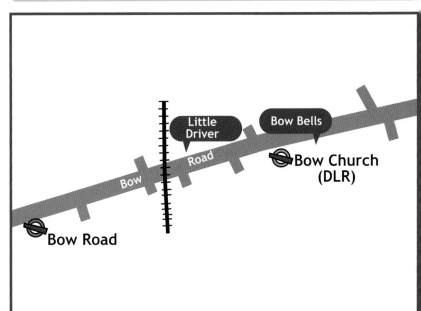

Bow Bells

RATING:

116 Bow Road

E3 3AA

020 8981 7317

It looks a bit dingy on the outside and the surrounding area is a bit offputting, but don't let that worry you. This is an excellent local. It has an interesting range of beers on the hand pumps and an extensive, value-for-money food menu. It also offers big-screen TV, pool, a function room and, curiously, a jukebox, which wasn't switched off even during the footy (surprisingly, it didn't spoil anything for anybody). An interesting mix of locals frequent the place and the service is prompt, friendly and attentive. Every so often a coachload of tourists pops into the place. We're not sure why. Maybe it's something to do with Bow Bells (except they're in the Wren church in Cheapside in the City). Nevertheless, the tourists like it too. They won't be disappointed: it's a top boozer.

FEATURES:

Little Driver

RATING:

125 Bow Road
E3 2AN

This smallish pub can get a bit noisy (or lively – depending on your point of view) and the big telly is sometimes intrusive, but it's still good for a reasonable pint in the East End. When the telly's not on, they usually have music, but it's not overpowering. They also have a pool table. Reasonable range of beers, genial staff and friendly locals make this a not unreasonable experience. Give it a go if you're in the area.

FEATURES:

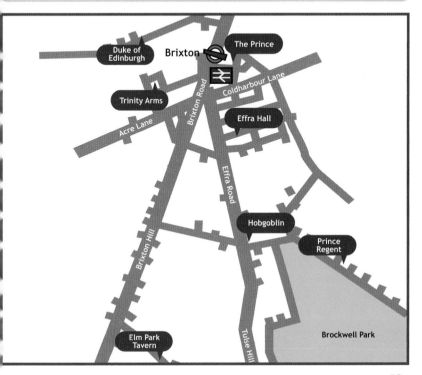

The Duke of Edinburgh

RATING:

204 Fearndale Road
SW9 8AG
020 7326 0301

Previously the sort of pub wedded to attracting the pre-clubbing crowd (think full-on banging techno on a weekday afternoon), the Duke of Edinburgh seems to have calmed down somewhat and is now putting in a bid to be everyone's favourite local. Despite the piss-lager-poor choice of beers, the service is friendly and the live DJ seems to have been replaced by a variety of tamer (and, presumably, more popular) entertainments, including a weekly pub quiz and pool competition. Add to that a beer garden, which Rabelais's characters would have felt happy in (translation: it's very, very big), complete with giant barbecue in summer, and you end up with a boozer that's really not bad at all.

FEATURES:    HANDY FOR: Brixton Academy

Effra Hall

RATING:

38a Kellet Road
SW2 1EB
020 7274 4180

A popular boozer that's worth the walk to get there. It's not the biggest pub in the land, but it manages to cram around the island bar a space for live music, a pool table and a wide cross section of Brixtonians. A lively night out guaranteed.

FEATURES:

Elm Park Tavern

76 Elm Park
SW2 2UB

Despite its unprepossessing exterior, the Elm Park Tavern is a comfortably shabby local boozer with a welcoming atmosphere. Tucked away on a quiet corner among Brixton Hill's myriad Victorian terraces, it boasts a clientele that is composed almost entirely of locals and it's rare that you won't find a seat, even during the raucous Thursday-night quiz, which is as close as this pub gets to being packed out. The back bar holds an unassuming television (a wall-sized screen is wheeled out for sporting events), and there's a jukebox in both rooms. The bar has a small range of both lager and bitter on tap, and service is friendly and unhurried. No food is served, although having a takeaway delivered to your table seems to be a popular alternative.

FEATURES:

Hobgoblin

RATING:

95 Effra Road
SW2 1DF
020 7501 9671

This place has long been uncertain whether it wants to be a club or a pub. A refit (which didn't change the appearance much) saw it veer further in the club direction. Its selling points are now definitely the regular DJs, late licences and comedy nights. Really it's now an entertainment venue, i.e. a big room with a pub attached, and it's certainly less of place to go for a quiet drink. That said, it does still have a large beer garden where on a summer Sunday afternoon you can enjoy the sun and traffic fumes. A hardworking mix, but singular and with a varied appeal.

FEATURES:

The Prince

RATING:

469 Brixton Road
SW9 8HH
020 7501 9061

Second relaunch in under a year for the old Prince of Wales, so will The Prince last longer than Harlem? On the basis of our visit it's probably got a chance. 'Gastro pub and club', this one's calling itself. We can't vouch for the 'club' but the 'gastro' part of the equation was pretty good, with a menu that didn't stray into the world of ostrich steak or an amuse of fennel. With little of note on tap, drink options include a long list of shooters and cocktails. There are big plans for this one (including talk of a private members' bar), so we'll keep an eye on it and see how things pan out (can things really get that swish with a KFC next door?). For the moment, though, worth a look.

FEATURES: HANDY FOR: Brixton Academy

Prince Regent

RATING:

69 Dulwich Road
SE24 0NJ
020 7274 1567

The Prince Regent has recently undergone something of a transformation and is now (hurrah!) a jolly nice place to have a drink in what could be thought of as a less than salubrious area. While it verges on middle-class gastropub territory, we were nonetheless impressed with the jugs of fresh flowers everywhere, swanky-looking dining area and tempting menu. There are second-hand books for sale in aid of the local Green Party, and, if all this is starting to sound a bit too right-on for you, you can escape outside with a beer (they have quite a nice selection of real ales and Belgian lagers, if you like that sort of thing) and eavesdrop on the yummy mummies. All in all, a great place for a lazy Sunday lunch, and there's a good pub quiz too, we hear. We say: bravo! Well done, that pub.

FEATURES:

Trinity Arms

RATING:

45 Trinity Gardens
SW9 8DR
020 7274 4544

If what you're after in Brixton is an unassuming pub rather than a style bar, this is probably your best bet. Off the main drag in a quiet Victorian square, it's a tad removed from the sights and smells of Brixton centralis. Well-kept beer, comfortable interior and a beer garden. A good local.

FEATURES:

Visitors' Award (Overall Winner) 2004

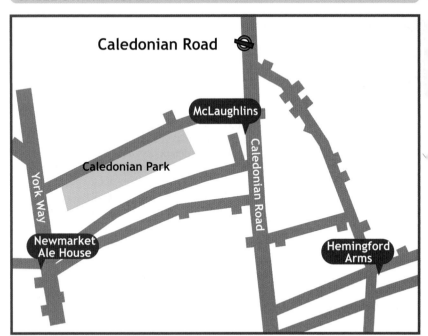

Caledonian Road

McLaughlins

Caledonian Park

Caledonian Road

York Way

Newmarket
Ale House

Hemingford
Arms

Hemingford Arms

RATING:

158 Hemingford Road
N1 1DF
020 7607 3303

Tucked away in the affluent niche of Barnsbury, the Hemingford Arms can be a pleasant spot for a drink. Its cosy interior has a plethora of objects hanging from the ceiling and on the walls: these include a set of hickory golf clubs, film posters, trumpets and the odd Methodist church sign. These appear to be a genuine assortment of oddities rather than, as so often elsewhere, a cynical effort to give the place a forced quirkiness. Five beers are available on the hand pumps in addition to the usual range of draught beer, and reasonable Thai food's on offer. The downside is the service, which can range from adequate to rude. Sadly, on our last visit we were kept waiting while seemingly every regular was served, regardless of the fact that they hadn't been waiting as long and when our time arrived the pints were thrown down in front of us with contempt.

FEATURES:

McLaughlins

RATING:

427 Caledonian Road
N7 9BG

Set among the *embourgeoisement* of the Cally Road, McLaughlins stands firm as all around it transforms into organic bakeries and holistic crystal shops. A nice little boozer, serving the usuals on tap, and, rather excitingly, Ireland's legendary Tayto Crisps, McLaughlins remains very much a traditional boozer, decked out in nice dark woods and spotlessly clean. There are plenty of screens available for the football and the racing on a Saturday, keeping their punters happy in the process. The place has a number of options in case football isn't your bag, with a pool table, dartboard and jukebox to keep you occupied. Cheery Irish fellas, burly off-duty cabbies from the local hackney carriage offices (who all seemed to have Tenerife tans on our visit) and a few random punters having a pint and a read of their papers keep the place lively, but not boisterous. Although we'd never set foot in the place, we were welcomed and cheerily accommodated by the locals, who didn't seem to mind some new faces in the place. Sitting very close to Pentonville Prison, all in all it wouldn't be a bad spot in which to have your first pint on release.

FEATURES:

The Newmarket Ale House

RATING:

17 York Way
N7 9QG
020 7485 4738

Perched at the top of York Way as it descends to King's Cross, the Newmarket bears signs of the redevelopments down the road. Proclaiming itself as an 'Art Deco Pub' might be stretching things a bit, but this one's managed that difficult trick of smartening itself up to attract new punters, while not doing anything too drastic to scare away the regulars. Not the greatest range of drink you'll ever see behind a bar, but the service was friendly enough, and, if the sport shown on the TV isn't to your satisfaction, you might find something of interest on the bookshelves at the back (everything from Henry Fielding to Stephen Jay Gould when we were last in).

FEATURES:

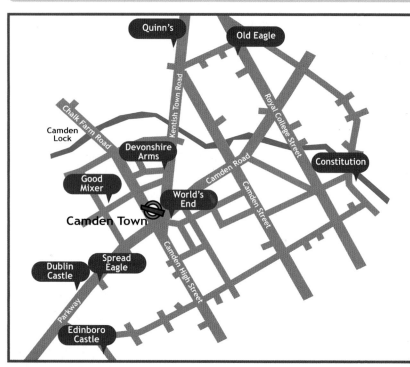

Quinn's

Old Eagle

Chalk Farm Road

Kentish Town Road

Royal College Street

Camden Lock

Devonshire Arms

Constitution

Good Mixer

Camden Road

World's End

Camden Street

Camden Town

Dublin Castle

Spread Eagle

Camden High Street

Parkway

Edinboro Castle

The Constitution

RATING:

42 St Pancras Way
NW1 0QT
020 7387 4805

The Constitution is predominantly a geezers' pub, hidden away from the market-going throngs and hence unmolested by gastropubism and similar twenty-first-century afflictions. The beer is well kept with Adnams and regular guest beers offered on the hand pumps by friendly bar staff. The clientele were friendly enough, but most of them were watching the match on the telly anyway. A good no-nonsense local.

FEATURES:

Devonshire Arms

RATING:

33 Kentish Town Road
NW1 8NL
020 7284 0562

You don't come here for the drink – this is one of Earth's last bastions of gothdom. If you're into that sort of thing you'll be happy (if that's the right word) here. They take their music very seriously, which suits a lot of the locals and the many goth tourists who come here (they're easy to spot: they're the ones who eye everyone else nervously). A bunch of older locals also drink here, adding a quaint touch of banality and accenting the doom-laden atmosphere of the rest of the clientele. It's strictly for the pierced (unless you're an older local), and there's a door policy in the evening, to prevent 'normals' coming in and diluting the atmosphere. Nevertheless, anywhere you get a pentagram drawn on the head of your Guinness is OK by us.

FEATURES:

The Dublin Castle

RATING:

94 Parkway
NW1 7AN
020 7485 1773

As other pubs move on, smarten up and strip down, the Dublin Castle remains. A hangover from the music scene of the eighties and nineties, this boozer attracts indie kids, rockers and tourists who come to convince themselves Camden isn't a shell of its former 'alternative' self. It's a definite weekend pub, and the small backroom has been a music venue for many a year and great shakes are made that Madness, among others, began their career here. We hasten to add that it also holds itself up as a good pub, too. Not one for a quiet night, this is a busy, raucous place and is a must for anyone looking for an antidote to predictable gastropubs or the All Bar One-type scene.

FEATURES:

Edinboro Castle

RATING:

57 Mornington Terrace

NW1 7RU

020 7255 9651

Well, the pool table has gone and the soft furnishings have been brought in, but it's still a decent enough pub. Slightly creeping to the gastro side of things, this one (like its near neighbour The Victoria) is still, though, first and foremost a pub. Add on a large beer garden (with a barbecue) and a pleasant atmosphere and you have a more relaxed drinking environment than you'll find in the pubs closer to Camden Market. And that *is* how you spell it.

FEATURES:

Good Mixer

RATING:

30 Inverness Street

NW1 7HJ

020 7916 6176

If you remember Menswear, chances are you've had a few jars in the Good Mixer; in the early 1990s, it was the Britpop crowd's boozer of choice. Things have moved on since then, but the Good Mixer has hardly changed. It's a bare place with a pretty limited choice of beers, relying more on its reputation than anything tangible to attract punters. The pool tables at the back are often occupied, but it might be worth dropping in if you fancy a game.

FEATURES:

Old Eagle

251 Royal College St
NW1 9LU
020 7482 6021

A warm and welcoming pub on any day but especially welcoming on a cold, wet, miserable day in November. Even though it's had the now traditional 'gastro' treatment (settees, stripped-down furniture, 'art' on the walls etc.), it's only a nod to the genre and the pub is largely unblemished by it. It's a genuine, friendly, local boozer that serves decent, well-priced drink and food. The beer's pretty good and the service is excellent – all in all, an offering that's rare in many locations, but especially welcome in Camden.

FEATURES:

Quinn's

RATING:

65 Kentish Town Road
NW1 8NY
020 7267 8240

Quinn's is a large, friendly pub boasting an amazing selection of beer on tap and in bottles. When we visited, a good atmosphere prevailed with some people watching football, some enjoying the Sunday roast, and others just chatting; the pub is spacious enough to accommodate all of these without difficulty.

FEATURES:

69

The Spread Eagle

RATING:

141 Albert Street

NW1 7NB

020 7267 1410

This is a very normal boozer for this area – not themed, not stripped out, not run down and, as a result, it can feel slightly out of place here in Camden. A decent pub, it's well looked after and up to Young's usual high standards – as are also the food and the drink – and a recent refit has smartened things up a tad (though the changes aren't too wholesale). Tellies keep you up to date with the sport and there are some comfy-looking corners to hide away in and some outdoor seating for when the sun comes out. Possibly the most un-Camden of all the pubs in NW1, the Spread Eagle is a safe bet for a couple of drinks.

FEATURES:

World's End

RATING:

174 Camden High Street

NW1 0NE

020 7482 1932

This rather large pub is really two pubs. The front is the original pub, with its cosy booths and fireplaces. The back is a later two-storey addition with a large central bar and balcony areas for sitting and watching the crowds. As it's directly over Camden's Underworld Club (they are both tied together), it can get very full if there's a band on, and consequently rowdy and rambunctious. Last time we were in was a Saturday night and it was a heaving mess. Six deep at the bar and so loud you can't hear yourself think – or order a drink. They do have bouncers on the door, but there was little sign of their turning anyone away – well, we got in. It's less uncomfortable during the day than at night, but there are better places nearby of an evening. Look upon it as Camden's answer to Disneyland and you're almost there.

FEATURES:

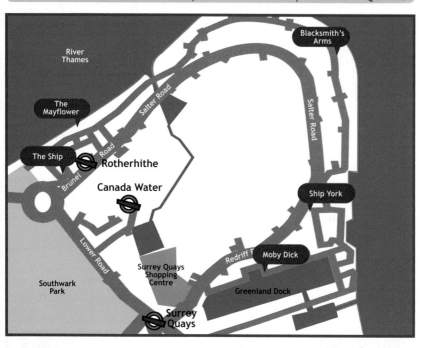

Blacksmith's Arms

RATING:

257 Rotherhithe Street

SE16 5EJ

020 7237 1349

This is a fine local and has served the area very well over the years. It hasn't been affected too much by the influx of people filling the many developments in the surrounding area over the last few years, although it's moved upmarket a little. This 'Tudor-bethan' pub has a nice oak-panelled 1930s interior, which hasn't been too messed about with, simply spruced up, giving it a clubby, comfortable air. Relaxed during the week – picking up refugees from the nearby Hilton – it does get rather busier at the weekend, when it's pretty much a local affair. There's a good range of well-kept Fuller's ales on the hand pumps, with a pretty reasonable wine list for those who aren't into pints, accompanied by an extensive Thai menu and some traditional pub grub.

FEATURES:

The Mayflower

RATING:

117 Rotherhithe Street
SE16 4NF
020 7237 4088

A tourist favourite, it's ancient, it's quirky, it's got a riverside terrace, a restaurant upstairs and it's surrounded by lots of old (historic, even) stuff, making the area around it look rather like a village. It's a pub favoured by Americans looking for their roots and if you sit on the terrace in summer you'll hear the word '*Mayflower*' time and time again from the river-tour boats' commentary as they chug past. It serves a decent pint, the food is pretty good and the service is usually fast, polite and friendly. A tourist favourite it may be, it's a favourite of ours too – other pubs could take lessons.

FEATURES:

Moby Dick

RATING:

6 Russell Place, Greenland Dock
SE16 7PL
020 7231 6719

This large pub on a dockside, just in from the river, hasn't really changed much in recent history, maybe edged upmarket a little along with the surrounding area. The food looks good, the beer's more than palatable with a good range of Fuller's excellent ales on tap (including Festival Mild when we were last in), and the wine list should cater for most tastes. Lovely place to spend a nice afternoon or evening, sitting outside and enjoying the sunshine reflecting off the water. It's the sort of pub that, if you're here, it's hard to leave, although that may be because everything's so far away.

FEATURES:

The Ship

RATING:

39 St Marychurch Street
SE16 4JE
020 7237 4103

A nice-looking boozer from around the thirties, it's a quiet, professional pub, serving its locals well. Obviously, Young's fare is on offer and when it's done well, as it is here, then that's OK with us. Busier in summer, owing to the outside seating and its proximity to the river. It's been tidied up and the fresh paint fairly gleams. It's a good family local pub and one we're happy to recommend.

FEATURES:

The Ship York

RATING:

Rotherhithe Street
SE16 5LJ

A locals' pub that was here well before the latest redevelopments (looks like it's a thirties building). This is a big place providing reasonable food and drink and decent, friendly service for its clientele. This pub is immaculate – the carpet is so clean you can eat off it and the owners (and the clientele) are obviously proud of it. The locals are friendly, the landlord and landlady are very welcoming, there are quizzes and so forth, and the beer's pretty decent. We like this pub for all these reasons and wish we lived nearby so it could be our local.

FEATURES:

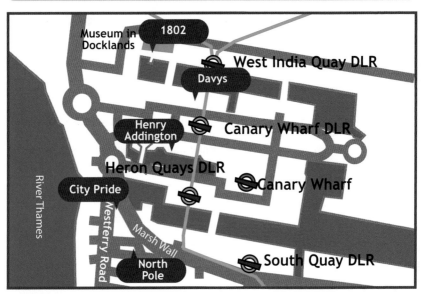

1802

Museum in Docklands No. 1 Warehouse
West India Quay
E14 4AL
0870 444 3886

It's not often that you'll decide to visit a museum for a pint, but, in the case of 1802, you might do just that. The place bills itself as 1802 Bar, Lounge and Dining, and 99% of the people who come here are here for the food – and pretty decent grub it is too. 1802's dockside location combined with decent weather can make a visit just for liquid refreshment and pleasant conversation a very worthwhile proposition. There are a few beers on tap and a large range of bottled beers from all over the world. Oenophiles are pretty well catered for with a decent, if pricey, wine list. The prices are high, but all purchases in the bar fund the museum. Word of warning: good weather can cause the quayside to be packed to bursting point with punters; at weekends it does tend to be quieter, although bank holidays can also see crowds return. With its waterside location, broad, traffic-free pavements and terraces with table service, West India Quay is one of the few London areas that truly emulates a Continental-style ambience. And, if cultural curiosity gets the better of you, the museum is well worth a visit.

FEATURES: HANDY FOR: Museum in Docklands

City Pride

RATING:

15 West Ferry Road
E14 8JH
020 7987 3516

This pub will be familiar to the sadistic among you who enjoy the self-inflicted punishment of the participants in the London Marathon. The course of the marathon winds its way around the pub, putting the pub in a prime viewing position. During this time, the pub is festooned and sports live music and other entertainment. For the rest of the year, it provides refreshment to the ever-increasing number of office workers in Canary Wharf and its environs, a job it does competently enough. A very extensive and cheapish menu is partner to the unremarkable range of beers (only one ale on the hand pumps) and wines on offer. It has a very large beer garden and terrace with views of Docklands and the river which, when the hurly-burly of Canary Wharf and the other quays gets too much for you, provide a welcome respite.

FEATURES:

Davy's

RATING:

31-35 Fisherman's Walk
E14 4DH
020 7363 6630

Davy's may well have been established in 1870, but the current manifestations of Davy's outlets do no more than précis Identikit Britain. You could well be in a Davy's, All Bar One, Fine Line or Pitcher & Piano and not know the difference (apart from a smattering of sawdust in the case of a Davy's), such is the predictability of the genre nowadays. Perhaps the only reason you would choose one over the other is geographical, but they're all located here anyway – so how to decide? For sure, Davy's has its Wallop, Lager and Bitter, but the quaint renaming of produce does not constitute a memorable drinking experience. Davy's is, indeed, a purveyor of fine wines and spirits and the service is universally good. But, when it comes to pub-going experiences, it's somewhat synthetic, a bit too olde-worlde for its own good and especially ironic when it's in a location like Canary Wharf. In summer when you get the sun on the north side of Canary Wharf, the waterside tables are worthwhile, but for the rest of the time you'll probably be here because someone else decreed it.

FEATURES:

Henry Addington

RATING:

Mackenzie Walk, 4 Canary Wharf
E14 4PH
020 7513 0921

Taken over by Nicholson's not long ago, this pub tries to be a bit of everything for the lads at Canary Wharf. It's got TVs (and projection screen) for the sport, a bit of a disco, a bit of lunchtime food and a waterside bit for when the weather's nice. It's not a particularly remarkable pub (although it did used to bill itself as having the second longest bar in England), but if you're nearby it's worth popping in for a swift half or two. It's not quite as 'City' as some of the nearby places and at the weekend it's a bit quieter than a lot of bars in the area. And, as it's Nicholson's, at least the standard of food and drink is pretty good.

FEATURES:

North Pole

RATING:

74 Manilla Street
E14 8LG
020 7987 5443

Quite simply, this is a top local. The service is polite, fast and friendly. It offers some fairly standard, but well-kept beers on the hand pumps – Pride, Pedigree etc. And everyone in the pub seems to know everyone else, but somehow they never seem to make you feel left out. An excellent preference to the unimaginative bardom in the dockside areas. Not open all the time (especially at weekends and, when we were in on a Saturday night, it was woefully empty).

HANDY FOR: Museum in Docklands

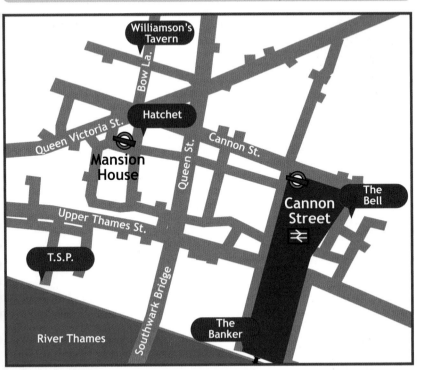

The Banker

2 Cousin Lane
EC4R 3TE
020 7283 5206

We weren't expecting this one, tucked, as it is, down a side street under the shadow of Cannon Street station, to be much of a revelation. We were wrong. Spacious pub, well lit, cracking conservatory area overlooking the river. And reasonable outside seating also with river views. OK, if you look too closely you have a freight-loading bay in your eye line but, hey, river views of London while having a few beers are not to be sniffed at. On a sunny day, the terrace is usually crowded if you don't get your beach towel out first thing. Recommend you sneak off to get there early if it's a nice day.

FEATURES:

The Bell

RATING:

29 Bush Lane
EC4R 0AN
020 7626 7560

Not so long ago, this was one of many old-style, untouched, City pubs, but now the Bell's something of an endangered species. Its tiny size means it gets packed to the gunwales at commuting times, but the service is prompt and polite and the range of real ale on the hand pumps is pretty well looked after. It claims to be one of the few houses that survived the Great Fire of London in 1666, and much of the original structure of the building survives. It was even a riverside pub when the Thames was wider. It's fairly modern inside now, though it's still half-timbered throughout. In any case, the time-warp interior décor is in keeping with the old-fashioned service and we don't want it to change a thing. Devotees of style bars and gastropubs won't be battering down the doors to get in, but if you want a pub that harks back to times past you should give it a go. The recent introduction of two TV screens has changed things somewhat, but not so much as you might expect. See it while you can and before the interior ends up in the Museum of London as an example of twentieth-century social history.

FEATURES:

The Hatchet

RATING:

28 Garlick Hill
EC4V 2BA
020 7236 0720

Lovely little pub that all too often gets very crowded at the customary lunch and pre-commute times. Outside of these hours, good beers and pleasant bar staff provide a welcome break form the hurly-burly of the City. Open at the usual City times during the week and afternoons on Saturday.

T.S.P. (The Samuel Pepys)

RATING:

Stew Lane, High Timber Street
EC4V 3PT
020 7634 9841

There was a Samuel Pepys here years ago, a bare-floorboards-and-oak-beams place in a Victorian warehouse. It was a dark place spread over a couple of floors, where the only view of the river was from a small balcony, which got laughably crowded in summer as people tried to get some air. Now the warehouse has been completely redeveloped, retaining the original shell, and the Pepys has been reinstated in more or less the same place with a number of improvements. The spit-and-sawdust has been replaced with a brighter, more contemporary interior, there's a lot more light and better views of the river, but still just the one balcony The place is decent enough. There are Cask Marque ales and Belgian beers on the pumps and a range of bottled beers. The emphasis is on food and wines now, catering for lunchtime punters from the City, and this is probably what you'd come here for. Yes, you can come here and just have a pint, but really this place is geared for the hungry.

FEATURES:

Williamson's Tavern

RATING:

1 Groveland Court, Bow Lane
EC4M 9EH
020 7248 5750

Whatever is said about this being London's oldest excise licence and a watering hole since shortly after the Great Fire, the reality is that most of the structure dates from the 1930s. But it's kept the magic. The location is superb – tucked in a courtyard off an alley from Bow Lane through the magnificent wrought-iron gates presented by William III after he'd enjoyed what must have been a particularly fine pint. It's basically two interlinked bars. The smaller front bar boasts probably the most uncomfortable benches ever designed. The back bar includes a separate dining area with decent food from snacks to full meals and charming staff dispensing the beers. It can get busy – and nowhere round here is safe from the City suit – but seats and a quietish corner can usually be found if required. Oh, and did we mention the ghosts? At least one long-serving barmaid flatly refuses to do evening shifts after one experience too many. And it's said that police-dog patrols have the devil's own job to persuade their canine chums to venture anywhere near the place.

FEATURES: HANDY FOR: St Paul's Cathedral

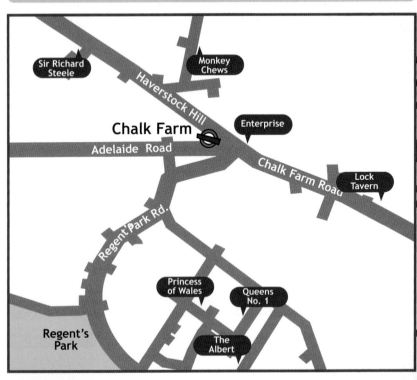

The Albert

RATING:

11 Princess Road
NW1 8JR
020 7722 1886

Not surprising for the area, the Albert is an old pub that had an upgrade a few years ago. With good, fresh food being served at inflated Primrose Hill prices, it would be easy to argue that this is a pub bordering on gastro territory. However, it's still distinctively a pub, even if the stripped interior and country-kitchen tables simply mean a slightly more modern version. Plenty of old-school locals still pop by and the atmosphere is unpretentious and welcoming. A great beer garden, complete with an apple tree in the middle, only adds to the Albert's charms. Relaxed and pleasant – it's a very good pub for this neck of the woods.

FEATURES:

The Enterprise

RATING:

2 Haverstock Hill

NW3 2BL

020 7485 2659

An honest pub with none of the pub theme-park style of décor you seem to get in this area. There's a strong Irish literary theme to the décor – pictures of numerous notables adorn the walls and there are poetry evenings continuing the literary tradition. A large band of regulars, supplemented by visitors to the upstairs events frequent this place, but it is a place where you could sit alone and quietly read a paper or have a full-on night out with your mates – this place takes it all in its stride. A decent range of drink is on offer, including stuff like Wieckse Witte and Affligem, and the service is OK too.

FEATURES:

Lock Tavern

RATING:

35 Chalk Farm Road

NW1 8AJ

020 7482 7163

Once an old spit-and-sawdust affair, it was bought by DJ Jon Carter and chums and is now more in keeping with the trendsetters of Camden. With its designer black interior, ever-changing DJ sets and a mix-and-match menu, the place could easily have ended up too self-consciously hip for it's own good. It hasn't, though. The bar staff know what they're doing and, even if there's an air of studied cool about some of the punters, they're not the sort of crowd who'll stare at you if you're not sporting an old-skool Adidas top. Plenty of room inside and outside (including a garden and roof terrace), but come early, as it gets filled to capacity at the weekend. All in all, a fine advert for the rejuvenation of old pubs. If only they kept hold of that MP3 jukebox. Oh, and the beer's good, too.

FEATURES:

Monkey Chews

RATING:

2 Queens Crescent
NW5 4EP
020 7267 6406

It would be a travesty to describe Monkey Chews as anything less than a really great place to spend an evening – the sort of place you can go, intending to have just a drink or two, and end up staying until closing time. It's a clever and modern take on the British pub, with friendly service, a decent array of drinks (cocktails a speciality), while the food served, both in the main bar area and in a more meal-oriented backroom, surpasses in quality the offerings of many a gastropub. The lighting is understated and there's a wide array of knick-knacks all around. The seating is proper seating, and comfortable too. The soundtrack was eclectic, with everything from Motown to Morricone, Marley to Morcheeba. The relative discretion in the way Monkey Chews presents itself counts heavily in its favour, as does its slightly hidden-away location on the boundaries between sleb-ville and ASBO-central. Regulars seem to love it, and so do we. All very impressive, it must be said.

FEATURES:

Reviewers' Award Winner 2005

Princess of Wales

RATING:

22 Chalcot Road
NW1 8LL
020 7722 0354

Somehow, the Princess of Wales was missed in the trendification of Primrose Hill and is definitely the better for it. This pub has it all: large windows at the front (which fold back for summer) and cosy nooks and crannies towards the back and in the basement. There is even a (sadly, underutilised) garden. The central bar creates a good focal point and the numerous pot plants are a nice touch. A fair selection of real ales can be found and the food is both the cheapest in the area and superb. It can attract the older locals, witnessed by the popularity of the Sunday-afternoon live jazz sessions, but also a younger crowd who have grown tired of the postmodern affairs that are all too common in the area. So, for people whose idea of going to the pub is all about style over substance, the Princess of Wales won't suit them. However, for those who want a warm, genuine pub and are trapped in the wilds of NW1, it's thoroughly recommended.

FEATURES:

Queens No. 1

RATING:

1 Edis Street
NW1 8LG
020 7786 3049

Apparently, this used to be a cosy local and one of the nicest traditional pubs in Primrose Hill. We never saw it then, because at some point it was deemed better to gut the place totally and start again. Despite this, there's a pleasant, warm and subtly modern feel about the place. Leather, wood and candles – the staples of many a modern pub – feature heavily here, but it's all done with a degree of individuality. The beer was fine and the (mainly Thai) food fairly reasonable. Try it if you're in the area, but watch out for their propensity to scatter one too many 'reserved' signs around.

FEATURES:

The Sir Richard Steele

RATING:

97 Haverstock Hill
NW3 4RL
020 7483 1261

A big old rangy place that's possibly the template for London pubs furnished with curios and knick-knacks (or junk to some). Even without the toy carts and animal heads looming down at you, there's also an old-master-style fresco on the ceiling to take in, too. Aside from the decoration, this is still a noteworthy pub: Thai food on offer, a beer garden for the summer and a piano in the corner for any impromptu singalongs (fittingly, the sheet music for a variety of music-hall tunes hangs on the wall). This one offers up a more traditional experience than the more loungey 'Hill' nearby, though the rather standoffish bar service we received when we last stopped by rather marred things. Shame. Let's hope it was a one-off.

FEATURES:

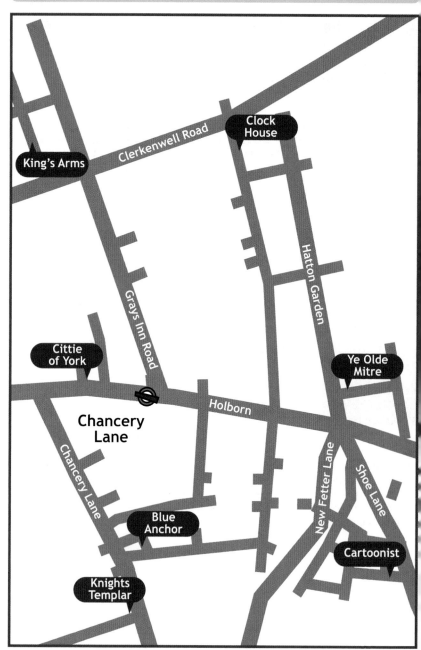

Blue Anchor

RATING:

Rolls Passage
EC4A 1HL
020 7430 2205

Not a bad pub, frequented by legal and financial types – hardly surprising, considering where it is. The beer's good with decent guest beers, pop on the box, food, sport on TV. While it gets busy at lunch and commuter times, it's actually very quiet and comfortable in the afternoon. And, as an added incentive to get you to go on Friday nights, they do karaoke. How can you say no to that?

FEATURES:

Cartoonist

RATING:

The Merchant Centre, Shoe Lane
EC4A 3JB
020 7353 2828

An odd pub slotted in the base of a office tower block, this pub offers nothing out of the ordinary other than the eponymous cartoons. This is hardly surprising given it is surrounded above and on all sides by law offices and supporting businesses - conservative is the watchword here. It's just a modern pub with pine floors, a downstairs bar cum function room, food, fairly loud music and a reasonable pint. It's really not one to go out of your way for, not even for the cartoons.

FEATURES:

Cittie of Yorke

RATING:

22 High Holborn
WC1V 6BS
020 7242 7670

A large, well-known, magnificent pub with a host of unusual architectural features – especially in the back bar, with its cubicle-like nooks and crannies and giant vats. Of particular interest is the fireplace in the centre of the room with its chimney and flue diverted under the floor and up the wall. Packed lunchtime and evenings with people associated with the nearby Inns of Court. Don't let that put you off, since it's worth a visit and it's much quieter at the weekends. The beer is just what you'd expect – this is a Sam Smith's pub, of course – and if you're a fan of Sam Smith's produce you won't be disappointed. The nonsmoking cellar bar is available for hire and, as often as not, is as full as the upstairs bars. There's food at lunchtimes, but it's not likely to set gastropub fans' pulses racing. You come here for the beer, the company and the surroundings.

FEATURES:

Clock House

RATING:

82 Leather lane
EC1N 7TR
020 7430 1123

A decent, well-looked-after Greene King pub. All the old favourites are there, Abbot and IPA among them. Its proximity to Leather Lane market means that it does a booming business when the market's on. At lunchtimes it's pretty packed, but in the evening it's a much more modest affair. The clientele is mostly regular locals, as the trendies go off to their favourite bars in the area. The service is friendly and there's a games room upstairs with a pool table and a TV, and TVs are dotted around the place downstairs for the footy. A reasonable choice if you're in the area.

FEATURES:

King's Arms

RATING:

11a Northington Street
WC1N 2JF
020 7405 9107

When we reviewed this pub in 2003, we awarded it three pints, stating it had the potential, with a bit of work, to become a four-pinter. There's been a bit of an overhaul, so how has the King's Arms fared? It's still a friendly, traditional, boozer, with cheery crowds spilling out on to the street at lunchtimes and in the early evenings. There's a reasonable selection of beers, Thai food is served most of the day and service is courteous and prompt. The quieter upstairs front room, popular with couples and small groups of friends, drinking or dining, is adorned with photographs by Frank Meadow Sutcliffe, depicting scenes in and around Victorian Whitby. There's also a fine view of one of the smartest Georgian streets in London. The upstairs backroom is a games room that packs an awful lot in without feeling cramped: two pool tables, a dartboard and table football. And not a teenager or hooded-top wearer in sight. The King's Arms has earned a coveted fourth pint.

FEATURES:

Knights Templar

RATING:

95 Chancery Lane
WC2A 1DT
020 7831 2660

A popular J D Wetherspoon pub in Chancery Lane, this used to be the Union Bank; the main banking hall forms a large, high-ceilinged bar choc-a-block at lunchtime with hungry lawyers and students from Kings College. A lovely old building but JDW haven't been as sympathetic with this as with others – nasty fruit-pattern carpet over the original tiling, plaster ceiling painted orange, poor murals of medieval scenes made to try to look as if they were charcoal drawings and the odd bit of charcoal-coloured marble dotted about. What it does have going for it is a little nonsmoking mezzanine that feels like a comfy middle-class Surrey anteroom. Food is tasty, though not as cheap as other Wetherspoon's pubs, but these punters can afford it. Most of the tables have high stools, so it's not that comfortable to eat here. But there is a discount, including a free pint if you want to eat after 2 p.m. And it's a free house, of course, with well-kept guest ales, and the staff are helpful and friendly. It's just there are better bank conversions in the Square Mile.

FEATURES:

Ye Olde Mitre Tavern

RATING:

1 Ely Court

EC1N 6SJ

020 7405 4751

This well-concealed pub (in a little yard just off Hatton Garden) can be an oasis in a manic area. Of course, like any pub too near the City, it also gets overrun at the usual times – lunch and immediately after work. The beers are well kept, usually a couple of decent real ales on the hand pumps; food is decent and the service is excellent. This is a genuine, old pub, quirky and atmospheric, replete with panelling and odd little nooks and crannies – and we hope it stays that way for ever. By the way, if you don't spot the sign on the lamppost in Hatton Garden pointing into the alleyway, you will walk straight past it.

FEATURES:

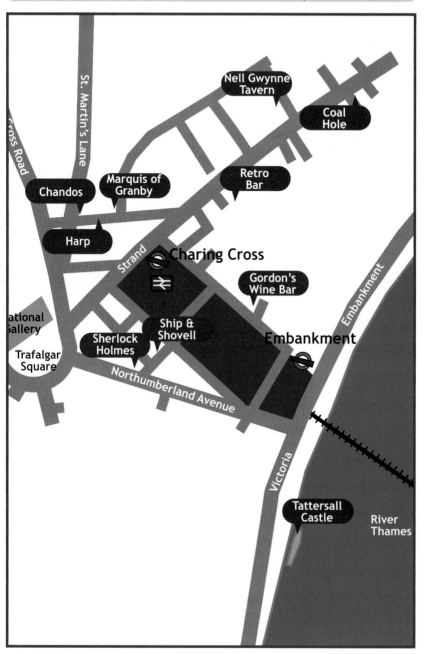

The Chandos

29 St Martin's Lane

WC2N 4ER

020 7836 1401

The Chandos is an attractive pub. The beer is Sam Smith's and is up to their usual standard; there is lots of room and an upstairs bar/restaurant with nice window seats. The pub suffers from its location, though. Perfectly placed to draw people from Charing Cross, St Martin's Lane and Trafalgar Square, consequently it's often uncomfortably packed. We advise you to visit one of the nearby pubs further away from the tourist hustle and bustle.

HANDY FOR: Trafalgar Square, National Gallery

Coal Hole

RATING:

91 Strand

WC2R 0DW

020 7379 9883

Probably the most famous pub in the area, the Coal Hole is pretty much unchanged over the years, although it has had its ups and downs. Built in a corner of the Savoy Hotel complex, the pub has a medieval (*circa* 1904) style of décor – dark beams, leaded lights, flagstone floors etc. – lending it a theatrical air, which not only fits with the fact it's next door to the Savoy Theatre, but is doubly apt given the past clientele. It being a Nicholson's pub, along with the splendid interior you get a good range of well-kept beers on the hand pumps – Bombardier, Landlord, Deuchars, Adnams – which you can try before you buy, and the service is good. As the pub is easy to find, expect it to be crowded at the usual times, with tourists, office workers and Covent Garden shoppers, who spill out into the alleyway down the side of the pub. There is some, but not much, relief on the pressure in the downstairs cellar bar. The crowd factor and the perennially over-amped PA – quiet conversation is not feasible – mean this pub gets a solid three pints, rather than the four it might otherwise merit.

Gordon's Wine Bar

RATING:

47 Villiers Street
WC2N 6NE
020 7930 1408

Not a pub, we know, but a wine bar with more charm and atmosphere than many of London's boozers (particularly those nearby). Gordon's is one of the most idiosyncratic drinking holes in town, its darkened alcoves a world away from your average pub interior. Yellowing newspapers from yesteryear adorn the walls, and candles plugged into dusty wine bottles provide the illumination. If Miss Havisham were in the licensing trade, this could have been the result. As for the choice of drinks, a wide range of both Old and New World wines is available, though port or sherry (decanted from barrels above the bar) often feels the most appropriate tipple. Given the proximity to Trafalgar Square, it's no wonder the place is sometimes standing-room-only (hence only a three-pint rating). So it's worth visiting at a quieter hour at the weekend to get a bit more space. Either that or get off work early and nab a table. Though take care entering from the side entrance – one false step and you'll be head first into the salad bar.

FEATURES:

Harp

RATING:

Chandos Place
WC2N 4HS
020 7836 0291

Given that drinking real ale in the middle of London can often result in a Wetherspoon experience, this little free house so close to Trafalgar Square comes as something of a surprise. The regular ales are Timothy Taylor Landlord, Harvey's and Black Sheep, with two guest beers also on offer. The pub's tasty sausage (there are several varieties to choose from) sandwiches do the business too. This one fills up most evenings but if you can find a seat, or catch it at a quieter time, it's worth a visit. Keep an eye out for the oil paintings – the one of a young James Mason is especially fine.

FEATURES:

HANDY FOR: Trafalgar Square

Marquis of Granby

RATING:

51–52 Chandos Place
WC2N 4HS
020 7836 7657

A quaint old place on an odd-shaped triangular plot that comes to a very sharp point at one end, so that the seating in this part of the pub gets very cosy. It is surprisingly rarely crowded – despite the hordes of passers-by who often look in through the long windows that front the place, yet they fail to enter. We suspect they were going on to rendezvous in the more usual Covent Garden haunts. The hand pumps dispense well-kept beers such as Pride, Adnams, Deuchars and Greene King IPA. There's agreeable pub grub and often a bit of space upstairs. It's built on the site of the Hole in the Wall – the pub where the highwayman Claude Duval was captured – and a refurbishment brightened the place up but didn't substantially affect the atmosphere. The open fire in winter is very welcome and goes very nicely with the Sunday papers and the Sunday roast.

FEATURES: HANDY FOR: Trafalgar Square

Nell Gwynne Tavern

RATING:

1–2 Bull Inn Court
WC2R 0NP
020 7240 5579

On the face of things an 'Olde Pubbe', the Nell Gwynne is not as touristy as its location and cosy size would make you think. Sure, it's dimly lit and makes the most of its historical associations, but it still has the feel of a locals' pub. Friendly staff, a good jukebox and decent fare add up to a decent, busy boozer. Even though it's about the size of a phone box inside, it's usually a better bet than some of the other tourist traps nearby. Hellish stairs to the toilets, though.

FEATURES:

Retro Bar

RATING:

2 George Court, Strand

WC2N 6HH

020 7321 2811

With a preponderance of standy-uppy, stripped-pine bars and corporate pseudo-olde-worlde places nearby, Retro Bar stands out by being just a little bit different. Tucked down a little alleyway, it's certainly more Camden than Charing Cross. An intimate arrangement of seats, a smattering of neon-lit knick-knacks, photos of rock stars and a great jukebox all add up to a place suited for either a swift weekday pint or a longer Saturday night. There was a gay-friendly crowd, but it was still pretty mixed, interspersed with only a smattering of suited office workers. Certainly, Retro Bar is worth seeking out if you're in the area and tired of the usual drinking places.

FEATURES:

Sherlock Holmes

RATING:

10–11 Northumberland Avenue

WC2N 5DA

020 7930 2644

You have to be a bit of a Sherlock Holmes to find this pub, as Baker Street is a good hansom cab's ride away from Northumberland Avenue. Nevertheless, the pub has plunged wholeheartedly into its chosen theme to please pub-going Conan Doyle fans with an entertaining diversion. The walls are adorned with innumerable Holmesian memorabilia, there's the 221B restaurant upstairs and the TV shows nonstop Sherlock Holmes movies and TV programmes – the colour on the TV being turned down to render even the newest TV programme in nostalgic black and white. The news is pretty good on the beer front with the likes of Speckled Hen and the pub's own Sherlock Holmes bitter on the hand pumps with plenty of wine and pub grub (albeit a little pricey) to round off the victuals. All competently and pleasantly served. However, this pub's USP appears to be of interest to only about half the clientele in here, the other half being civil servants and other officerati from roundabout. As themed tourist pubs go, this is one of the better ones.

FEATURES: HANDY FOR: Trafalgar Square

fancyapint?

The Ship & Shovell

RATING:

1–3 Craven Passage
WC2N 5PH
020 7839 1311

Claiming to be 'the only London pub in two halves', the Ship & Shovell is a good pub in an area short of them. Its pleasant red and black façade, adorned with street lanterns, presents a mirror image across the narrow passage. Each half of the pub has its own bar, serving an interesting range of draughts, including Badger Best and IPA, Tanglefoot, Sussex and JB Pilsner. Due to its proximity to the railway and tube stations, the pub tends to be busy in the evenings but it's also possible to enjoy a standing drink outside in the passageway; no matter how crowded it gets, this pub always has a good atmosphere to it.

FEATURES: *Visitors' Award Winner 2005*

Tattersall Castle

RATING:

Kings Reach, Victoria Embankment
SW1A 2HR
020 7839 6548

The Tattersall Castle has a fine riverside location, situated almost opposite the London Eye. It's a vast place with plenty of seats on the upper deck, and more downstairs inside the boat. If you fancy a drink on the river, you might well give it a try, but bear in mind the expensive bar prices. The mixed clientele lends the place a strange atmosphere, added to by the gentle swaying of the boat. A decent and varied menu is available and a nightclub starts in the evening for those who feel like dancing (open until 2 a.m. on Thursdays and 3 a.m. on Friday and Saturday). Be warned, though: there may be a few drunken sailors down there.

FEATURES: HANDY FOR: Houses of Parliament, Downing Street, Whitehall

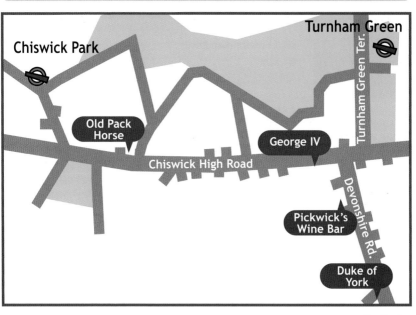

Turnham Green

Chiswick Park

Turnham Green Ter.

Old Pack Horse

George IV

Chiswick High Road

Devonshire Rd.

Pickwick's Wine Bar

Duke of York

Duke of York

RATING:

107 Devonshire Road
W4 2HU
020 8994 2118

Although Café Rouge and All Bar One are probably the most representative of Chiswick High Road's drinking opportunities, dip down Devonshire Road and you'll find a solid old pub still plying its trade. A fine local in a residential area, the Duke of York serves up Fuller's ales to its regulars and has a rather untouched feel about it. There's no indication it's due for a gastro relaunch any time soon – long may that be the case.

FEATURES:

George IV

RATING:

185 Chiswick High Road

W4 2DR

020 8994 4624

Great big Fuller's pub, that with its (relative) proximity to Turnham Green tube is a good place to use as a meeting point. Inside, there's the usual Fuller's ales, loads of space (including a balcony and a beer garden) and a clientele pretty similar to the All Bar One next door. Expect it to be packed to the rafters when there's a big match on, but this one does its best to provide a somewhat alternative range of entertainment for its punters: there are regular comedy nights on Fridays and Saturdays, and the pub also plays host to screenings by the Chiswick Film Society. We've had some good and some bad experiences in this pub, though, hence our rather average two-pint rating.

FEATURES:

The Old Pack Horse

RATING:

434 Chiswick High Road

W4 5TF

020 8994 2872

A good, solid pub. Has a sleepy feel out of hours, but picks up at nights when a mixed bunch of locals fill the place out. The old-fashioned interior has some plush leather sofas dotted about, and, with the beer being brewed down the road, you're sure of a decent pint. The Thai kitchen at the back comes recommended too. One of the best pubs in the area.

FEATURES:

CHISWICK PARK/TURNHAM GREEN

Pickwick's Wine Bar

RATING:

13 Devonshire Road
W4 2EU
020 8747 1824

Sometimes, just sometimes, a place comes along that restores your faith in the art of running a pub. Pickwick's – one of Chiswick's last independent bars – was apparently saved some years ago from being turned into a restaurant by a wealthy philanthropic regular who has kept it pretty much the same since. Inside the place is vaguely reminiscent of an understated German or Dutch bar, complete with wooden-beamed walls and ceilings, as well as German beer on tap. There didn't appear to be any food on offer and it seemed to have limited opening hours, but this didn't matter. Some of the stack-'em-high-and-sell-'em-cheap chains should take lessons from the welcome people received that night – warm and genuine, not just reserved for the regulars, but to greet new faces too. On our visit, the owner even cleared space by the open fire for us to warm up after we'd arrived soaked from the cold winter rain; it was so cosy, it almost felt as if we were in someone's front room in the country. This one certainly stands out from the rather Identikit pubs and bars in W4.

FEATURES:

CLAPHAM COMMON/CLAPHAM NORTH

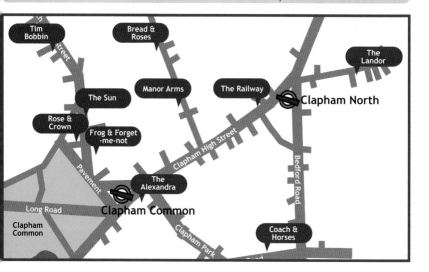

The Alexandra

14 Clapham Common South Side
SW4 7AA
020 7627 5102

Not a bad place, this one. It's a large pub with some rather eccentric (but appealing) décor. Outside it's an unpretentious Victorian pub, but inside it's crammed with various old pieces of farm kit, shop tills, printing presses and some ancient pub games etc. all scattered around – highly entertaining to look at or tinker with after you've had a few. Speaking of which, the service is excellent and you'll catch the eye of more than one member of the bar staff while buying a round. The upstairs 'Balcony Bar' sports big screens, for, er, sports and indeed the pub promotes sporting events up here. In case your legs aren't up to it, there are loads of smaller screens downstairs too. Overall the clientele are mostly younger locals, but thankfully you won't be assailed by the braying of the stereotypical Clapham dweller. A good pub for a quiet drink and especially popular for big footy matches, it's a very welcome presence among the wine bars in this locale.

FEATURES:

Bread & Roses

68 Clapham Manor Street
SW4 6DZ
020 7498 1779

As its name signifies, the Bread & Roses has strong links with socialism, and it's owned by the trade-union-backed Workers Beer Company. But working-class style it isn't. If images of flat caps and Northern club comics come to mind, you're in for a disappointment. This place is very 21st century and cool. There may be five hand pumps offering traditional ales, but there's also a good wine list and an impressive array of spirits if you're in a cocktail mood. The food is pretty swish and reasonably priced and the music's decent. There's usually something on here – a regular pub quiz and a photography competition – if you need something more than drink, food and a relaxed vibe. If pubs were newspapers, you feel this one might be the *Observer* – a bit Sunday supplement to look at, but sincere.

FEATURES:

Coach & Horses

RATING:

173–175 Clapham Park Road
SW4 7EX
020 7622 3815

Another boozer that's been cleaned up, had a decent menu installed and set out to attract a new clientele. The Coach & Horses has some good beer on tap such as Old Speckled Hen, Adnams and London Pride. There's a variety of food on offer at around £7 (including 2-4-1 burgers), and outside seats for summer drinking and traffic watching. On our visit, a smart weekend crowd read the papers quietly while the bar staff kept themselves amused by putting on lots of Sinatra tunes. For those into football, there's a big TV to keep you posted.

FEATURES:

Frog & Forget-Me-Not

RATING:

32 The Pavement, Clapham Old Town
SW4 0JE
020 7622 5230

A popular Clapham pub that manages to border into loungey bar territory, but without succumbing to the pretensions of the area. The sofas are old and knackered, but have more charm to them than your usual bar furnishings. The food is Thai during the week, but it's worth a look on Sunday if you're after a huge roast, but make sure you get there early to get a table – oh, and the paper napkins are ideal for post-blowout doodling. For when the weather's nice there's a roof terrace, where, for a change, you can rise above the pavement. Not as trendy as some of Clapham's bars, though more appealing than some of its pubs. We like it.

FEATURES:

The Landor

RATING:

70 Landor Road

SW9 9PH

020 7274 4386

Just what you want when wandering the wastelands where Brixton and Clapham merge. This welcoming place offers eccentric decoration, a theatre upstairs, a good range of drinks – Harvey's, Abbott, Pride, IPA – and a genial atmosphere. Be sure to give a look to the beer garden – a welcoming spot, with a mural and an overgrown street lamp to keep you company. In case that isn't enough, Sunday nights have an intelligent-looking pub quiz, too. Hard to fault really. So we won't.

FEATURES:

Manor Arms

RATING:

128 Clapham Manor Street

SW4 6ED

020 7622 8856

A traditional pub just off the High Street and just off the radar of the younger crowd who throng the main street of a weekend. It's a friendly place and offers a pretty decent range of beer on the hand pumps. Its small size (even with the tent out the back in the beer garden) means that the tellies tend to dominate when there's a sporting event on, but the atmosphere is jovial and the beer is good and you can't say fairer than that.

FEATURES:

The Railway

RATING:

18 Clapham High Street
SW4 7UR
020 7622 4077

Clapham High Street on a Saturday night is a scene no different from many, repeated on provincial CCTV screens around the country on a weekend evening. The streets are thronged with the local bright young things, ducking from bar to bar hell-bent on having a good time. And the Railway blends in perfectly with this scene. The moment you walk in you are assailed by a cacophonous blast of people screaming over the top of sound system. Upstairs it was slightly calmer, and here you merely had to shout. It is quieter at other times, but 'relaxed vibe' is not a description we'd apply at any time. There is a Thai menu and Sunday roasts too – a Clapham formula it seems – but, when it's standing room only, you're unlikely to indulge. As to the drink on offer, you'd really come here only if you're a fan of shots or brightly coloured confections – the beer available being Grolsch, Carling, Caffrey's and Guinness.

Rose & Crown

RATING:

2 The Polygon
SW4 0JG
020 7720 8265

We had our fears for this one. The longstanding landlord and landlady had waved farewell and we thought they would take all the charm of their idiosyncratic real-ale Mecca with them. However, despite the changes in décor (out goes the privacy of the old booths, in come some more tables and chairs and some enlarged photos of Ye Olde Clapham), there's still the essence of the old pub here. The beers still have the regularly rotating guests of old (as well as Greene King and are decently kept), to entice any passing ale fans in. Devotees to fizzy beer will appreciate the choice of Budweiser (the Czech stuff), Kronenbourg and Stella. That and the ATM in the pub make a reassuring combo. The pub grub still seems good value, while an eye cast at the wine list was a temptation hard to resist. And, even with new management, the old claim of the Rose & Crown being 'Clapham's only traditional pub' still has a certain truth in it.

FEATURES:

The Sun

RATING:

47 Old Town
SW4 0JL
020 7622 4980

You'll love or hate this one. The crowds that gather to enjoy sun and lager here testify to its popularity with the young of Clapham and beyond. Inside and out, it's a pleasant spot to while away an afternoon, with a large bright main bar. The yard bar opens only occasionally, while the upstairs bar is usually open evenings, and sports real gas fires in winter. There's a pleasant artiness about the place and a curious fresco upstairs. The Thai food is recommended, and lunch for a fiver is a decent promise too. Well, that's the good bit. A limited range of beers at hefty prices, with Guinness and Staropramen on offer. Towards the end of the week the place is often so rammed you'll make slow progress at the bar, which soon spoils your night. The staff don't wear blinkers, but they might as well. This pub has entertained Clapham's young for years, but until they sort out watering them reliably too, it'll be staying a two-pinter for us. Shame, but we doubt it'll stop the summer crowds.

FEATURES:

Tim Bobbin

RATING:

1–3 Lillieshall Road
SW4 0LN
020 7738 8953

Renovated a few years back now, this pub has settled down to a life somewhere between aspirational gastropub and local boozer. Given its location in a residential side street in Clapham, this is probably the only way it could survive, but it seems to work quite well. The beers are not bad at all, with guest ales, and, though the food's pretty dear, it's of a good quality and the service is good, too. The range of spirits is excellent and the décor is pleasant, if a bit of a mixture. The clientele consists of locals by daytime, with the more stereotypical Cla'am dweller of an evening and at weekends. And on our last visit the locals would have made Roger Melly blush, but they're amiable enough and the atmosphere is generally quieter than the rowdier bars in the area. Oh, if you are wondering who Tim Bobbin was, you'll see from his sketches of eighteenth-century London images that'll show anyone in doubt what real binge-drinking used to be like (they seemed to be rather good at it then).

FEATURES:

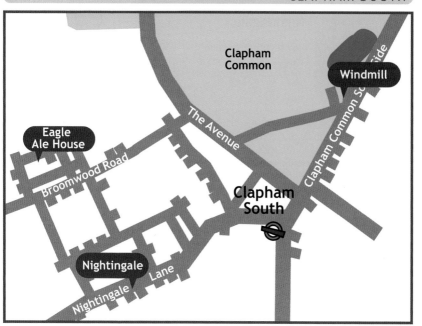

Clapham
Common

Windmill

The Avenue

Eagle
Ale House

Broomwood Road

Clapham Common Southside

Clapham
South

Nightingale
Lane

Nightingale

The Eagle Ale House

RATING:

104 Chatham Road
SW11 6HG
020 7228 2328

A pleasing discovery between Wandsworth Common and Clapham Junction, here's a local pub with an independent spirit about it. The beer's pretty decent with Landlord, Regatta and Unicorn, for example (there are regular guests), on the hand pumps – just the thing to wash down a Sunday roast. With a stack of board games available, and some tables inbuilt with chess and backgammon tops, the place is ideal for an afternoon of slothful drinking. That said, the empty champagne bottles on the bookshelves suggest it's pretty handy for a night of excess, too – maybe in the marquee you can hire out the back. Worth giving it a look if you're in the area.

FEATURES:

Nightingale

97 Nightingale Lane
SW12 8NX
020 8673 1637

When an area gentrifies there's usually an impact on the local pubs. Round these parts the rise in house prices has seen pubs remodelling themselves with lounge-style interiors, or, as in the case of the Surrey Tavern, being shut down to make way for luxury flats. For remaining true to its boozer roots, then, this Nightingale is indeed a rare bird. Devotees of gastropubs won't be setting foot over the threshold until there's at least one lunchtime option featuring balsamic vinegar; the rest of us will make do with a pub that plays to the traditional pleasures of good beer, bantering locals and an atmosphere conducive to knocking a few back. And, given the pub is big on collecting for charity (photos of all the guide dogs the pub has raised money for take up a whole wall), the punters seem a decent lot as well. All in all, a fine little pub.

FEATURES:

Windmill on the Common

Clapham Common South Side
SW4 9DE
020 8673 4578

What with a bar, lounge, restaurant, conservatory and plenty of tables outside, there's enough room here for anyone who ambles in from Clapham Common. However, given its large size, it does sometimes feels a bit dead, especially on warm days when most of its customers get their drinks and then head for the Common. This means that, if you want to enjoy a drink outdoors but still on the premises, you will have your pints poured into plastic glasses. You can hardly blame them, as either the council or the glass bill will have made this necessary. Also, being a hotel (and the fact that the beer garden borders the hotel car park) can give the place the feel of a Midlands travel tavern. Those criticisms aside, the usual Young's fare is on offer and it's a handy meeting place before you head elsewhere. The Windmill was given a lick of paint not so long ago and we can report the restaurant is much more appealing since the previous buffet arrangement was finally terminated.

FEATURES:

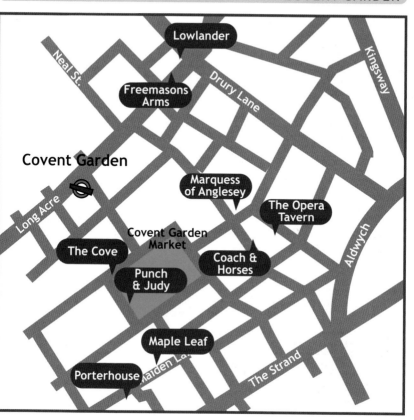

Lowlander

Neal St.

Kingsway

Drury Lane

Freemasons Arms

Covent Garden

Long Acre

Marquess of Anglesey

The Opera Tavern

Aldwych

Covent Garden Market

The Cove

Coach & Horses

Punch & Judy

Maple Leaf

Maiden Lane

Porterhouse

The Strand

Coach & Horses

RATING:

42 Wellington Street

WC2E 7BD

020 7240 0553

Excellent Guinness and friendly service put this pub above many others in Covent Garden. You can usually find a seat inside, even when people are crowding the pavement, which in this area is no mean feat. The Gaelic sport pictures on the walls let you know that this is an Irish pub without shoving it down your throat. If you're thirsty in theatreland, come on down.

FEATURES:

105

The Cove

RATING:

The Piazza

WC2E 8RB

020 7836 7880

Once upon a time this was probably the world's (well, London's, anyway) only Cornish theme pub. Now it has a sister pub on the King's Road. Like that one, this pub sells Cornish ale from the St Austell Brewery and delicious (and good-value) pasties from an impressively large menu. The chairs are comfortable and the balcony is great to watch the 'entertainers' below. It's let down by cramped toilets and Europop on the jukebox, but it's still ten thousand times better than the place opposite.

FEATURES:

Freemasons Arms

RATING:

81–82 Long Acre

WC2E 9NG

020 7836 3115

This is one of the better Covent Garden pubs. It bears up to the strain of office-worker and tourist crowds quite well. A recent lick of paint has brightened the place up, but not affected it in any other way. It's not worth making a special journey to visit it, but it's a useful meeting place if you're in the area. Standard Shepherd Neame fare served pleasantly and promptly. If you sit in the back you'll notice a good few historic footy photos around the wall and a sign proclaiming, 'The Football Association was founded here in 1863.' A bit of history for you.

FEATURES:

Lowlander

36 Drury Lane
WC2B 5RR
020 7379 7446

This is a top-notch establishment for those of us who like to sample different beers, especially Belgian ones – fourteen different Belgian beers on tap and more than thirty in bottles, albeit at a thoroughly Covent Garden price. The Lowlander likes to bill itself as a grand café of the Low Countries, and so does wines, coffee and food. It can get more than a bit busy, so, if you are coming along in the evening time, try to get there early or phone in advance to reserve a table. And when it's busy it's bloody noisy.

FEATURES:

Maple Leaf

RATING:

41 Maiden Lane
WC2E 7LJ
020 7240 2843

No prizes for guessing the theme of this pub. *Sacre bleu! C'est Canada*! You don't have to drink Molson, watch the ice hockey or wear a checked shirt to come here, but, if you haven't got an interest in things Canadian, you'll naturally find yourself in the minority. The staff are attentive (although service can be slow when it's crowded), and more untypical beers, wines and spirits are also on offer. It's one of those Covent Garden fixtures that are pretty much unchanged over the years.

FEATURES:

COVENT GARDEN

Marquess of Anglesey

39 Bow Street
WC2E 7AU
020 7240 3216

The worst time to visit this pub is at 6.30 on Friday night in summer. It will be absolutely packed with tourists, office workers celebrating the end of another week and people on their way out for the night. The rest of the time it's just full. It's an easy place to find (hence a useful rendezvous), and it's not too bad a pub in itself despite the All Bar One look – it's a Young's pub after all – but the endless tides of people coming in and out don't make this the place for a relaxing pint. No surprise to see all of Young's beers on tap here, though we weren't expecting the extra pump dispensing Pimm's...

Opera Tavern

RATING:

23 Catherine Street
WC2B 5JS
020 7379 9832

This has been a jolly little pub for ages and continues to be so. It does get crowded with tourists and theatregoers, but when the bell goes in the theatres for the next performance the place empties as if it had just received a bomb threat, so don't be alarmed if you and your mates are suddenly the only people left in the place. The upstairs room gives some relief from the crowds when it's not being used for a private function. There are decent beers on the hand pumps and the service is excellent. This is one of the better pubs in the area.

Porterhouse

RATING:

21 Maiden Lane
WC2E 7NA
020 7379 7917

Very often we like to bring you a choice little hideaway, an undiscovered gem with a few enchanting flaws. But we also have to concede that, if a place is really popular, chances are they're doing something right. Porterhouse is a brewing company in Dublin that has opened its own select chain of pubs. There aren't many in the chain – quality rather than quantity is the watchword. The Porterhouse in Maiden Lane is a massive boozer and expensively decorated in brewery brass and antique doodads and yet is designed full of cosy nooks for you and your chums to hide away in. All nine house beers are brewed in Dublin to their own recipes – three stouts (including a miraculous oyster stout), three real ales and three lagers. Responsible pub reviewers would, of course, never suggest that you try a pint of each one in one night. But they're all good (ahem). One lift entrance and toilets offer some disabled access. Tasteful live music, decent food, a patio (where those who want to be seen can be) and the location in the heart of London's theatre and eating district mean this pub is very busy. But they've done their research, they know what the 'craic' is – it's another word for a niche.

FEATURES:

Punch & Judy

RATING:

The Market Piazza
WC2E 8RF
020 7379 0923

Some things never change and the Punch & Judy is one of them. It always was a terrible place, especially on Friday and Saturday nights, full of pissed-up day trippers and tourists who stumble into the place and seemingly find it impossible to leave unless they've drunk a few gallons and started a punch-up. We could go on at length, but we'd better not. Suffice it to say we can think of no good reason to visit this place. Sorry, one thing has changed – it doesn't smell of vomit any more.

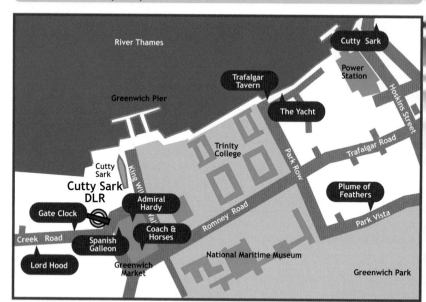

River Thames

Cutty Sark

Power Station

Hoskins Street

Trafalgar Tavern

Greenwich Pier

The Yacht

Trinity College

Trafalgar Road

Park Row

Cutty Sark

Plume of Feathers

Cutty Sark DLR

Gate Clock

Admiral Hardy

Romney Road

Park Vista

Coach & Horses

King William

Creek Road

Spanish Galleon

Lord Hood

Greenwich Market

National Maritime Museum

Greenwich Park

Admiral Hardy

RATING:

7 College Approach
....
SE10 9HY
....
020 8858 6452
....

This place has two things going for it: a better-than-usual range of booze on offer and its location. It also has two major things working against it: its clientele and its location. Situated in the heart of Greenwich market, this pub will inevitably be popular: it's easy to find and it's a handy refuelling stop after a day spent inspecting the pricey tat on offer all around it. And in the evenings – especially towards the weekend – it's popular with kids out on the town (well, Greenwich, anyway) with their mates. It tried to be different for a while, with its food shop and foodie menu, but in the end bowed to the pressure: out went the shop and the menu; in came the 'lounge bar' features and a pretty standard menu. And the crowds followed. So, despite the drink – there's a good range of real ales on offer, with regular guest beers – it's not really our sort of place any longer, more's the pity. But who can blame the owners for cashing in?

FEATURES: 🎵 ☁   **HANDY FOR:** Cutty Sark, National Maritime Museum

The Coach & Horses

RATING:

13 Greenwich Market
SE10 9HZ
020 8293 0880

The old Coach & Horses in the market was given the inevitable stripped-out gastropub treatment and, we feel, it probably deserved it – the old one was never up to much. The beer and food are good, e.g. Speckled Hen and guest beers on the hand pumps, accompanied by a range of Continentals such as Amstel and Paulaner. It's quite comfy with its settees, easy chairs and newspapers. The music is decent and there's a relaxed vibe when it's not crowded, although if it's warm enough you can always sit outside. Prices are tourist high, which some may find offputting, but there are enough well-off locals to fill the place on a Saturday night. Market days will see it packed with tourists and shoppers and on Friday and Saturday nights younger locals having a few pre-club drinks.

FEATURES:

Cutty Sark Tavern

RATING:

Ballast Quay
SE10 9PD
020 8858 3146

Confusingly, this pub is not as near to the Cutty Sark as you'd imagine. There are quite a few pubs a lot nearer that would probably better qualify for the name. Still, once you get to it (it's a five-minute walk downriver), you'll find that it's a jolly decent place. The Georgian building and the riverside terrace are what make it worthwhile coming here. And there are fine beers to be enjoyed here too – such as Tribute, Broadside and Tiger. The service is polite and very prompt and copes admirably with the crowds as they flock down here on a warm summer's evening (when we get them). Off season, it's a very nice place for a pint or two with its excellent views and relaxed atmosphere, but the freneticism of the summer months removes some of the shine. However, such is the way with many tourist pubs. Well worth a visit, though.

FEATURES: HANDY FOR: National Maritime Museum

The Gate Clock

RATING:

Creek Road

SE10 9RB

020 8269 2000

With all the charm and intimacy of an airport departure lounge, this place is designed to pack them in. It's part of the new development around the Cutty Sark DLR station and Wetherspoon have opened up what surely must be one of their profitable branches here. Packed with a surprising number of locals (you'd expect mainly tourists here), this place will never fail to draw in punters. You can enjoy a pint and diesel particulates on the terrace out front, or have a very cheap meal and a few cheap drinks inside. Not one for the pub connoisseur, but, if you're drinking on a budget in the area, this is the one for you.

FEATURES: HANDY FOR: Cutty Sark

Lord Hood

RATING:

300 Creek Road

SE10 9SW

020 8858 1836

Despite its proximity to central Greenwich, the Lord Hood is firmly a locals' pub. Although a little scruffy around the edges, it has a genuineness lacking in many of the tourist-oriented places nearby. There's nothing unusual in the way of drink here and only pub grub in terms of food, but, if it's just a pint you want, it might be worth a go. The Hood has recently been threatened with demolition. With the demise of the Cricketers in 2005, the Hood is now the last locals' pub in central Greenwich and it would be a shame to see it disappear.

FEATURES:

Plume of Feathers

RATING:

19 Park Vista
SE10 9LZ
020 8858 1661

Established in 1691, the Plume of Feathers has a lovely tiled exterior and outdoor seating to the front and rear. Inside, the walls are packed with pictures and nautical ephemera, and the fireplace adds to the cosy atmosphere. Attracting locals, walkers and some tourists, the place gets packed and buzzes with a lively, congenial atmosphere. The Plume serves good pub grub, with a decent Sunday roast, which you can have in the restaurant area at the back or in the bar area. Adnams and Fuller's ales are among the beers behind the bar and the service is excellent. Turnover is pretty brisk at lunchtimes, so, if you can't get a table immediately, wait a short while – it's worth it. There's also a children's play area where the kids can disappear, leaving you to sup your pint in peace, although occasionally customers don't avail themselves of this facility, to the annoyance of the people around them. We like this pub – it's the best in the area.

FEATURES: **HANDY FOR:** National Maritime Museum

Spanish Galleon

RATING:

48 Greenwich Church Street
SE10 9BL
020 8858 3664

Even the most unobservant will find this place, bang opposite one of the exits to the DLR, yet, curiously, until quite recently, it was largely ignored by the people who throng the area day and night. However, the Spanish Galleon's unpopularity now seems to be a thing of the past. Where once it used to be the place for a spot of quiet refreshment, it's now elbow to elbow with people yelling at each other and the bar staff, especially on Friday and Saturday nights. The beer and food haven't changed much – the beer's Shepherd Neame – but, alas, this is not of the quality we've come to expect of Shepherd Neame pubs. We suppose nowadays it doesn't really need to try; the competition certainly doesn't appear to– the name of the game is to bang it out as quickly as possible. Par for the course in these parts.

FEATURES:

Trafalgar Tavern

RATING:

Park Row

SE10 9NW

020 8858 2909

Anybody who's ever been to Greenwich knows the Trafalgar. It's a huge, handsome pub, well in keeping with its grand and historic surroundings. It's right on the river with views to the north and, as a result, is incredibly popular. We usually visit this pub when we're meeting people who are new to the area and then we have to move on. It's not the pub's fault, but the tourist crowds, seemingly packed floor to ceiling, cause us to repair to other establishments, should we require quiet conversation – you'd do the same in any tourist haunt in any city. The restaurant has a reputation for good food, although we haven't eaten here (blame the crowds again), and the beers are pretty well kept, but it's all a little pricey – hardly a surprise, given where it is. It's now expanded into the street and on to the riverside to provide more tables and seating, such is its popularity.

FEATURES: HANDY FOR: Cutty Sark

The Yacht

RATING:

5 Crane Street

SE10 9NP

020 8858 0175

The Yacht is often a better choice than the Trafalgar a couple of doors down, as it tends to be less crowded. The beer is good (usually two or three real ales) and there's a reasonable wine list of mostly New World varieties. There's a range of reasonably priced food, too, with main courses for less than £10, and the pub has a welcoming atmosphere. However, it can get crowded here at weekends, when families come for lunch. If you're lucky enough to get a window table, a view from Borthwick Wharf in Deptford around to the Millennium Dome awaits. The Yacht may not be the best pub in Greenwich, but it's a decent boozer all the same.

FEATURES: HANDY FOR: Cutty Sark, National Maritime Museum

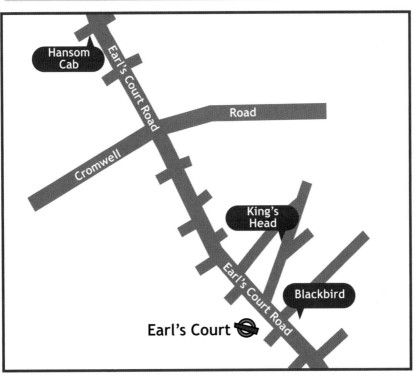

Blackbird

RATING: ▮▮▯

209 Earl's Court Road
SW5 9AN
020 7835 1855

Not an outstanding pub but it's probably your safest bet on the Earl's Court Road. Since it's a Fuller's Ale and Pie House, it's no surprise that the food and drink are of a good quality. That's really the pub's strength and what pulls in the customers (including many of the guests from the nearby hotels). There are a couple of screens for the sport, a further draw for many of the punters here. You can do far worse, not many metres from here.

HANDY FOR: Earl's Court

The Hansom Cab

RATING:

86 Earl's Court Road

W8 6EG

020 7795 4821

Another pub that's been refitted by Mitchells & Butlers and another pub that's been improved as a result. There's a fine range of options behind the bar (Adnams and other ales on the hand pumps as well as some Belgian beers) and a spruced-up interior in which to enjoy them. As with many other M&B pubs – the Washington in NW3 springs to mind – the refit has managed to combine with good effect smart furniture with traditional pub glasswork. It all adds up to a very decent little pub, and one patronised by a fair range of drinkers. As pubs go in this neck of the woods, it's one of the best. Just watch out for the rather too boisterous groups who take advantage of the late licence and you won't go far wrong here.

FEATURES:

King's Head

RATING:

17 Hogarth Place

SW5 0QT

020 7244 5931

Once upon a time this was an old-fashioned backstreet boozer, but times have changed and it's been revamped with lounge and gastro touches. Taken on its own merits it's not bad at all: there's decent beer on the hand pumps, plenty of Belgian bottles in the fridge and enough space to enjoy them in and, when you consider where this pub is, it makes the package all the more remarkable. To entertain you there are quizzes, sport on the telly and a fish tank has been promised. Well worth the detour, we say.

FEATURES: HANDY FOR: Earl's Court

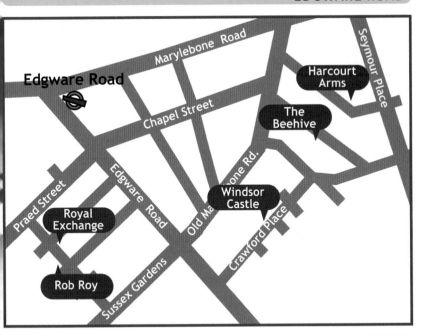

The Beehive

7 Homer Street

W1H 4NJ

020 7262 6581

Marylebone is home to some of the friendliest pubs in London and this one is a prime example. Perhaps conversation is induced by the small interior – it's hard to avoid speaking to your fellow drinkers when there's so little space. On offer are an average, but decent, range of beers, but it's the cheery atmosphere that makes it worth coming along to sample.

FEATURES:

Harcourt Arms

RATING:

32 Harcourt Street

W1H 4HX

020 7723 6634

The Harcourt Arms belongs to a nexus of great pubs in the Marylebone Baker Street area, and has pretty much everything you could ask for in such a place. It's very welcoming, clean and well maintained, serves a decent selection of beers, including Pride and Adnams, as well as a monthly guest ale, and has a good beer garden. Many of the pubs in this area have their own little eccentricities or things that make them that little bit different. While lacking in strange memorabilia or acting as a meeting place of odd societies, the Harcourt proudly boasts a link with the area's Swedish community. If you don't fancy sitting in the main bar, what about the Svenska Salongen situated at the back? You can also be served Swedish ciders by the Swedish bar staff. They also show Swedish sport, if that's your thing – and that's when the place can get really crowded. When the ice hockey's on the box, if Forlunda or HV 71 means nothing to you, forget it. But, overall, a pub that goes from strength to strength.

FEATURES:

Rob Roy

RATING:

8 Sale Place

W2 1PH

020 7262 6403

You may have gathered that the Rob Roy is a Scottish pub. Although it has Caledonian 80 and Calders on draught, you're unlikely to hear too many Scots voices here, as the place sometimes seems more popular with Australians. But all that changes on big-match days, when the place becomes tighter than an Aberdonian's wallet. On such occasions it's wall-to-wall expat Scots. Not for the faint-hearted – especially if Scotland are tackling one of football's 'lesser nations' …

FEATURES:

Royal Exchange

RATING:

26 Sale Place
W2 1PU
020 7723 3781

A long time ago, when we didn't know any better, we would often arrive at Paddington after a long journey and wonder where on earth we could go for a decent pint before the pubs closed. And we'd end up in a pretty dismal sort of place, only because we could see a pub sign beckoning us from the station. If only we'd known about the Royal Exchange. A five-minute walk from Paddington station gets you to a fine, traditional boozer of the old school. Serving real ales, hot and cold Guinness, Murphy's and a bunch of other traditional tipples, this place is a real, down-to-earth, honest pub. The atmosphere is friendly, as is the service, the food is proper pub grub and the pub hasn't been renovated to within an inch of its former life. If you want to visit an example of a pub as they used to be (and as we remember them), you'd better get here, before someone decides it's worth 'improving'.

FEATURES:

Windsor Castle

RATING:

27–29 Crawford Place
W1H 4LQ
020 7723 4371

This is certainly one of the oddest pubs you'll ever drink in, and it's a real treat. Once inside, you enter an Aladdin's cave of royal/celebrity photos (including a signed one of Pelé), glass cabinets and generally enough gewgaws to fill every gift shop in Blackpool. Even the ceiling is covered in plates in display cases. As for the beers, there's not a huge selection – just as well, as the pub is intoxicating enough in itself – but there are decent hand-pumped ales. It's a friendly place too and it's on the itinerary of many a tourist, but an influx of newcomers does nothing to upset the ambience (unlike a few places we can think of). It also offers pretty decent Thai food, and, in case all that isn't enough for you, the pub is home to the Handlebar Club. Excellent.

FEATURES:

Reviewers' Award Winner 2005

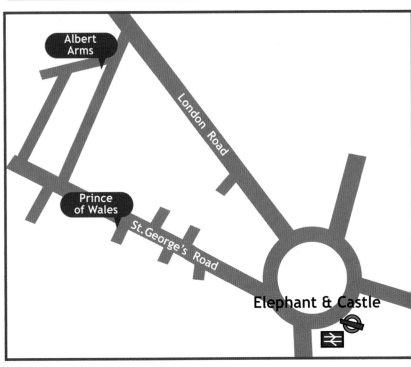

Albert Arms

RATING:

1 Gladstone Street
SE1 6EY
020 7928 6517

Off the main roads that dominate the area, the Albert Arms is a neat two-room pub with a bit of character. Beer mats, brass kettles and other ephemera decorate the walls. Reasonably priced pub grub is on offer and a few wines, with Greene King IPA and Leffe on the taps. Its proximity to South Bank University means some student clientele, but it's got a regular local crowd who are genial enough. Still, this pub has got things going for it and we'll be back.

FEATURES: HANDY FOR: Imperial War Museum

Prince of Wales

RATING:

51 St George's Road
SE1 6ER
020 7582 9696

This is a traditional boozer and very much a locals' pub, which looks more like a working men's club than anything else. And, despite the England flags everywhere, it has more than a hint of Irishness about it – and the Gaelic football on the telly last time we were in did nothing to dispel this feeling. Even so, everyone seemed quite content and fairly friendly when we were there. If you don't live nearby, there is probably no reason you would go here, but, if you stumble out of the Imperial War Museum in the wrong direction, it's all right for a pint. With two fairly large rooms and a large outside area at the back, there is plenty of space, especially in summer. It does pub food, and everything costs a fiver. What we're most intrigued by is the offer of 'Sunday Roast to take away' – beef, pork or lamb. No mucking about – it knows exactly what it's there for.

FEATURES:    HANDY FOR: Imperial War Museum

EMBANKMENT – see Charing Cross, pg 89

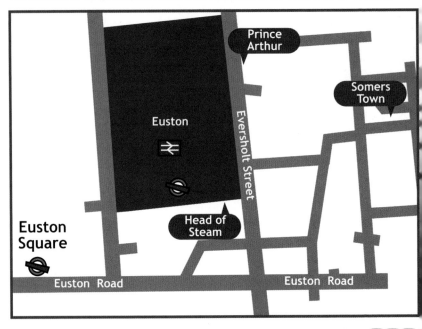

Head of Steam

RATING:

1 Eversholt Street
NW1 1DN
020 7388 2221

Once one of the most notable free houses in London, this one's now been bought up by Fuller's. For the moment, not too much has changed. As you'd expect, there are more of Fuller's beers on tap than before, though there's still room for a couple of guests (including that Head of Steam perennial, Hopback's Summer Lightning). The atmosphere seems relatively unchanged, too, with the pub still attracting a variety of commuters. We'll keep our eye on this one and see if Fuller's get itchy for a redesign. For the moment, though, this one's still an above-average pub – a rarity so close to a mainline station.

FEATURES:

Prince Arthur

RATING:

80–82 Eversholt Street
NW1 1BX
020 7387 2165

This place just goes from strength to strength. Formerly one of the most depressing licensed establishments in London, the Prince Arthur has been gradually transformed into one of those magical places that you just don't want to leave. Fantastic staff and, even better, table service (so you don't even need to drag yourself the short distance to the bar), delicious and reasonably priced Thai food available when you really need it (when you realise you're there for the night – again), and a variety of ear-pleasing tunes you thought could only be found on the best pub jukebox in the world. All these elements and more combine to offer one of the best pubs in the area. A plea to management: please don't change it.

FEATURES: *Reviewers' Award – Most Improved 2004*

Somers Town Coffee House

RATING:

60 Chalton Street
NW1 1HS
020 7691 9136

An establishment with a bit of history, having once been a meeting place for Huguenot intellectuals to catch up on events and drink coffee. More recently, however, the fortunes of the Coffee House (its caffeine-related vocation more or less sidelined) have seemed to track the misfortunes of the surrounding neighbourhood, caught as it is between three main railway lines and located on the disfavoured side of the Euston Road. However, perhaps with an eye to the future, or to the workers of the various companies that have taken up residence nearby, the Coffee House has undergone a major refurbishment to become a really rather smart gastropub. Lots of polished wood and subtle lighting, and a few of the cosy-looking, high-backed cushioned seats are very reminiscent of those that used to be found in the single-compartment portions of trains. It's quite spacious, with a central island bar, and retains the feel of a proper (if upmarket) pub. One side is given over explicitly to dining, the other for both drinking and eating. There are a few hand pumps for real ales, although only one was working on our visit, but also some other interesting beers. The food we sampled was pretty good, too, although relatively expensive. The bar staff were friendly, and the music playing was funky but unobtrusive.

FEATURES:

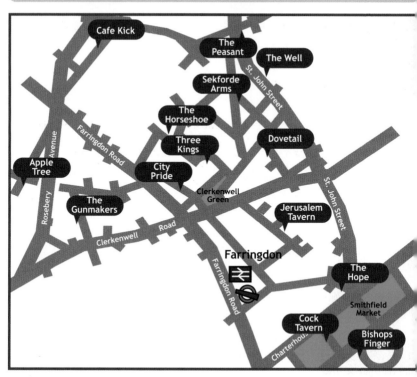

The Apple Tree

RATING:

45 Mount Pleasant
WC1X 0AE
020 7837 2365

The Apple Tree is no longer the posties' favourite that it once was, having gone more upmarket, like much of the surrounding neighbourhood. What's more, the pub now has both the décor and prices to match this *embourgeoisement*. There's rather an abundance of arty things (prints, paintings, sculptures) on the walls as well as the occasional sofa, and there's a gastro-food menu. As well as being expensive, the pub is fairly expansive, and service is friendly and often surprisingly prompt, even when there's quite a crowd in. Even after the refurbishment and restyling, though, this remains a proper pub, and only the most ignorant philistine or hardline class warrior would describe it as pretentious. A solid three-pinter.

FEATURES:

Bishops Finger

9 West Smithfield

EC1A 9JR

020 7248 2341

An old favourite in Smithfield, this one's had a bit of a café-style makeover of late, though nothing too serious to degrade the feel of a pub in such an earthy bit of London. A good range of Shepherd Neame ales to work your way through and a decent range of pub food to fill up on while drinking (though with Smithfield meat market across the road you'd expect nothing else). Some fine old cartoons and drawings decorate the walls and add to the pleasant air of the place. It gets pretty crowded and smoky at the usual business times, but is, nevertheless, a decent three-pinter.

FEATURES:

Café Kick

43 Exmouth Market

EC1R 4QL

020 7837 8077

OK, we're probably pushing the description of 'pub' with this one. Exmouth Market's trendy table football (or 'fussball', we're informed) bar is not the place we'd usually be found researching on behalf of our esteemed users; and on first glance it's obvious why. Looking like a beacon for all sorts of Hoxtonian tomfoolery, we expected the 'café' to be a showcase of the latest in trainer and 'ironic' haircut fashions. We were, we have to say, pleasantly surprised to see this was not solely the case. The place has a general Portuguese-Brazilian atmosphere to it, maybe due to the preponderance of Portuguese beers and some dangerous (particularly in happy hour) caipirinhas. We soon found ourselves quite enjoying gnawing on an olive or two, washed down with a mouthful of Sagres, and were even more surprised to find ourselves indulging in what we believe to be called 'a tournament' on the footy tables. However, the first person who says it has a 'chilled-out, laid-back kind of vibe' gets a K-Swiss in the mush. And we're not talking about cocktails now.

FEATURES:

City Pride

RATING:

28 Farringdon Lane
EC1R 3AU
020 7608 0615

Very pleasant Fuller's pub in the heart of Clerkenwell. It serves a good pint (Pride, Adnams, ESB), not a bad crowd, and has the added advantage of being able to open up most of the front of the pub, which is nice in hot weather. Doesn't get too crowded, even when all around are packed to the gunwales – and there's a room upstairs to expand into if it does – and it still has enough of a clientele to give it atmosphere. Nice.

FEATURES:

Cock Tavern

RATING:

East Poultry Avenue
EC1A 9LH
020 7248 2918

We were taken aback when we passed by here and saw signs advertising 'Live Jazz'. Given that the pub used to shut up shop of an afternoon, the fact that it was even open at night – let alone showcasing live music – took us a bit by surprise. We knew Smithfield's future is far from secure but had this bastion of bloodied butchers been homogenised for the local loft dwellers? Well, if you give it a look early morning you won't see too many changes. Located in the bowels of Smithfield Market, the Cock comes across as a comfortable cross between a pub and a greasy-spoon café, with a snug bar on one side, a pub dining space on the other and a café-style area separating them. The fact that it's underground adds a nefarious edge to your drinking; that it's in Smithfield means you can start on the sauce at a very early hour – although, with the new licensing laws, that frisson has now disappeared. Around early afternoon, the Cock used to shut up shop. That's where the changes begin, since, now that it stays open, there's a handover in the kitchen and a more upmarket lunchtime menu offered. Before the area becomes just like any other (there's already a Starbucks and Pizza Express around the corner), take a trip here. To see it at its best, though, grit your teeth, set the alarm clock and visit before 9 a.m. Your vegetarian friends might not approve but this irreplaceable bit of London is worth making the effort to see before it possibly goes.

FEATURES:

The Dovetail Bar

RATING:

9 Jerusalem Passage
EC1V 4JP
020 7490 7321

This place specialises in things Belgian, mainly beer, moules etc., but also Continental stuff such as Genevers. There are a good number of Belgian beers on the pumps and a very extensive range of bottled Belgian beers. The Dovetail does a pretty good impression of being Antwerp rather than London and is a refreshing change from the relentless tide of bars and gastropubs. The food and service are decent and priced for the area – i.e. not cheap, but not too expensive, either. It gets pretty popular towards the end of the week with people who work in the area. Well worth seeking out if you want something different and can't afford Eurostar.

FEATURES:

Gunmakers

RATING:

13 Eyre Street Hill
EC1R 5ET
020 7278 1022

Clerkenwell is underrated as a place to go pubbing – being predominantly a designer's paradise of bars and clubs – but there are a good few pubs that reward you for following up on that instinct that says, 'I wonder what's down that side road.' The Gunmakers was always one of those that hit the spot, and it continues to do so. It's a small front-room bar with two tables, followed by a parlour decorated in student-union green with attendant red PVC benches, and a backroom full of tables for two. It's patronised by one or two local firms, possibly at the expense of the curious explorer. And the loos let them down a bit (we needn't go into details, right?). The good news is it's still very good for food – pub grub, certainly, but with genuine flair, well presented and reasonably priced. They do decent grog, too (Bombardier and IPA were both well kept), and it still feels like a local with a friendly greeting.

FEATURES:

The Hope

94 Cowcross Street
EC1M 6BH
020 7250 1442

This old early-opening pub in the heart of Smithfield meat market has serviced the traders here for many a year. It retains a few of its original features, and the well-kept beer and genial bar staff make it a good place to meet and have a couple of drinks. It also has a critically acclaimed restaurant on the first floor. Quiet enough of an evening. Be warned, though, that it often closes early (8.30–9-ish most nights – well, you would too if you opened at six in the morning). However, if you like a place with a bit of activity and a comfortable atmosphere, or like the idea of a Guinness with your breakfast, you could do a great deal worse than the early-opening Hope.

FEATURES:

The Horseshoe

24 Clerkenwell Close
EC1R 0AG
020 7253 6068

That London term 'village' for often apparently undifferentiated bits of the capital suddenly makes sense when you slip away from the trendies cluttering up Clerkenwell Green and find yourself a hundred yards and – possibly – a hundred years away. The Horseshoe could sit happily in any true village, jostling with the church and duck pond. Externally, it's sixteenth-century quaint and tiny – but inside it runs back further than you would expect, to give quite a long bar area and a separate eating section. Décor is pretty basic and it's got no airs and graces – rather you have Greene King IPA or Sharps Cornish Coaster at £2.40 a pint and pie and mash at £3.95. And the two dartboards are obviously well used. A lunchtime group seemed regularly to get their exit doubles at the first time of asking – and when was the last time you saw a treble top scored in a local boozer? The little beer garden is probably a great suntrap – well, at least for an hour or so either side of noon, as the towering buildings around make it feel rather like sitting inside a cooling tower. And the revolt against modernism shows quite nicely in the framed daily newspaper in the gents' – it had been last updated four months before.

FEATURES:

Jerusalem Tavern

RATING:

Britton Street
EC1M 5NA
020 7490 4281

No stranger to those who have an interest in good public houses, the Jerusalem Tavern is a serious contender for nomination as one of the best pubs in London. Converted from a fabulous-looking eighteenth-century clockmaker's shop, it's the only pub in London owned by the Suffolk-based St Peter's Brewery. So you can usually expect to see their complete range of excellent award-winning ales, both in bottles and on tap. The place is tiny and the only negative we can attribute here is that it gets seriously busy quite often. After work it is predictably bad, with the lucky winners being the first two-dozen local workers to arrive from their offices; but the crowds do die down towards closing time. Overall, if you're lucky enough to find some free seats, the Dickensian feel of the place is perfect for a cosy winter's evening of warming ale and good conversation. Highly recommended.

FEATURES:

The Peasant

RATING:

240 St John Street
EC1V 9PH
020 7336 7726

The Peasant is a grand former gin palace turned upmarket gastropub, which languishes in the middle of Clerkenwell, surrounded by an uneasy mix of Victorian townhouses and council estates. Like many gastropubs, it's unsure of how to strike an even pub–restaurant balance, indicated by the wine glasses and cutlery on a scattering of ground-floor tables, in addition to the upstairs restaurant. Still, its aim in life appears to err towards minimal pretension and, due to the pub's size, there's plenty of space to sit and have a well-kept pint, while possibly enjoying one of the (expensive) bar snacks. With a relaxed atmosphere, friendly service and a tastefully refurbished interior (which retains many wonderful original features), The Peasant is a more traditional and comfortable alternative to the nearby bar The Well.

FEATURES:

Sekforde Arms

RATING:

34 Sekforde Street
EC1R 0HA
020 7253 3251

A very pleasant Young's pub in an old residential area just off Clerkenwell Road. Of course, it's all residential round here nowadays, with all the warehouse conversions and new apartment blocks going up, but this is the real deal. We'd hazard a guess that it's been like this round here from very early in the nineteenth century. The service is friendly, the beer very well kept and the food unpretentious (and without the pretentious price tag). This pub fits very comfortably with its surroundings. It's a genuine local and hardly anyone seems to know about it.

FEATURES:

Three Kings

RATING:

7 Clerkenwell Close
EC1R 0DY
020 7253 0483

A lively pub in trendy designer land. Despite the garish signage, this pub is a pretty solid, traditional local. It serves a good range of beers and wines, offers good service and has a lively clientele. Not being the biggest of places, its only real drawback is its popularity on Thursday and Friday nights, when the crowds spill out on to the street in preparation for their weekend nights out. Earlier on in the week it's quieter and easier to get served. This is definitely one of the better pubs in the area.

FEATURES:

The Well

RATING:

180 St John's Street
EC1V 4JY
020 7251 9363

This place really needs no introduction. It's one of the earlier trendy bars in the area and has appeared in countless pub and bar guides before. It gets pretty crowded at the end of the week, especially in summer, and that's when it can often be better to go elsewhere. But, if the crowds are thinner and your wallet's up to it, it's not a bad place at all. The drink's interesting – Continental beers on the pumps such as Hoegaarden, Leffe Blonde and Paulaner Weiss bier – the wine list is OK, the gastro-type food is decent and the service is good. Look out for the fish tanks in the basement bar, too.

FEATURES:

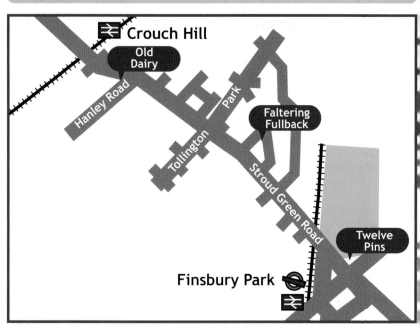

Faltering Fullback

RATING:

19 Perth Road
N4 3HB
020 7272 5834

Hidden away on a backstreet just north of Finsbury Park, the Faltering Fullback is a distinctly better alternative than any other pub within the vicinity of the station. It stocks an impressive range of draught and bottled beers, and has a friendly, laid-back local atmosphere. There's also an impressively cavernous backroom full of picnic tables and a pool table that appears to attract a younger crowd than the front area. In keeping with its name, the pub regularly screens football and rugby, though it's pretty unobtrusive and quite possible to enjoy your drink if you're not interested in the game. Recommended.

FEATURES:

The Old Dairy

RATING:

1–3 Crouch Hill
N4 4AP
020 7263 3337

This is a huge pub, which, although usually busy, always seems to have a table free. It has loads of little rooms, nooks and corners, so it's quite possible to have a romantic drink for two without noticing the rowdy group of rugby players in another section. It's quite an unusual building – it used to be a dairy, after all – and the fantastic exterior crenellations and painted decoration are easily matched by the lovely tile work in some of the rooms inside. The range of beer is well kept and the food is tasty too. Oh, and on Friday nights the pub plays host to the indie-oriented Cow Club.

FEATURES:

The Twelve Pins

RATING:

263 Seven Sisters Road
N4 2DE
020 8809 0192

The sheer size of The Twelve Pins and its proximity to Finsbury Park station limit its appeal a little, but it's not really so bad. The interior is quite magnificent, if a little careworn, a good example of a Victorian pub interior. The varied mix of punters seem oblivious of its charms, content to drink quietly and keep themselves to themselves, and there's a decent drop of Guinness to be had here. The pub shows Gaelic football and hurling matches, and has regular appearances by Irish bands – it gets lively when Banjaxed are on.

FEATURES:

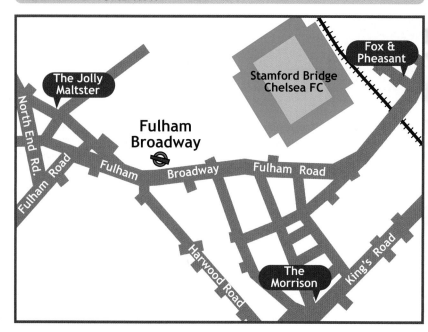

The Jolly Maltster

North End Rd.

Fulham Road

Fulham Broadway

Stamford Bridge Chelsea FC

Fox & Pheasant

Fulham Broadway

Fulham Road

Harwood Road

King's Road

The Morrison

Fox & Pheasant

RATING:

1 Billing Road
SW10 9UJ
020 7352 2943

Unless you're of the Chelsea persuasion, you'll probably stay clear of this one when there's a game on at Stamford Bridge. At any other time, though, it's worth a look if you like your pubs cut from the same traditional cloth as Knightsbridge's Nag's Head or Barons Court's Colton Arms. Like those two, the Fox & Pheasant is a small affair, managing to fit a dartboard and a TV screen into its classic low-ceilinged pub interior. There are some seats out the back and there's a small lunchtime menu (weekdays only) to nosh while you sample their Greene King ales. An untouched gem in an area where most of the pubs chase after the latest trends, it's the sort of old boozer where it's no great surprise to find a signed Britt Ekland picture behind the bar.

FEATURES:

The Jolly Maltster

RATING:

17 Vanston Place
SW6 1AY
020 7385 3593

A pretty ordinary pub most of the time, it comes into its own on two occasions – match days and karaoke nights. When Chelsea play at home, the Jolly Maltster is on the wrong (or right, depending on your point of view) side of the tube station for fans heading towards the match, and consequently doesn't get half as rammed as other pubs in the area. But the real reason that people come here is for the karaoke – and they love it. The booze is pretty standard – a place for a contemplative pint and the crossword it ain't, but the locals seem very happy with it.

FEATURES:

The Morrison

RATING:

648 King's Road
SW6 2DU
020 7610 9859

A sleek and stylish newcomer to this end of the King's Road, this one's the sort of place almost custom built for this neck of the woods. All soft furnishings and chill-out sounds on the stereo, it's a touch above your usual loungey hangout, purely from the fine service offered from the friendly staff. Best of all, despite its being Irish-owned, there's no recourse to plastering 'Cead Mile Failte' all over the place. There's probably a market for an O'Neill's All Bar One hybrid (with 'Colcannon risotto' on the menu probably), but thankfully this isn't an attempt at it. Decent Guinness, fair menu as well, though perhaps the wine list isn't as wide-ranging as you'd expect. A few plasma screens are dotted about for the rugby and football, though escape from that in the summer months comes in the form of a beer garden at the back. Good stuff.

FEATURES:

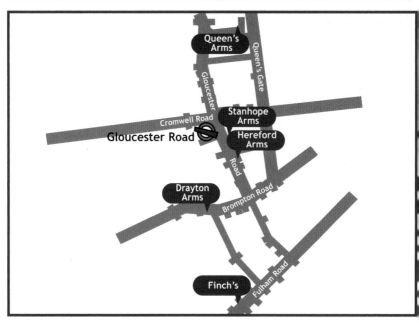

Drayton Arms

153 Old Brompton Road
SW5 0LJ
020 7835 2301

A Victorian pub with some nice touches of interior detail, now setting its stall out as a loungey sort of place. That may explain the frankly ridiculous numbers of chair styles on offer here. Still, the slight amateurish shtick on the furniture is part of the charm of this place, marking it apart from a branded pub-chain affair. Plenty of space for the mainly young clientele, though they appeared on our visit to be laid back and relaxed rather than achingly stylish trendsetters. Enough goodies behind the bar to cover all tastes, and, if you're after entertainment, it comes in the form of DJs through the week and live music on Sundays. Not a bad pub for the area.

FEATURES:

Finch's

RATING:

190 Fulham Road
SW10 9PN
020 7351 5043

Young's have done an excellent job of retaining the lovely Victorian interior of this light and airy pub – the tiled walls are particularly stunning. There's a big-screen TV, so it buzzes more when there's a game on, but this is a perfectly agreeable place for a couple of drinks of an afternoon. And, for the sake of variety, it's good to see a pub (as opposed to a bar) managing to eke out an existence on the Fulham Road.

FEATURES:

Hereford Arms

RATING:

127 Gloucester Road
SW7 4TE
020 7370 4988

Not surprisingly for the area, this is very much a pub for the tourists – the flags of all nations festooned around the place are a bit of a giveaway. It's been given the old-rustic-pub-interior-décor treatment, which is a bit of a shame, since the old place was OK – a normal boozer, but a bit shabby. It's also a pretty big place, serves decent enough food and drink and is not too badly priced, given the area. Service was friendly, although it was pretty quiet last time we were in. We wonder what the service would be like with a few coach parties in there. While the committed pub goer might spend more effort looking for something a little less formulaic, if you're thirsty and/or hungry and in the neighbourhood, you might as well pop in.

FEATURES:

Queen's Arms

RATING:

30 Queens Gate Mews
SW7 5QL
020 7581 7741

This pub is tucked out of sight in a small mews not far from Hyde Park. The surrounding colleges explain the student population, but that's not the whole story. It's also a good place to meet before going to see something at the Albert Hall and shows the effects of major events such as the Proms, spilling out into the hapless mews. It was done up a while back and is no longer the dark boozer it used to be. The menu is a bit gastro, but what we saw looked good – and not more than a tenner a plate. They also have specials every day and Sunday roast from lunchtime until 8.30 in the evening! A lively place, good guest beers and a selection of Belgian beer (had a raspberry one on when we were in last). The harried staff manage to stay friendly even after a long evening. It's less busy during the day and at weekends, which makes it a good spot to meet in Kensington, if a little off the beaten track.

FEATURES: HANDY FOR: Royal Albert Hall   *Visitors' Award Winner 2005*

Stanhope Arms

RATING:

97 Gloucester Road
SW7 4SS
020 7373 4192

A reasonable pub for a quick pint and an ideal place to meet before going to the Albert Hall or other attractions nearby (though leave enough time to get there!). Standard pub fare, both beer and food. Friendly and attentive bar staff and well-kept beer help make it. It can fill up with tourists, as it is in the heart of tourist-hotel land, but the televisions encourage locals and office workers in for the sport.

FEATURES: HANDY FOR: Royal Albert Hall

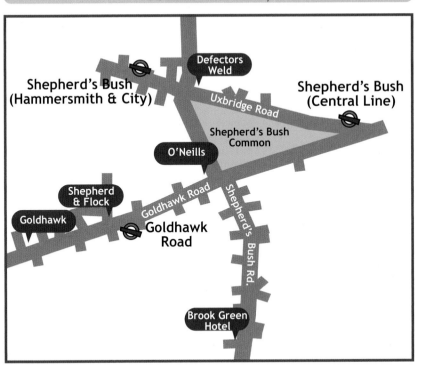

Brook Green Hotel

RATING:

170 Shepherd's Road
W6 7PB
020 7603 2516

A large, handsome Young's pub that manages to fit in post-work office staff, canny locals and trendy west Londoners, and leave no one disappointed. We like the beer, the lounge-style interior – recently redecorated with a little care and consideration for the old building – and the fact that, even on a busy Friday night, we eventually got a seat. The space downstairs is known on Fridays as Brooks Blues Bar, so, if you find yourself in W6 with a hellhound on your trail, make sure to stop by. The pub also comes in handy for a pre-gig drink if you're heading from Hammersmith up to the Shepherd's Bush Empire.

FEATURES:

The Defectors Weld

RATING:

170 Uxbridge Road

W12 8AA

020 8749 0008

When pubs are taken over and revamped, it can result in much weeping and wailing, but that's not the case here. The last pub at this address – an outlet for the bargain-bin bar chain Edward's – won't be missed by too many drinkers. It's been replaced by something a lot more in keeping with both the gradual gentrification of the area and also the needs of folk meeting for a pint before a gig at the Shepherd's Bush Empire. Following on from the same owners' reworked Lock Tavern in Camden, here is a professionally loungey pub, where a set of DJ decks is as essential as a supply of bottled Leffe. Even though the first floor is primarily a dining space, a couple of leather armchairs provide the opportunity for some Rowley Birkin-style remembrances. The whole enterprise does have an enforced air of cool to it (note the copies of *Sleazenation* artfully arranged on a side table), but as a pre-gig drinking and eating spot it does the job (though don't expect to have too much money left for a drink at the Empire). We're not so sure it'll appeal to the pre-match QPR fans quite as much though. As for the oblique name, we're still not 100 per cent sure, but the picture of Cambridge KGB man Kim Philby on the stairs must have something to do with it.

FEATURES:

Reviewers' Award - best newcomer 2005

The Goldhawk

RATING:

122 Goldhawk Road

W12 8HH

020 8576 6921

Making a deliberate attempt to appeal to a clientele different from all the Irish boozers round these parts is this loungey pub. All squishy furnishings and laid-back sounds, it's hardly one to make a beeline for if you want a big party, but it does serve a need in this neck of the woods if you want a drink but don't fancy watching the racing from Fairyhouse. With decent ales on the hand pumps, Continental beers on tap (including, for example, Sleeman's), a fair wine list, cocktails, modern pub food (and Sunday roast) and arguably the cleanest pub toilets on the Goldhawk Road, this pub's a pleasant place to while away an afternoon.

O'Neill's

RATING:

Goldhawk Road
W12 8QD
020 8746 1288

A cut above your usual O'Neill's, this one's for music lovers and sport fans. For music lovers, we're not talking about DJs, live music or a great jukebox, but the fact that it is right next door to the Shepherd's Bush Empire and is the obvious place for the pre-gig meet (and to ingest something other than Carling). For sport fans there are screens dotted all over the pub and big screen too, so you're always close to the action. For the thirsty, there's Guinness, of course, plus the excellent Budvar on tap.

FEATURES:

Shepherd & Flock

RATING:

84 Goldhawk Road
W12 8HA
020 8743 4046

A narrow little Irish pub that serves the need of the local community and anyone else with a hankering for Setanta Sports. Newcomers may well be treated to a stop-and-stare from the locals, though nothing that's too offputting. If the pubs on the Kilburn High Road are getting too trendy for you, you may want to give it a look.

FEATURES:

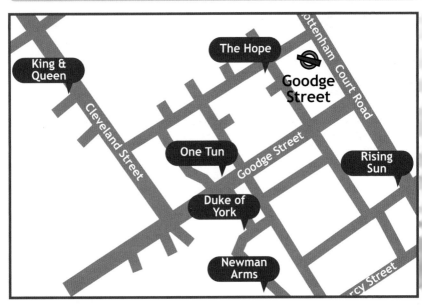

Duke of York

RATING:

47 Rathbone Street
W1T 1NQ
020 7636 7065

Why is it that so many of the traditional pubs that we really like just don't stack up on paper? Your passing American tourist will be baffled as to why this cramped, slightly grubby, feature-free drinks vendor is an automatic three-pinter. It's small – with no more than four dozen punters in, all the stools round the semi-island bar are taken and the handful of tables are fully occupied. It doesn't appear to do non-liquid refreshment. The board outside which advertises 'terrestrial' sport – so look elsewhere for the Saturn Korfball league – on two screens even suggests you bring your own food while you watch it. Bring spyglasses, too, as the high-level screens are probably no bigger than the one in your kitchen. But it's a proper London boozer. Some impressive traditional pub mirrors and apparently genuine Victorian prints and portraits scatter the walls. IPA, Abbot and Speckled Hen are professionally served and the mix of local workers – white- and blue-collar – makes it feel like a local that has been there for ever.

FEATURES:

The Hope

RATING:

15 Tottenham Street
W1T 2AW
020 7637 0896

This is a decent enough pub and the beer's drinkable. It gets busy between quitting time and mid-evening – sometimes getting packed with students and local workers. It's not surprising, as they've got outside tables for enjoying a good evening. There's nothing really remarkable about the pub itself, but the staff are friendly and accommodating. It's a good pub if you're here at the right time, otherwise it can be a little dead. A reasonable place to meet if you're in the area.

FEATURES:

King & Queen

RATING:

1 Foley Street
W1W 6DL
020 7636 5619

A lot of the pubs between Warren Street and Goodge Street are moderate drinking holes, but this one sticks out. It's a bit off the main drag, but a Friday-night visit found it to be one of the most popular pubs in the area. It attracts a fair mix of punters, the beers (especially Adnams and now the excellent St Austell Tribute) are well kept and a jovial atmosphere pervades. The bar staff are prompt and friendly and aren't overawed by big crowds at the bar. It's perhaps one worth sampling on a quieter night – a winter's evening drinking next to the fire is something we're looking forward too. Fine brass till, too.

FEATURES:

Newman Arms

RATING:

23 Rathbone Street
W1T 1NQ
020 7636 1127

This is another old favourite. It's had a lick of paint and lost some of the eccentricity that it used to define it, the upstairs Pie Room is no longer the haven from the heaving masses downstairs that it used to be, but it's still a good pub. And frankly, while we have a soft spot for grubby pubs, grubbiness doesn't bring in the punters. So we have to commend the landlady's hard work to improve the pub and make it more convivial whilst still keeping it a pub – it would be easy to make it into a trendy bar and try to make as much as possible from expensive lager and overpriced cocktails. While we'll miss the old version, some things have to move with the times.The beer's still good, with Adnam's Bitter and London Pride on when we were in last, and if you haven't tried it, the Addlestone's Cloudy Cider is a cut above normal pub ciders. The pies upstairs are probably the best pies in London, with organic and free range ingredients wherever possible - apparently they can tell you which farm the meat came from. On the people front, the veteran bar staff continue to pour a decent pint, and are generally convivial and act pleased to see punters coming in. Where else in this area can you get toasties for £1.50? The only thing you need to be aware of is it will get tremendously busy at office quitting time, but wait a while and you will get a seat. A sometime sanctuary in Fitzrovia.

FEATURES:

One Tun

RATING:

58–60 Goodge Street
W1T 4LZ
020 7209 4105

Even though it's been tidied up and smartened (and we have to say we like it, as it's not gone over the top), it's still a decent enough Young's pub, featuring all the usual Young's stuff and pleasant service. Beyond the fact that it's looking smarter, we can't see what's changed. It has two attributes worth mentioning: it's heavily into sport (not a recent bandwagon thing by the way), so all the big sporting events are catered for; and it has a quiz every Tuesday evening, with drink prizes (which must be consumed on the evening). And jolly good fun it is too.

FEATURES:

Rising Sun

RATING:

46 Tottenham Court Road
W1T 2ED
020 7636 6530

With its impressive Victorian exterior, this easy-to-find place is a popular pub on Tottenham Court Road and a safer bet for a drink than some of the other pubs in the area. It's had another makeover on the outside, but it's also got a decent pub interior to match. With five beers on the hand pumps, reasonable wine list and an updated menu, you'll find it to be a reliable place for a pint and a bit of grub. One obvious sign of their main clientele is the sign on the bar that says 'Student discount 3 p.m. – closed, Monday to Thursday' and '4 pint jugs available'. It's not bad during the day, just try to be out by 3 p.m. if you have an aversion to students.

FEATURES:

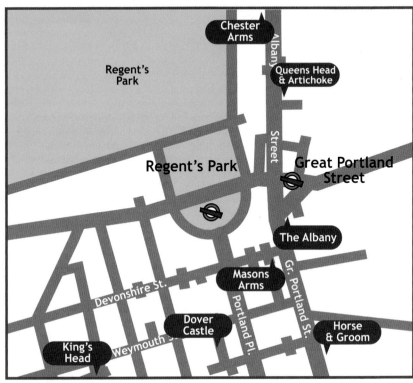

Regent's Park

Chester Arms

Queens Head & Artichoke

Regent's Park

Great Portland Street

The Albany

Masons Arms

Devonshire St.

Dover Castle

King's Head

Weymouth

Horse & Groom

The Albany

RATING:

240 Great Portland Street
W1W 5QU
020 7387 0221

Now firmly established (having replaced a Firkin pub), the Albany is a pretty decent pub. The beer is fine with a selection of guest ales on the hand pumps as well as Leffe and Hoegaarden for those in a Continental mood. The service is good and there's a stronger emphasis on food (lunch and evening snacks). But we just wish pubs would get beyond seventies and eighties furniture and butcher's-block tables when they're being done up. We've done postmodern, we've done post-ironic, let's think of something new. Also well established, the basement is known as Lowdown and has comedy on every night, interspersed with regular club nights.

FEATURES:

Chester Arms

RATING:

87 Albany Street
NW1 4BT
020 7681 6017

Perhaps not as stately as the Regency architecture that surrounds it, this is still quite a cosy little boozer with a pleasant air. It attracts strong support from the local rugby club, even though the small interior doesn't suggest it's a venue for rugger-bugger exploits. There's an emphasis on sports coverage and the food looks fairly homely. If the sight of too many joggers in Regent's Park is driving you to drink, this one is a handy port of call.

FEATURES: HANDY FOR: Regent's Park Zoo

Dover Castle

RATING:

43 Weymouth Mews
W1G 7EH
020 7580 4412

A fine old Sam Smith's pub tucked away in a mews, just away from the hustle and bustle of Marylebone Road and Portland Place. It rarely gets crowded and, if you like Sam's produce, is just the place to put your feet up, and read a good book or ponder eternity. It's on the tourist map but it's so difficult to find that very few manage to get here.

FEATURES:

Horse & Groom

RATING:

128 Great Portland Street
W1W 6PX
020 7580 4726

This is a beautiful-looking Victorian pub with plenty of original tile work. Usual for W1, the Sam Smith's own-brand drinks range is on offer. The bar is split into three sections, none huge. The front is predominantly standing room and high tables, the middle area has table footy and darts and the backroom is the most civilised – a seating area, complete with skylight. There also seems to be an upstairs bar, too. On our Friday-night visit, although busy, it was probably the only pub in Fitzrovia that wasn't packed like a rush-hour tube train – it was actually possible to get a seat. Definitely an advantage for after-work drinks, but it points to possibly being frighteningly quiet at other times. It's possible the pub's position – most other pubs in the area occupy imposing corner plots – means it blends in with the anonymous shops on Great Portland Street too much. Certainly a shame, as it's a pub with plenty of potential.

FEATURES:

King's Head

RATING:

13 Westmoreland Street
W1G 8PJ
020 7835 2201

A quiet local in the posh West End dormitory bit between Marylebone Road and Oxford Street. It's a Greene King pub so the beer is decent, there's champers by the glass (we did say it's in a posh area) and Sunday lunch, too. One or two celebs who live nearby use this as a local. You wouldn't make a special journey to get here, but it's handy for a quiet pint if you're in the area.

FEATURES:

The Masons Arms

RATING:

8 Devonshire Street
W1W 5EA
020 7580 6501

Tucked away near Great Portland Street tube, the Masons Arms is a solid well-kept pub worthy of a visit. The beer and service are excellent and the food pretty decent, too. A variety of masonic (in an architectural sense) paraphernalia adorns the walls, and subdued orange lights create a pleasant, relaxing atmosphere.

FEATURES:

The Queen's Head & Artichoke

RATING:

30–32 Albany Street
NW1 4EA
020 7916 6206

Nestling behind the back of the Royal College of Physicians, this place is handy for the Indian food nirvana of Drummond Street. It's packed during lunchtime and in the evenings, with the upstairs restaurant doing a booming business as well. The bar also serves an extensive tapas menu and daily specials, though we wouldn't classify them as cheap. There are some good ales on the pumps, which are well kept. The place looks like a Continental café and if you can bag one of the capacious sofas you may well feel tempted to stay a while and hold forth on questions of existence and philosophy.

FEATURES: HANDY FOR: Regent's Park Zoo

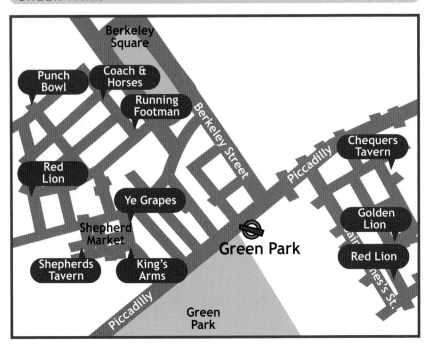

Berkeley Square

Punch Bowl

Coach & Horses

Running Footman

Berkeley Street

Chequers Tavern

Piccadilly

Red Lion

Ye Grapes

Shepherd Market

Green Park

Golden Lion

Red Lion

Shepherds Tavern

King's Arms

Piccadilly

Green Park

Chequers Tavern

RATING: 🍺🍺🍺

16 Duke Street
SW1Y 6DB
020 7930 4007

Another small St James's pub. Usually the quietest pub in this neck of the woods, it means more chance to get a seat. It gets the basics right, with good real ales, including Brakspear and a simple but cheap food menu. The service was very good and they clearly take pride in running their pub – we even noticed the landlord cleaning all the brass at closing time. However, what made us continue our night here, rather than move elsewhere, was the music. Uniformly good, it ranged from Roxy Music through to the Clash, with some eighties and nineties classics thrown in. A good, solid boozer.

FEATURES:

Coach & Horses

RATING:

5 Hill Street
....
W1J 5LD
....
020 7355 0300
....

A very nice little pub indeed, set in rather posh surroundings, it has a well-looked-after interior, with enough old bits remaining to give it a genteel sort of feel without making it look like a museum. As it's a Shepherd Neame place, the beer is pretty good and so is the rest of the booze, and the prices aren't bad, given where it is. There's a pretty extensive food menu, with vegetarians well catered for, again at decent prices, and the service is excellent. Everybody seems to know everybody in this pub (including the bar people) and it doesn't take an Einstein to work out why they keep coming back. It can get rather crowded after work towards the end of the week – understandable but inconvenient if you're looking for a quiet pint. It's a pity it's not open on Saturday and Sunday – but then it's a pretty quiet around here at the weekends and it probably wouldn't have as much atmosphere. You can hire the pub at the weekend, though, so you could create your own.

FEATURES: HANDY FOR: The Royal Academy

Golden Lion

RATING:

25 King Street
....
SW1Y 6QY
....
020 7925 0007
....

While its interior may not quite match its exuberant exterior, this one's worth popping into should you find yourself idle in St James's with no club membership to fall back on. The Nicholson's chain pride themselves on their traditional food and drink selection, though the local office clientele keep this one from being too much of a tourist 'Ye Olde Pubbe'. The upstairs is now no-smoking, but, if you fancy a unique bird's-eye view of local life, try to bag the two chairs outside on the balcony.

FEATURES:

The King's Arms

RATING:

2 Shepherd Market
W1J 7QB
020 7629 0416

Another popular establishment in the pub-heavy Shepherd Market. This one, although not bad, offers nothing out of the ordinary, although a recent refurbishment has improved the menu and brought the pub up to date. On summer evenings it often gets crowded with people spilling outside the front, like most of the other pubs in the locality. With a rather bland interior, plus average beer and food, it's probably one for a quick pint rather than a long evening.

FEATURES:

The Punch Bowl

RATING:

41 Farm Street
W1J 5RP
020 7493 6841

A quiet old pub in the backstreets of Mayfair. The interior has been opened out a little, but it's still got an olde-worlde charm that you don't get much of these days – especially in these parts. It's just that little bit harder to find and as a result tends to be quieter when all the surrounding pubs are mobbed. Nevertheless, it's still a deservedly popular place, with a friendly bunch of regulars. It serves a decent pint – Speccy, Bombardier, Courage Best – and the service is friendly. There's lunchtime food, which is when it tends to be busier.

FEATURES:

The Red Lion

RATING:

Waverton Street
W1J 5QN
020 7499 1307

This place is steadily improving in our estimation, returning to the decent boozer it used to be in the not-so-distant past. There's a range of good beers on the hand pumps and they're well kept. The service is OK, as is the pub grub, and the wine list is pretty decent and cheap (especially for the area). The self-important suits whom we used to find offputting still frequent the place and crowd the place out just after work, but they tend to go home earlyish. The taxi rat run outside is still on the go – so an alfresco drink in summer is still laced with particulates and accompanied by the clatter of diesels. But at quieter times – usually later in the evening – this pub's certainly a pleasant place to be.

FEATURES:

The Red Lion (Crown Passage)

RATING:

23 Crown Passage, King Street
SW1Y 6PP
020 7930 4141

Tucked away down a gaslit side street in Mayfair, this is a charming boozer. Its age and location may suggest a soulless dive aimed purely at tourists, but by and large this is as genuine and as genial a pub as you'll find. The TV is seldom switched on and there's no music, but what you do get is well-kept beer (Adnams, Bass), a cracking selection of whiskies and excellent sandwiches, all served up by some of the politest bar staff in town. It also helps that many of the punters – from businessmen to builders – are up for a natter. Granted, it can get very busy on weeknights (try for a seat upstairs if so) but it's a handy hideaway of a Saturday. If you're after a warm and comfortable pub, give it a look. (Closed Sunday.)

FEATURES:

Running Footman

RATING:

5 Charles Street
W1J 5DE
020 7499 2988

Basic no-frills pub that does the simple things fairly well (decent pint, cheap pub grub) – but it's just a little unatmospheric for its Mayfair surroundings. We were intrigued by the 'Ben Nevis Burger' on our last visit – we can only imagine how big it must be! It's got three beers on tap, some that look to be guests, and the rest of the menu seems fairly reasonable pub grub. Not one to go out of your way for necessarily, but not bad.

FEATURES:

Shepherds Tavern

RATING:

50 Hertford Street
W1J 7ST
020 7499 3017

Not a bad little pub – built in 1735 and still going strong. Does food during the day and there is a separate dining room upstairs for a more comprehensive menu. The steak baguette is quite tasty, and the ale was equally good – a nice spot for a few afternoon pints if you are in the area. Quite a cosy atmosphere and not usually as crowded as other pubs in the area.

FEATURES:

Ye Grapes

RATING: 🍺🍺🍺

16 Shepherd Market

W1J 7QQ

020 7499 1563

Quite a nice big old pub that has an eccentric collection of olde-worlde knick-knacks and a cosy sort of loved and lived-in feel. Six beers on the hand pumps, the usual wines and lagers and a real fire round off the experience. Usually very crowded in summer when the local workers cram into the market after work – you can try the upstairs lounge but even that fills very quickly. Winter is less frenetic, but not by much. A pretty reasonable sort of boozer overall.

GREENWICH (DLR)

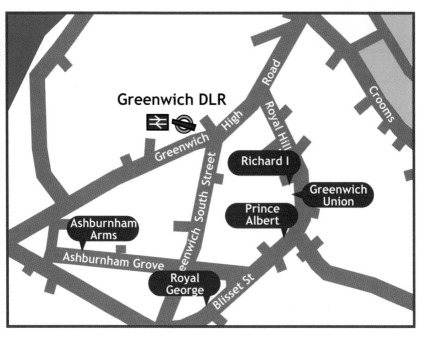

Ashburnham Arms

RATING:

25 Ashburnham Grove

SE10 8UH

020 8692 2007

Hidden just a few minutes away from the bustle of central Greenwich, the Ashburnham Arms is an excellent place to draw breath over a pint or two. It's situated on a quiet street in a very pleasant part of Greenwich and has a fine beer garden in case you fancy a drink outside. It's had a makeover recently – farewell to the bar billiards table, hello arty prints and lounge-style décor. We preferred its previous look, to be honest. Nonetheless, the usual range of excellent Shepherd Neame beers on tap remains and the Ashburnham is still a good pub.

FEATURES:

The Greenwich Union

RATING:

56 Royal Hill

SE10 8RT

020 8692 6258

Opening up next door to a fine pub like the Richard I can't have been easy, but the Greenwich Union pulled it off. It's a smart, spacious place that's modern and has a relaxed vibe. The bar offers a unique range of superb beer from the nearby Meantime Brewery, including raspberry beer, blonde ale and chocolate stout. When we were unable to make up our minds, a friendly barmaid gave us some free samples of different beers – excellent service matched by the enthusiasm of the staff for their wares. If the draught beers don't tempt you, try the good selection of bottled beer in the fridge. A varied gastro-esque menu has main courses for around £8. Greenwich Union is somewhere that you could happily bring friends who aren't really into pubs. The only negative can be the abundance of parents and pushchairs around at the weekends, so, if kids don't induce a warm sentimental glow, then you might choose to do your boozing elsewhere at these times. This is really nitpicking, though, as the Greenwich Union is a top place.

FEATURES:

Visitors' Award 2004

Prince Albert

RATING:

72 Royal Hill

SE10 8RT

020 8333 6512

The Prince Albert's walls are covered in nautical pictures and ephemera, yet you won't find too many tourists or museum-goers here. The pub has a down-to-earth feel that we like for its honesty and hospitality. The big-screen TV is handy for sports events and there always seems to be a good atmosphere. When other Royal Hill pubs are crowded, we often end up here, drinking with the friendly, older local crowd.

FEATURES: HANDY FOR: National Maritime Museum

Richard I

RATING:

52 Royal Hill

SE10 8RT

020 8692 2996

This place has always been a good pub, though more recently we've felt it to be slipping a little and knocked it back a pint. However, our last few visits have found it with an excellent atmosphere on both Friday night and Sunday afternoon, so we reinstated our original rating. It does excellent Young's beer, the service is polite and prompt and the food comes recommended as well. On warmer days, the large beer garden pulls in the punters, so leaving a bit more space inside (though the place is never empty). The regulars come in all shapes and sizes and come across as a friendly lot. There are plenty of pubs in this little area of Greenwich, but this one's still among the pick of them for us.

FEATURES: HANDY FOR: Old Royal Observatory

The Royal George

RATING:

2 Blissett Street

SE10 8UP

020 8692 1949

An excellent little local, next to one of the biggest fire stations we've seen. The colleagues of Captain Flack, Barney McGrew, Dibble et al. were not in evidence when we visited, but what we did get was a warm and friendly welcome. It's a Shepherd Neame pub, so fine pints of Master Brew and Spitfire were available. Attractive stained-glass windows at the front, ship models and tankards give the pub's interior character. Recommended.

FEATURES:

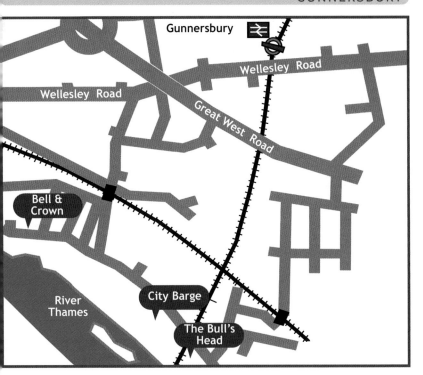

Gunnersbury

Wellesley Road

Wellesley Road

Great West Road

Bell & Crown

River Thames

City Barge

The Bull's Head

Bell & Crown

RATING:

11–13 Thames Road, Strand on the Green

W4 3PL

020 8994 4164

If you fancy a riverside stroll and a couple of drinks, the three pubs on Strand on the Green certainly fit the bill. Start at Kew Bridge and the Bell & Crown will be the first one you come to. Probably the biggest and busiest of the three, it's a safe, dependable Fuller's pub. The beer tastes good, the food looks fine and there's a comfortable air of repose to the place. It's the sort of place you take your folks to when they visit London – nothing flash, just a decent pub.

FEATURES:

GUNNERSBURY

The Bull's Head

RATING:

15 Strand On The Green
W4 3PQ
020 8994 1204

It's been gone a few years now, but we still have fond memories of the sticky-floored boozer this once was. Probably such a thing was thought uncouth for such a prime site and, after a sprucing up, it became a Chef & Brewer pub. And so it remains, and, try as we like, we just can't warm to the place. The wide range of real ales certainly appeals but a good pub needs more than that. It's olde-worlde but overly so: like many other Chef & Brewer pubs, it has a slight air of artificiality that takes hold. This one seems geared more for punters after food rather than stopping in for a drink and a chat. It's a perfectly pleasant enough pub, but we've tried and we just can't find this one's heart and soul. Jazz nights on Sunday evenings, though.

FEATURES:

The City Barge

RATING:

27 Strand On The Green
W4 3PH
020 8994 2148

Halfway between the Bell & Crown and the Bull's Head, in both distance and style, appears the City Barge, a titchy drinking den that's tried to tidy itself up a little (there's loungey furniture at the back). Thankfully, it retains a good atmosphere and is arguably the most publike establishment on this little stretch of the river, with particularly warm and friendly service from the bar staff. Ideal for a cosy winter warmer or a summer cooler, it's one that's ideal for a slow afternoon of easygoing imbibing.

FEATURES:

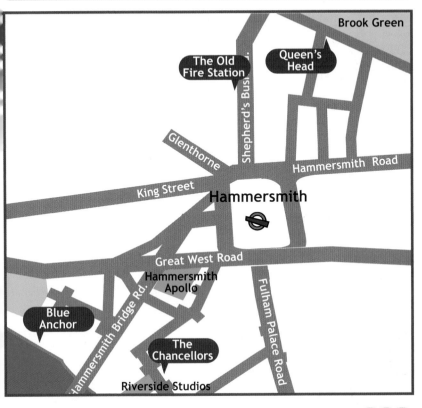

Blue Anchor

RATING:

13 Lower Mall
W6 9DJ
020 8748 5774

Maybe we caught it when they were all messing about on the river, but this pub seemed surprisingly devoid of rowers. It has a small downstairs and an upstairs function room/dining room, the stairs to which are hidden by the side of the bar. Decorated with many an old photograph of the area, it's a pleasant place to while away a Sunday afternoon in. But, if you are lulled to sleep by the 1930s jazz CDs, don't say we didn't warn you. Thai food at weekends.

FEATURES:

The Chancellors

RATING:

25 Crisp Road

W6 9RL

020 8748 2600

Directly opposite Riverside Studios yet a world away from media-land, the Chancellors is a fine little boozer. A warm and friendly place, this pub attracts a large mix of punters who all get looked after by a wonderfully attentive landlady. An unpretentious pub with a good atmosphere (and great toasties), this is a real gem. Snacks on the bar on Sunday lunchtimes, too.

FEATURES: HANDY FOR: Riverside Studios

The Old Fire Station

RATING:

244 Shepherds Bush Road

W6 79L

020 8222 8453

If, like us, you prefer sitting with a pint in a cosy pub, perhaps with a real fire in the background and a pub quiz planned for later that evening, you may be tempted to walk straight past the Old Fire Station. However, to do so would be to miss a treat. The building itself is interesting – it was until recently (you've guessed it) the local fire station and is full of period Victorian features (even if the tiles do make it look a bit like a swimming pool). Friendly staff serve an array of draught beers, including comparative rarities such as New Zealand's Steinlager, and the fire-station theme is kept throughout – from the sections on the pub-grub menu to the innovative gents' urinals. Well worth a look for something a bit different.

FEATURES:

The Queen's Head

13 Brook Green
W6 7BL
020 7603 3174

Tiny from the outside, enormous on the inside, this is another old coaching inn, so there's a long history on the menu and plenty of copper stuff. Chef & Brewer, the company who own it, specialise in big local pubs that do food and are aimed at non-teenaged drinkers and families. They haven't strayed from the formula here, and so, weirdly, this does not feel like a London pub but like a successful country boozer. The result isn't too bad. The food looks fine, though a little frilly, and, because the old bits are actually old and the pub is made up of what were once adjoining smaller rooms, there is a genuine cosiness to the place. It's worth a look on a warm day, too, as the beer garden is one of the largest in town. Courage Best and Directors are your choices on tap.

FEATURES:

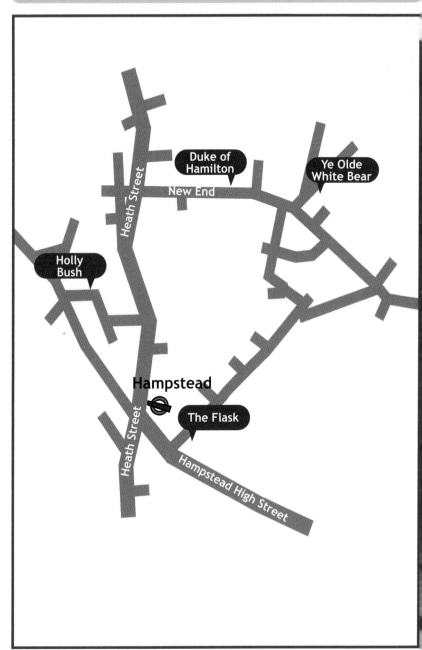

Duke of Hamilton

RATING:

23–25 New End

NW3 1JD

020 7794 0258

Not the most famous pub in Hampstead but arguably one of the friendliest, the Duke of Hamilton is an amiable local, which you soon warm to. It has an excellent barman and one or two regulars who are always up for a chat. They pride themselves on their wide selection of real ales, which usually include some well-kept seasonal choices. With a relaxed unpretentious atmosphere, it's the sort of pub you wish was your local. Go see.

FEATURES:

The Flask

RATING:

14 Flask Walk

NW3 1HE

020 7435 4580

One of the most popular pubs in Hampstead with both locals and tourists, this is a very solid rather than spectacular boozer. Its design is Victorian, with banquettes in the lounge, a decorated screen separating the public bar, and a modern conservatory at the back. The usual Young's beers are on tap, and the staff are friendly enough. Don't come here for a hectic Saturday night out, but, if you want a warm and friendly pub for a few jars and a chat, give it a go.

FEATURES:

Holly Bush

RATING:

22 Holly Mount

NW3 6SG

020 7435 2892

Beauty is a rare and precious thing in this world and it is even rarer and more precious in a public house. The Holly Bush is one of the older pubs in London, dating from the time when Hampstead was a country town. Inside this listed building, its stripped wooden interior and slightly ramshackle atmosphere lend it the charming aspect of a nineteenth-century coaching inn. That said, it can get a little crowded at times (although we have spent many a Saturday afternoon and evening here without suffering unduly) and some of the punters do seem like parodies of *Guardian* readers. But there is something deeply fine about this place – maybe the history, maybe the wooden booths and log fire, or maybe the good beers – that engenders wit and conviviality. Just avoid the rather bland renovation in the backroom.

FEATURES:

Ye Olde White Bear

RATING:

Well Road

NW3 1LJ

020 7435 3758

It's far from easy to pinpoint the finest public house in Hampstead, such is the strength and breadth of the competition, but Ye Olde White Bear is certainly in the running. It's comfortable and friendly, has board games and a good selection of beers, and there's decent food that, although not particularly cheap, is certainly neither the most expensive nor the most pretentious in the neighbourhood. A splendid establishment.

FEATURES:

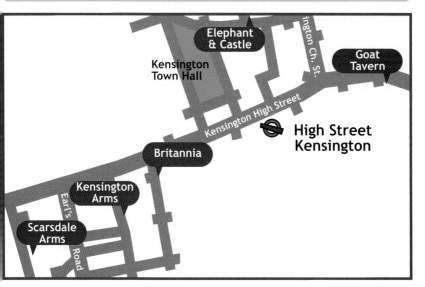

Elephant & Castle

Goat Tavern

Kensington Town Hall

ington Ch. St.

Kensington High Street

High Street Kensington

Britannia

Kensington Arms

Earl's

Scarsdale Arms

Road

The Britannia

RATING:

1 Allen Street

W8 6UX

020 7937 6905

Jumping somewhat belatedly on the gastro bandwagon, the Britannia is an early attempt from Young's to cash in on the beer-and-expensive-grub trade. In our opinion there was nothing much wrong with the old place. It may have needed a lick of paint, but it was a dark, cosy place, and the atmosphere was helped enormously by three real fires. Whether it was a response to competition or an attempt to increase margins, the pub's recently been modernised. Thankfully, the fires are still there, but the décor of the place has been considerably brightened up. Young's excellent beers have been supplemented by Continental invaders. And then there's the appearance of extensive drinks lists – starting with champagne, naturally – on the tables. Brewing appears to have been marginalised in favour of dining, and it all sits together rather uncomfortably for us. In the past, the glow of the fires fostered the illusion of warmth, but now they're mostly cosmetic detail. The old regulars are still there, but it feels like there should be a much younger crowd here now. We're not against modernisation in the slightest, but we really expect more empathy from the owners of our top pub of 2005.

FEATURES:

167

Elephant & Castle

RATING:

Holland St

W8 4LT

020 7368 0901

A welcome refuge in the quiet backstreets two minutes from High Street, Kensington, the Elephant & Castle's multi-award-winning flower-festooned façade almost hides this small and homely pub. Though it's been taken over by Nicholson's, it's not the normal routine for their pubs. The beer and service are good and the atmosphere is usually pretty lively (though a bit 'OK, yah' at times). The food is very good, and not Nicholson's usual menu, with daily menu choices and specials, and not too expensive, either. It used to be that, whenever there was a hint of sunshine, the locals deserted the bar for the tiny front garden, spilling out on to the street, but there must have been complaints from the neighbours, as the signs make it clear that drinking on the pavements isn't allowed. Still, it's got a lot going for it and it's worth a look in.

FEATURES:

Goat Tavern

RATING:

3a Kensington High Street, London

W8 5NP

020 7937 1213

When a pub lays claim to 300 years of history you would be entitled to expect olde-worlde charm and bags of character. Unfortunately, with the Goat Tavern you get only an average, at best, tourist pub for those unable to find their way off the High Street. On first impression it looks so welcoming, with natural light filtering into the front of the bar through a large bay window. The three tables here do provide a pleasant enough place to sit, though make sure you don't get hungry. Food is served only in the dining area, so we had to squeeze on to the end of a table, leaving the front section deserted. The Goat also needs to improve its service – getting a drink requires plenty of patience, even when no one else appears to be waiting.

FEATURES:

Kensington Arms

RATING:

41 Abingdon Road
W8 6AH

We always had a soft spot for this one. It wasn't flash, it wasn't foodie and it certainly wasn't what you'd expect off the side of High Street, Kensington. We thought such a regular boozer wouldn't be long for this world and it wasn't, as – just like its near neighbour the Britannia – it's been remodelled and upgraded. The makeover has produced a stark and bright interior, reminiscent of style bars from the turn of the (21st) century. The one aspect that's remained the same is the multiscreens for the sport, though they're now clustered around the bar, leaving the back of the pub as a dining space. The pub has strong Cornish connections now, with landscapes photos on the wall, Cornish beers behind the bar and a Cornish menu. Those beers are from Sharp's Brewery, and they're rare sights in London. All in all, an intriguing mix, but it's one that's won us over. And you can fairly say – unlike many pubs that claim the accolade – there's nothing quite like this one around. Though did we really see the Cornish Pasty on the menu priced at £8?

FEATURES:

Scarsdale Arms

RATING:

23a Edwardes Square
W8 6HE
020 7937 1811

Offering the sort of olde-worlde experience you'd expect in this neck of the woods, the Scarsdale Arms is a cut above most of the nearby pubs. The darkened interior evokes a genuine atmosphere, as does the intriguing history of the place (it was reputedly built as living quarters for the officers of Napoleon's conquering army). Rather than being a full-on gastropub, it's first and foremost a pub, yet one with very good food. It also sports a restaurant space at the back in case you're after a grander dining experience. Over the years, plenty of punters have done so, if the empty champagne bottles that ring the walls of the pub are anything to go by. Rather similar in style and clientele to the Grenadier in Knightsbridge (though this pub is a tad larger), it has a refined feel that is upmarket yet not ostentatious. Busy all days of the week, but definitely worth a look.

FEATURES:

Visitors' Award (overall Winner) 2005

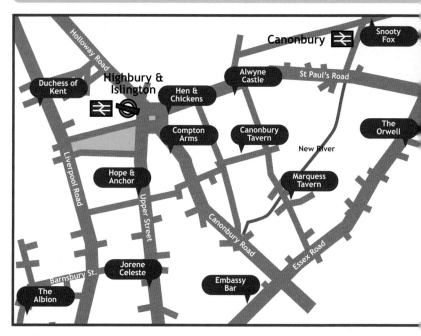

The Albion

RATING:

10 Thornhill Road
N1 1HW
020 7607 7450

A large, pleasant pub in Barnsbury. It does reasonable beer and a lot of food, and has most things people want from a pub. It's had a lick of paint, a few sofas and a new menu, but it's still a nice old place and has a large beer garden at the rear and outdoor seating at the front, so you can usually manage to stay in the sun (if we get any). The people are decent and the kids don't get too out of hand, but it's all just a little bit too leafy to get the old juices flowing. Nice for a quietish pint, but only if you're in the area.

FEATURES:

Alwyne Castle

RATING:

St Paul's Road

N1 2LY

020 7288 9861

Formerly a very average boozer, the Alwyne Castle has been given the trendy bar makeover and now it has many trademark features of early-twenty-first-century conversions (polished wooden floor, comfy sofas, overpriced food menu). But it also has a great fireplace and mercifully no polished chrome fittings. Service is friendly, there is good London Pride on draught and the atmosphere is more akin to that of a pub than a bar. All Bar One might learn something here.

FEATURES:

Canonbury Tavern

RATING:

21 Canonbury Place

N1 2NS

020 7288 9881

We often feel that the pubs in Highbury are a little disappointing. It's a pretty affluent area and there are loads of handsome Victorian buildings, but somehow the Highbury pub experience doesn't amount to much. Of course there are a couple of notable exceptions, but on the whole it's not a great area for the professional pub goer. The Canonbury breaks this rule. While it's not a great pub, it's a pretty decent one. It's old, large, got a beer garden, serves a decent range of pumped and bottled beers – with quite a few Belgians in there – does decent grub and has a large grown-ups' play area off to one side (pool, pinball etc.). The beer garden is only for grown-ups too. It's one hell of a lot more popular than it used to be and we're not surprised.

FEATURES:

The Compton Arms

RATING:

4 Compton Avenue

N1 2XD

020 7359 6883

We've always had the impression that this pub likes to think it's somewhere out in the wilds of Surrey or Sussex and, come to that, so do the locals. But that's OK. It certainly does look after its beer really well and has an extensive and ever-changing range of interesting bitters on the hand pumps. However, it's a tiny place that fills up very, very easily, though the street outside and the beer garden at the back do their best to cope with the overflow. Decent pub grub, a wide range of punters and the sort of traditional pub atmosphere you won't find on Upper Street. A fine place.

FEATURES:

Duchess of Kent

RATING:

141 Liverpool Road

N7 8PR

020 7609 7104

Geronimo specialise in doing up boozers to match their gentrified surroundings. No surprises, then, to find one of the newer additions to their group in the 'Highbury borders' (Holloway). There's certainly been a bit of time and money spent on this one and a bit of thought too. Though it's a narrow, L-shaped pub, some wall mirrors at the back give it a greater sense of space. The lurid paint job has been toned down, thankfully, and the paintings seem to have changed to something more subtle – seem to be guest artists. There's good thinking on display behind the bar: as well as the lengthy wine list, some German beers (Bitburger and Prince Ludwig when we last looked in) jostle for space with Aspall's cider, Adnams and Timothy Taylor Landlord. Oh, and the typeface on the exterior is reminiscent of a Double Diamond label. Probably unintentional, though.

FEATURES:

Embassy Bar

RATING:

119 Essex Road
N1 2SN
020 7226 7901

Along with the nearby Social, Embassy was one of the original Islington bars to give the kids an alternative to the nearby scary boozers and insipid chain pubs. While others have taken their time to catch up – with mixed results – Embassy remains popular. With its stylish, almost too darkly illuminated interior and red flock wallpaper (which made an appearance when flock wallpaper was still uncool), it's easy to forget you're actually sitting in grey Essex Road. Surprisingly, drinks aren't extortionate and the DJs are often interesting and varied. On weekdays it's a satisfying and lively place to have a drink, if you arrive early enough to get seats. However, at weekends, it gets very busy and with the allure of a dance floor in the basement it essentially becomes a club, complete with an entry fee after 9 p.m. Not to everyone's taste, this is a fine example of the kind of bar we often find is done badly.

FEATURES:

Hen & Chickens

RATING:

109 St Paul's Road
N1 2NA
020 7359 1030

This small pub on the northeast corner of Highbury roundabout is a fairly unremarkable pub that serves moderately good beer in moderately good surroundings. It does, however, open later than many nearby places and has a great comedy theatre upstairs, which has witnessed the birth of many a famous comedian's career. The seating has been marginally improved since our last visit, but is predominantly high-level, in no small part to accommodate the pre- and post-theatre crowds. As such, the place feels a little transitory, but at least attempts to gain repeat custom with an eclectic jukebox and frequent live music acts in the main bar. There are certainly far worse places to visit this close to Highbury and Islington tube, but it's probably not worth a major detour unless you're coming to see some comedy, or it's after 11 p.m. and you're thirsty for a couple more.

FEATURES:

Hope & Anchor

RATING:

207 Upper Street

N1 1RL

020 7354 1312

Well, this pub may be in 'trendy' Islington and it may try to pitch to a new crowd, but the soundtrack gives the game away – the Pixies and New Order on the jukebox are for the cognoscenti or for those willing to learn. This always was a music pub and always will be. The beer is OK, but nothing out of the ordinary, but if that's all you came here for you're missing a serious trick.

FEATURES:

Jorene Celeste

RATING:

153 Upper Street

N1 1RA

020 7226 0808

Older Islingtonians will remember this as the Royal Mail, but now it's another Upper Street watering hole straddling bar and pub territory. We have to say, however, it's rather more appealing than some of its neighbours. The mandatory stripped-out sofa interior is in place, but the addition of plants, mirrors and paintings puts across a rather luxurious old Colonial feel (to which the Middle Eastern bar food only adds). If only it were Noël Coward on the gramophone and not Justin Timberlake.

Marquess Tavern

RATING:

32 Canonbury Street

N1 2TB

020 7354 2975

Off the beaten track, but surprisingly near Essex Road's bars, lies the Marquess Tavern. A magnificent unspoilt Victorian building, it boasts a comfortable front bar with original wood panelling and a back room which claims an impressively high ceiling. With a recent change of management, however, its unsurprising to discover the emphasis has shifted towards gastro, with the aforementioned back room transformed into a dining room. An expensive dining room at that: prices hover in the mid-teens, excluding side dishes at additional cost. Still, service remains down-to-earth and an impressive range of Young's bottled beers can also be found. However, some work will be needed to attract the affluent crowd they seek in a pub which has traditionally consisted of regulars from the nearby housing estate. Its backstreet location also means Islington's weekend visitors simply won't see it.

FEATURES:

The Orwell

RATING:

382 Essex Road

N1 3PF

020 7359 4651

This one's gone through plenty of changes and is in new hands yet again. Previously the lounge bar Light House, other incarnations have included the George Orwell and, in the dim and distant past, it was one of those insalubrious looking pubs with accommodation that used to gather along roads like Essex Road. Most recently it was a DJ bar but for the latest incarnation it's still early days, so any change of direction is unclear. The jukebox has gone, the emphasis at the bar is now on premium brands, while the small courtyard at the back was still being renovated on our last visit. The decor's nothing if not interesting, with wallpaper last seen covering a school textbook in the 1980s. All good stuff, but with its rather off-putting location this one will do well to outlast its short-lived predecessors. If it sticks to its guns though, it might just manage it.

FEATURES:

The Snooty Fox

RATING:

75 Grosvenor Avenue

N5 2NN

020 7354 0094

Loungey pubs are so common these days that they have to try really hard to stand out. DJ nights? Been there. Open-mike sessions? Old hat. Quiz? Yawn. All these are in place at the Snooty Fox, yet there's still a freshness and originality to the place. Perhaps it stems from the pub's old-fashioned vinyl jukebox: there are not many of them left in London, probably because relying on A and B sides of singles can result in a rather odd selection of tracks (if you have a burning desire to hear the instrumental dub-mix B-side of Bowie's 'Absolute Beginners' be sure to stop by). Despite – or possibly because of – such a soundtrack, when we first visited here the staff were playing their own tunes. Given the quality of their selections, perhaps the jukebox should be switched off more often: from classical to jazz to 'Wichita Lineman', the choices were faultless for a lazy Saturday afternoon, as were the well-kept beers. Even though pine nuts feature on the menu we're not in the realms of gastro pretence, rather well-done pub grub. There are also some stylish touches on the décor front: the wooden cabinet for the spirit bottles was a particular favourite, and it's hard to be critical of a bar where posters of Debbie Harry and Marianne Faithfull adorn the walls. The early part of the week can find it too quiet here, so for the moment we're recommending the Snooty Fox as ideal for a lazy weekend afternoon.

FEATURES:

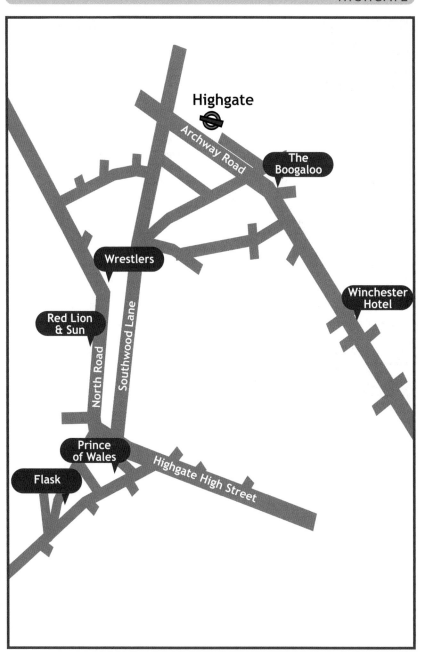

The Boogaloo

RATING:

312 Archway Road

N6 5AT

020 8340 2928

It's from the people who brought you Filthy McNasty's, so it was no surprise on our first visit to see that a selection of the CDs on the jukebox had been picked by Shane McGowan (spotted sitting at the bar when we dropped in) and Spider Stacey. And what a jukebox it is: if you've waited for a pub where you can select Captain Beefheart or Pere Ubu instead of picking your way through *Now! 5,000,000*, you should pay it a visit. A pleasant barman served up a fair range of drinks but there was no sign of any food on our visit. Not always a sticking point but, if you have the word 'kitchen' etched on your front window, you're leading hungry passers-by rather far up the garden path. The (fairly) regular quiz night will test the grey matter, and, as with Filthy's, expect literary nights every so often. It's not far off a cool record shop with a bar in the corner – not a bad thing in our book. It's open only in the evenings during the week, and from 2 p.m. at weekends.

FEATURES:

The Flask

RATING:

77 Highgate West Hill

N6 6BU

020 8348 7346

The Flask has been one of the traditional top boozers for many years, it seems. For those of you who aren't aware of its history, the Flask is an old, old place that has a number of small rooms knocked together to create a rambling olde-worlde experience in that posh olde-worlde village that is Highgate. It still does a range of decent hand-pulled beers, including a number of guest ales, and is strong on beers from Belgium and Germany. The pub is now one of Mitchells & Butlers unbranded pubs, though the introduction of loungey furnishings isn't as strong here as in most of their other pubs (not surprising given the aged interior). Still, a modern edge has been grafted on to the front of the pub for the summer – gazebo-esque structures that keep out the rain and are decorated with mirrors and paintings. It's the most famous pub in Highgate and, as a result, this one can get packed out at weekends. Visit it at a more irregular time, or get there early, to get the most out of it.

FEATURES:

Prince of Wales

RATING:

53 Highgate High Street

N6 5JX

020 8340 0445

The Flask seems to get all the attention round these parts, though we're not complaining, since it usually means more space in this one. The olde-worlde interior may not be as rambling as the Flask's, but it's certainly on the right side of cosy. Plenty of beers on tap and the menu is of Thai and Laos origin; it promises a good Sunday roast as well. The sort of villagey pub you'd expect in this villagey part of London, it's a fine local with a well-loved feel to the place. A small terrace at the back opens out on to where the old ponds used to be. Shame they're not still there, though if they were the pub would be almost too good to be true.

FEATURES:

Red Lion & Sun

RATING:

25 North Road

N6 4BE

020 8340 1780

The Red Lion & Sun's unintentionally ironic sign proclaiming the place to be 'Highgate's Best Kept Secret' is gone, but little else has changed since our last visit. Often overlooked in favour of the Flask and others on the main village road, it has a few added extras that the neighbouring pubs don't pick up on. Live music seems to be a speciality here and every evening offers something. There are piano nights, knees-up singalong revelry, Irish music and (in keeping with Highgate's refined air) a jazz night. A cultured feel is also evident from the well-thumbed paperbacks beside the bar, although we weren't sure whether they were for public perusal. The more standard pub features seemed in good working order, too, particularly the filling pub food. Less of a locals' place than on previous visits (the regulars don't eye newcomers suspiciously any more), this is a solid three-pinter.

FEATURES:

The Winchester Hotel

RATING:

206 Archway Road
N6 5BA
020 8374 1690

The first thing that hits you when you enter this pub (not a pint glass, thankfully) is the verdant nature of the place. It's home to an array of soothing plants, comfy leather sofas and unobtrusive blinds shielding you from the hot sun and traffic whizzing past on Archway Road. Unlike many pubs of late, it's been done up, but not done over. The Winchester remains very much a Proper Pub. It's got plenty of tables, a nicely sized bar where it should be and a bit of a games area. It's got a 'quiet corner' for those looking for a more intimate pub experience, and a beer garden too. What more could you ask for? Food, of course. It does big white plates of food, laden with some right good grub, very much of the lamb shank, fresh fish and huge pastas variety. It's not cheap, but you're not spending a tenner on pine nuts and spaghetti. The clientele are a good mix of locals, reflecting the cosmopolitan mix of the area with fashionistas and fitters happily taking up the same floor space.

FEATURES:

The Wrestlers

RATING:

98 North Road
N6 4AA
020 8340 4297

The sort of pub that always seems dark even on the sunniest days, the Wrestlers is a bit of a find in Highgate. Decked out in dark wood, with minimal lighting and a stunning inglenook fireplace, it offers punters the opportunity to step up to a set of mounted antlers and participate in its biannual 'Swearing on the Horns', dating back to 1635 (the pub itself started life in 1547). Don't worry if you're not too sure of what's expected of you: full details are displayed beside the horns. Ceremonials aside, this is a fine boozer, with plenty to tempt on the drinks front, food at weekends, and Wotsits for snack fans. There's plenty of space available, with comfy sofas to the front, proper pub furniture in the back and seating in the conservatory as well. It's the sort of place that offers an excellent selection of food and has the racing, not the footy, on TV of a Saturday afternoon – a fine place to enjoy a pint in. However, it does close weekday afternoons, since it's a bit too quiet to keep open.

FEATURES:

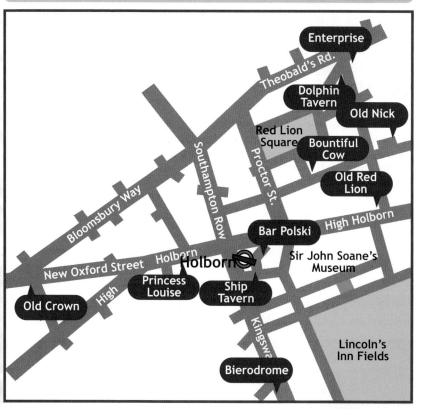

Bar Polski

11 Little Turnstile
WC1V 7DX
020 7831 9679

The name is Polish (as in 'coming from Poland', not that stuff you clean a table with). This place is great – a selection of Polish beers and vodkas are served by friendly, interested staff who will laugh at your pronunciation of the Polish names. The food is cheap and filling, too. The décor's not up to much and the music (bland Europop) was a bit loud on our last visit, but that's more than made up for by the friendly atmosphere, tasty beer and sheer randomness of the place.

FEATURES:

Bierodrome

RATING:

67 Kingsway
WC2B 6TD
020 7242 7469

Anyone familiar with the Belgo concept will find few surprises here. As with the other bars in the chain, a vast array of beers can be found: white beers, dark beers, Trappist ales and the fashionable fruit beers are all in evidence. The food is reasonable, especially considering the alcohol prices, and the long-running 6–8 p.m. food offer is deservedly popular. It's a shame, then, that the ambience leaves something to be desired. When it's quiet, the design makes the place feel soulless, but, once the after-work crowd from the nearby legal offices descends, it becomes incredibly busy and noisy and gains an unfortunate air of pretension. The idea of selling a large selection of Belgian beers is no longer the novelty it was in 1999, and there are now plenty of places to experience the beer without having to endure the atmosphere here.

FEATURES:

The Bountiful Cow

RATING:

51 Eagle Street
WC1R 4AP
020 7404 0200

Always heartening to report a pub rising from the dead, so farewell, then, Overdraughts, hello new proprietor and welcome to the Bountiful Cow. Fans of the Seven Stars on Carey Street take note, as this one shares both an owner and a devotion to the Suffolk beers of Adnams. The interior, too, takes its cue from that pub, being both small and having walls decorated with old movie posters. That they're for cowboy films illustrates the emphasis here on burgers, steaks and all things bovine-related (vegetarians look away now). So, perhaps more steakhouse than boozer, then, but at least we're not talking one of those touristy Aberdeen Angus abominations. And at least the independent nature of this one marks it out as a cut above the 'Midtown' rebranding that Holborn's been inflicted with. Anyway, it's just a relief to see this one rescued from oblivion.

FEATURES:

Dolphin Tavern

RATING:

Red Lion Street

WC1R 4PF

020 7831 6298

A decent small place tucked slightly out of the way in Holborn, the Dolphin Tavern is but a step from the far more wholesome – and thoroughly wonderful and wonderfully unique – Conway Hall, home of the South Place Ethical Society in Red Lion Square since 1929. It's a nice contrast in a way: you can be assured that, while the Socialist Workers' Party are discussing rising working-class militancy in Conway Hall, the working class are actually enjoying a well-earned pint in the Dolphin. Gets packed at times, but it's only a little place, so that's to be expected. The beer is well kept, and there's usually a couple of real ales on (Pride and Young's when we were last there). The service was very prompt and friendly too. Not a bad little place by any means.

The Enterprise

RATING:

38 Red Lion Street

WC1R 4PN

020 7269 5901

A lick of paint and a bit of care and attention and the Enterprise is a revived pub. Cask Marque ales are on offer, there's plenty of choice for those who don't fancy something pumped by hand, there's a beer garden out the back and comfy settees for those who prefer not to perch on bar stools. The grub is refreshingly unpretentious but served only lunchtimes and early evening. Although its popularity is increasing, it still tends to be quieter than the other pubs in the area, and it's very quiet at the weekends – it's closed.

FEATURES:

Old Crown

33 New Oxford Street
WC1A 1BH
020 7836 9121

This once pleasant arty little pub with twenties-style livery, and pizzas delivered from over the road, has had a total makeover. Gone is the light airy feel and in comes a dark and more serious affair. Outside now lacks a name, with the only decoration being a small '33', presumably for the postman. We were assured it is indeed still the Old Crown, but it's hard to say whether its lack of a name is an attempt to be minimalist-cool, or whether the signwriter has (so far) let them down. Inside, flock wallpaper lines the panels of the bar, behind which distressed exposed brickwork is highlighted by subtle lighting. The curved leather bench seating looks beautiful and it's a shame it was two inches too narrow and three inches too high to be comfortable. In reality, there was nothing wrong with the old place, but its new incarnation isn't too bad, either.

FEATURES: HANDY FOR: British Museum

Old Nick

21–22 Sandland Street
WC1R 4PZ
020 7430 9503

A couple of years ago when the Old Nick reopened after a period of closure, bigger and better than before, we breathed a collective sigh of relief. The place obviously had money lavished on it and happily the décor and ethos were of a good traditional British pub. Sure enough, it gained an award from our good selves. Sadly, since this inaugural high point, it seems the owners have taken their eye off the ball. It's overly bright inside, and our weekend night visit not only found all the beers off but the doors wide open, making it as cold inside as it was out. It was also considered acceptable to get a head start on moving stock and spraying bleach everywhere at 9.45 p.m. rather than wait until closing time. This could be a fine pub but is now, in a nutshell, supremely disappointing.

FEATURES: *Reviewers' Award – Best Renovation 2004*

Old Red Lion

72 High Holborn
WC1V 6LS
020 7405 1748

A pretty decent place, with a good, well-kept range of Greene King beers. The service is prompt and friendly and there's an upstairs bar that you can escape to if it gets crowded downstairs. The building itself is a fine old Victorian pub that's been well looked after and worth popping into if you're in the area.

FEATURES:

Princess Louise

RATING:

208–209 High Holborn
WC1V 7BW
020 7405 8816

Many visitors to London get to know this pub, mostly for its famous Victorian gin-palace interior and its handy location close to Holborn tube. It used to be quite a beer bore's pub, but now it's a Sam Smith's, so there are no surprises (pleasant or otherwise) about the food and drink on offer. It tends to get very packed at the usual times (just after 5.15 as a rule), but it's well worth a visit just to see the gents' toilets (sorry, ladies). It was apparently voted Most Beautiful Pub in London in the last few years – we'd say it's hard to disagree.

FEATURES:

Ship Tavern

RATING:

12 Gate Street

WC2A 3HP

020 7405 1992

Small pub frequented by those who know the shortcut that misses out the corner where Holborn station is. Amazingly, it's been refurbished relatively recently, but the designers have eschewed the tired 'chrome and pine' look and redecorated it to look … just like a proper pub! For this alone it's worth visiting. When you add in well-kept draft beers (Speckled Hen and Bombardier when we visited), pork pies and Scotch eggs for sale behind the bar (£1.50 each, with a bowl of pickle), friendly service, a relaxed atmosphere and the fact you can usually find a seat in here, it becomes high up on the list if you're in this area.

HANDY FOR: Sir John Soane's Museum

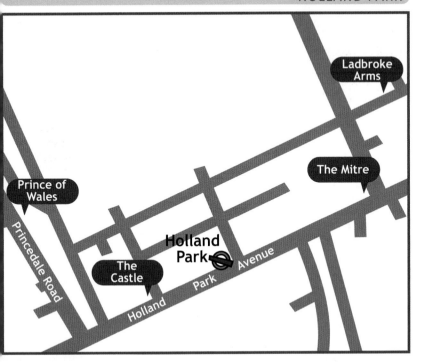

The Castle

RATING:

100 Holland Park Ave
W11 4UA
020 7313 9301

We were pretty scathing about the place after its gastro refit a few years ago, but it has settled down now and improved somewhat. It's got a decent range of booze, the menu's decent (although it does do fish-finger sandwiches with lime mayo, when everyone knows it should be salad cream, ketchup or, ideally, both) and the service is prompt and friendly. It's also not as pricey as many of the places around. It can get crowded towards the weekend, especially as it's on the main drag, but, if you can find a seat, it's not a bad place for a pint or two.

Ladbroke Arms

RATING:

54 Ladbroke Road
W11 3NW
020 7727 6648

Although a pretty good pub, it's gone the gastro route and the emphasis now is definitely on the dining. However, it's still possible (and worthwhile) to pop in for a pint where you'll find the service to be pretty good and will find decent, well-kept beer – Greene King IPA and Adnams – on the hand pumps. There's also an extensive range of wines and spirits on offer – including a bunch of decent single malts – so the accompaniment and digestif are nicely taken care of. The food is pretty good, too. On a warm summer's day, it should be nice to sit out the front of this place and sip your pint with a good book or a couple of mates, but everyone else in the area usually has the same idea – so you'll soon find yourself elbow-to-elbow with the braying hordes. When it's quiet, it's great; when it's not, it's not. *C'est la vie.*

FEATURES:

The Mitre

RATING:

40 Holland Park Avenue
W11 3QY
020 7727 6332

Well, this was a cavernous pub a little bit further out of Notting Hill, which has gone through a number of changes over the years. But now it's nailed its gastro colours to the mast, describing itself as a 'pub and restaurant', and pulls no punches, aiming to out-gastro any competition in the neighbourhood. The menu looks great, but it's not cheap. And, while it's got a couple of beers on the bar, it's got a selection of lagers that would make Continental bars envious. The changed focus from pub to eatery has made the drinking side of things suffer a little, in our opinion. Still, a prime example of how to do gastro – puts the pale imitators to shame.

FEATURES:

Prince of Wales

RATING:

14 Princedale Road
W11 4NJ
020 7313 9321

Well, it was due for an update, looking somewhat tired and in need of TLC, so this pub's refit was not much of surprise to us. The style of refurb wasn't much of a surprise, either, being an unoriginal nod to gastropubdom. However, it is *de rigueur* for the area (actually for a pub refit almost anywhere nowadays), so the seventies light fittings, the colour scheme and the furniture will probably be very comforting and familiar for the contemporary pub goer. It is, however, a jolly decent boozer, with a more imaginative range of beers on offer – Fuller's Chiswick and Abbey Ales' Bellringer, for example, on the hand pumps, Continentals on the ornate pumps and the usual keg stuff discreetly hidden away. The wine list is decent if you favour the New World and there are plenty of spirits in case you're thinking of fuelling up for a night out. The tiny TV won't set sports fans' pulses racing, but we'd hazard a guess they're not the POW's main market. Disappointingly, the rather splendid beer garden and BBQ closes at 7 p.m. – apparently it doesn't meet the local residents' approval – but it does make a pleasant place for an alfresco pint earlier in the day. All in all, a decent, if pricey, posh local.

FEATURES:

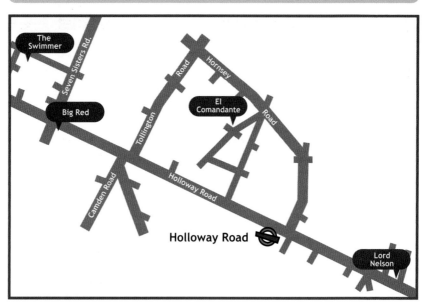

Big Red

RATING:

385 Holloway Road
N7 0RY
020 7609 6662

This pub is a favourite haunt of students from the nearby university and one of the best places to meet on the Holloway Road. The subtly lit interior is dominated by a large rectangular bar, which is surrounded on three sides by seating, including several cosy booths and a number of sofas. At the far end stand four pool tables and a pinball machine. Previously, Big Red hosted live bands but now the stage has gone, to be replaced by more sofas, while a giant projector screen hangs above them ready to show football. This doesn't seem to have drastically affected their clientele and it is as busy as ever at the weekend. Without entertainment from the stage the jukebox becomes the centre of attention and it doesn't disappoint, that's as long as you like rock. The only negative we can think of is that the bar staff, although efficient, tend to look aggrieved when you interrupt them by doing something audacious such as ordering a pint. They have to deal with more of that now, as Big Red has a late licence.

FEATURES:

El Comandante

RATING:

10 Annette Road

N7 6ET

020 7697 0895

In an area mixed with an odd blend of high-end gastro pubs, lager-lad bars and rough locals, to wander the backstreets of Holloway and discover this little place was a joy. It was formerly the Lord Palmerston, still visibly embossed on the windows, but there is no obvious name to the place until you see the small poster in the window. And that just about sums up El Comandante – a triumph of simplicity that goes a long way to prove that sometimes less is more. Essentially, this is a Cuban bar in an old pub. All that's been done in the way of updating was to splash round a fresh lick of paint and put up some huge Che Guevara posters. Throw in a couple of large pot plants, San Miguel on tap and some authentic Spanish Cuban music on the jukebox – and that's it. Yet, with only these few touches and a warm welcome from the Latin landlord, if it hadn't been for the greyness of N7 outside, you could've almost imagined you were in Cuba. If nothing else, it puts most of the other – more popular – Cuban bars to shame. *Viva la revolución!*

FEATURES:

The Lord Nelson

RATING:

100 Holloway Road

N7 8JE

020 7609 0670

Authentic Irish pub (albeit with a Thai menu) which specialises in live music and showing the hurling and the Gaelic football. It's a decent enough place that caters for a different audience from the student pubs in the area. Expect country dancing here on a Saturday night and a Wolfe Tones gig every six months or so.

FEATURES:

Swimmer at the Grafton Arms

RATING:

13 Eburne Road
N7 6AR
020 7281 4632

While it can be easy to criticise gastropubs, when the emphasis is still on the pub rather than the gastro, they're often hard to fault. The Swimmer is a good example. A smart and professional establishment, it's still first and a foremost a pub – and a good one at that. There's a range of Ridley's beers on tap, a fair wine list and excellent service. Add on a jukebox for which the word 'eclectic' was devised, and you have the sort of watering hole that, even if you're not ordering swordfish steak off the menu, you can still feel at home in. It's also pretty handy for the Odeon round the corner.

FEATURES:

HYDE PARK CORNER

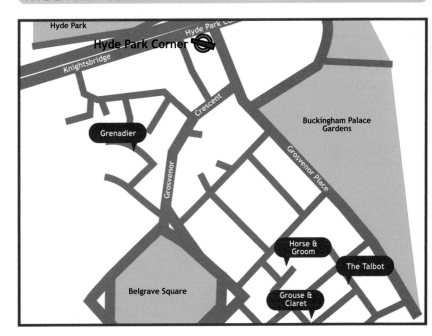

Grenadier

RATING:

18 Wilton Row
SW1X 7NR
020 7235 3074

The Ritchies used to pop in here every now and again apparently (Guy and Madonna, not Shane). But don't let that put you off. This is another one of those small Knightsbridge pubs you would expect to find in the middle of Suffolk, but maybe not the middle of London. As you'd expect from the name, military memorabilia hangs from the walls of both the bar and the small dining area at the back, and there is an air of old-fashioned gentility about the place. Unfortunately, the stuck-up nature of some of the clientele can be a bit offputting, but the professional staff and the general ambience of the pub make up for it. It's a small place, so a visit out of peak times is recommended if you want to get a seat.

FEATURES:

Grouse & Claret

RATING:

14–15 Little Chester Street
SW1X 7AP
020 7235 3438

Larger than a lot of the other pubs in Belgravia, this one still manages to attain the smart atmosphere you would expect of the area. It's made up of saloon and public bars, with a separate cellar bar and upstairs restaurant. The Fursty Ferret and Sussex beers were well kept, and the food counter offered a standard selection of fare. The only pub we know that has an illustration of a grouse shoot above the front door, it's the sort of place where a copy of the *Daily Telegraph* makes for fitting reading material.

FEATURES:

Horse & Groom

RATING:

7 Groom Place
SW1X 7BA
020 7235 6980

Another Belgravia pub in another mews, this small Shepherd Neame establishment is everything you might wish for in a local – if you're lucky enough to live in SW1. This small, wood-panelled bar might be described by some as scruffy, but 'well worn' is a better description. The beers were well kept, wine list interesting, the service friendly and (although possibly out of character for its location) a rather tempting cocktail list was also available. You can even sit back and enjoy a packet of dried elk sausages with your pint, too. The mix of clientele meant neither feeling as if you were invading a sacrosanct local (like some other nearby pubs), nor being swept along in the throng of the after-work and tourist crowd all too common in nearby Victoria. Recommended.

FEATURES:

The Talbot

RATING:

1 Little Chester Street, Belgravia
SW1X 7AL
020 7235 1639

Tucked away off a blink-and-you-miss-it mews, The Talbot is one of the less traditional pubs in the area. It's a big place, with plenty of standing room and seating both inside and out, but its character clearly suffers from the lack of imagination put into its hotel-lobby carpet and magnolia-wall refit. Of course, things like carpet patterns don't matter to the less fussy after-work crowd it's aiming at. Nevertheless, the food menu was extensive and there was the bonus of probably the only cash machine within a ten-minute radius. Although it's not bad by any means, with two rather good pubs only a stone's throw away, the incentive to stay for more than a couple is limited.

FEATURES:

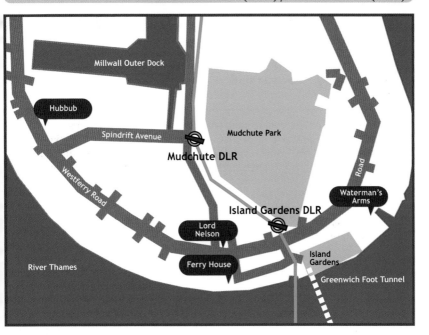

Millwall Outer Dock

Hubbub

Spindrift Avenue

Mudchute Park

Mudchute DLR

Westferry Road

Road

Waterman's Arms

Island Gardens DLR

Lord Nelson

Island Gardens

River Thames

Ferry House

Greenwich Foot Tunnel

The Ferry House

RATING:

26 Ferry Street
E14 3DT
020 7537 9587

The ferry to Greenwich has gone but the Ferry House still stands. It may appear a rather rough-hewn locals' pub from the outside, but it still offers a touch more colour and atmosphere than the modern bars around Canary Wharf. Here you sense 'redesigning the bar' means getting in a few new CDs for the jukebox. Apart from a new TV, the pub appears unchanged from the days when cargo ships were offloading at Millwall dock. It also sports a pub rarity – an old 'London Fives' dartboard. A genial barman is on hand to pull the pints and banter with the regulars.

FEATURES:

Hubbub

RATING:

269 Westferry Road

E14 3RS

020 7515 5577

Housed in a former Victorian chapel, which is now an arts centre (The Space), Hubbub is located upstairs. It's a cosy, gaslit place with excellent food and a decent range of drinks – wines, spirits, cocktails and coffees, if not real ales (only Guinness, 1664 and Foster's on the pumps, for instance). On our visit, young and older Docklanders wined and dined to a Coltrane jazz odyssey in comfy chairs. In an otherwise dull location, you can see why they come here. Late bar (midnight) Thursday to Saturday.

FEATURES:

Lord Nelson

RATING:

1 Manchester Road

E14 3BD

020 7987 1970

A great local pub, it's got a pool table, sport on the big-screen TV, quiz nights, darts and almost anything else you'd care to mention. They do a good range of food, the beer's decent and the staff are very friendly and helpful. This is one of the places that go out of their way to make everyone welcome, putting things on for the regulars all the time. Children are welcome before 7 p.m. and quiz nights are great fun and very popular. As well as the usual newspapers etc. at weekends, you get the *Eye* and the *Economist* – things really are changing on the Island. Showing how a local should be run, the Lord Nelson is definitely worth looking out for if you're in the area.

FEATURES:

The Watermans Arms

RATING:

1 Glenaffric Avenue

E14 3BW

020 7093 2883

Despite the relentless move upmarket as the City spreads eastwards, there are still a few old boozers left in these parts, and the Watermans Arms is one of the best of them. Solid in all departments, it's a popular one with both locals and any visitors who've stumbled across it while looking for that famous view of Greenwich. It's a rangy old place, made famous by a previous landlord, Dan Farson, and, while there's a fair-sized Indian restaurant section at the side. Oh, like the Ferry House pub down the road, they use an old-style 'London Fives' dartboard (just in case you've got your arrows handy). Well-kept beers, Irish whiskies and a pool table are some of the other features. Add on the mandatory 'solid-gold sixties' compilation airing from the CD player and a huge beer garden and you have a steady three-pinter.

FEATURES:

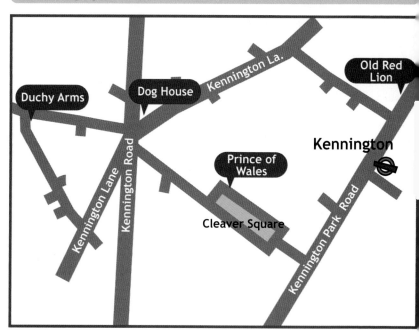

Dog House

Kennington Cross, 293 Kennington Road
SE11 6BY
020 7820 9310

Slightly more bar than pub, this one affords a relaxing environment in an often fraught neck of the woods. Its positioning on Kennington Cross, coupled with the large windows, offers a fine vantage point for a spot of people-watching. Well established as one of the smarter venues in the area, the Dog House feels comfortable in its skin, not one of those newly madeover pubs still thick with the whiff of varnish. Expect many of your fellow patrons to be here for the food but if you fancy a couple of lazy drinks in pleasant surroundings you'll find this one more than suffices.

FEATURES:  HANDY FOR: The Oval

Duchy Arms

RATING:

63 Sancroft Street
SE11 5UG
020 7735 6340

Forgive the estate-agent speak, but Sancroft Street contains some highly desirable properties, both period and modern. We're not sure if the boys and girls of Foxtons et al. make much of the street's pub, but this is the sort of amenity we wouldn't mind at the bottom of our road. A friendly and old-fashioned local, the Duchy Arms doesn't do too much out of the ordinary: Sky Sports dominates in one bar; darts and pool in the other. Its range of drinks is conventional enough but what raises this one out of the ordinary is the merry atmosphere on display. We won't kid you on that newcomers are greeted with a warm handshake and a free go on the pool table, rather that the locals are having such a good time enjoying themselves they'll hardly notice any newbies on their patch. Seems a decent arrangement to us.

FEATURES:

Old Red Lion

RATING:

42 Kennington Park Road
SE11 4RS
020 7735 3529

This is a mock-Tudor pub from the 1930s, and the rarity value rises by the year. Well serviced by its regulars, it's well worth the jaunt south if you want to check out a pub style slowly being realised as something worth preserving. Unlike many Red Lion pubs, this one plays the (Lion Rampant) Scottish card through its décor. Misty-eyed Jacobites should note the large-scale picture on the wall of Bonnie Prince Charlie arriving at Arisaig in 1745 – ideal if a spot of drinking the King o'er the water is your thing. It's certainly a locals' local, but one whose interior raises it above the average.

FEATURES:

KENNINGTON

Prince of Wales

48 Cleaver Square
SE11 4EA
020 7735 9916

RATING:

Cleaver Square is a beautifully preserved square, which, in Kennington, stands out 'like a tarantula on a slice of angel cake' (thank you, Raymond Chandler). The Prince of Wales lives up to its location too. It's a relaxed place with some good beer (Spitfire, Oranjeboom and others) to quench thirsts, a decent wine list and excellent food. We enjoyed their brie salad ciabatta on a previous visit, and, as well as the daily specials, expect homemade pasta dishes and Smithfield sausage and mash meals for around £6. The excellent music on the stereo is just a bonus.

FEATURES:

KENSAL GREEN

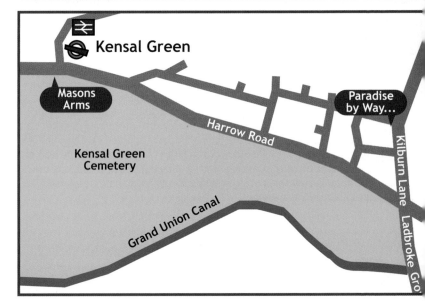

Masons Arms

RATING:

665 Harrow Road

NW10 5NU

020 8960 2278

Well, the Taylor Walker sign has gone and the QPR shirt has been replaced on the wall with sepia shots of olde-worlde Kensal Green – all signs the Masons Arms has been made over. The old place was rather ramshackle, but its worn carpet, solid-gold sixties jukebox and old-timer clientele held a place in our affection. Arguably, the refit has enhanced the Victorian interior and the new pub still plays host to some of the old punters. Heartening, too, that, despite the makeover, this one is still a pub first and foremost, unlike its reworked and gastrofied local rivals. With the dartboard, bar billiards and pool table upstairs, competitive types are kept happy. Sensible pub grub and a decent array of drinks fill in the rest. As pub refits go, this one gets the thumbs-up – though if only they kept the old jukebox: we were itching to choose something from 'Classic Irish Colleens' to blank out the noodly jazz-funk on our last visit.

FEATURES:

Paradise by Way of Kensal Green

RATING:

19 Kilburn Lane

W10 4AE

020 8969 0098

Befitting a pub that takes its name from a G K Chesterton poem, there's a deliberately idiosyncratic feel to this place. With sanded floorboards and Louis XIV-style furniture, it's almost gastropub as envisaged by Changing Rooms. If ever a hostelry was crying out for a chaise longue, it's this one. The restaurant at the back seemed your standard gastro dining room (with a Eurasian menu), so we investigated upstairs, where the alignment of floors and staircases brought the work of Escher to mind. Our revelries were spoiled by one child too many running about the place – offspring of the life-styling professionals who make up most of the clientele. We stuck to Spitfire on our visit, though a glass of absinthe might have been more in keeping with the environs. A bit too knowing, perhaps, but, if your local pub is proving too pedestrian, seek it out.

FEATURES:

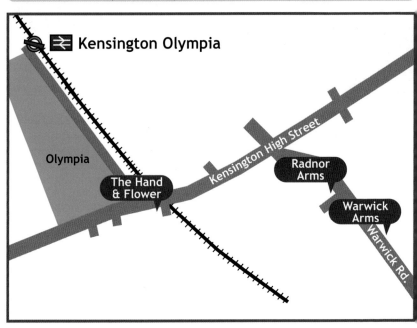

Kensington Olympia

Olympia

Kensington High Street

The Hand & Flower

Radnor Arms

Warwick Arms

Warwick Rd.

Hand & Flower Hotel

RATING:

1 Hammersmith Road
W14 8XJ
020 7371 4105

Situated on prime pub territory opposite Olympia Exhibition Hall, this place, it's safe to say, will never be short of customers when there's a trade fair on across the road. It's had a makeover to a style bar with muted colours and trendy lighting as well as serving decent coffee. The big tellies and sport listings are prominent, and there's a crowd of regulars coming in to watch it. They do decent food, including traditional Sunday roast, reasonably priced too. With decent beer on the taps, and rotating guest beers, it looks as if they're making a good go of things.

FEATURES: HANDY FOR: Olympia

Radnor Arms

RATING:

247 Warwick Road
W14 8PX
020 7602 7708

This lovely little pub in Kensington has apparently been trading since 1862, but there appeared to have been some doubt about its future – there was a bit of a media blow-up about it, started by CAMRA, with a petition and everything, and it looks like it might have worked. It's a great place for a quiet pint of an afternoon. The backroom, with its comfy sofa, is good for chilling out (if there isn't a darts match on), with a huge fish tank to watch. You'll probably be joined by the pub dog and cat, who spent a lot of the time we were last there in a state of unconsciousness. The well-kept beers include Everard's Tiger as a regular, and Skinners was on as a guest last time we were in. It does get busy at lunch and commuting times, however. And, even though the petition appears to have been successful, go and visit it anyway – our continued custom means its continued existence. It would be a shame to lose another great pub.

FEATURES: HANDY FOR: Olympia

Warwick Arms

RATING:

160 Warwick Road
W14 8PS
020 7603 3560

With champagne bottles around the windows and some choice memorabilia on the walls, here's a pub staking a claim for a refined clientele. A rather relaxed and easygoing place, it's the sort of pub ideally suited to an afternoon of slothful drinking (hardly a chore with a good range of Fuller's beers on tap). We've also heard good things about the Indian food on offer, but, as yet, we've yet to sample it for ourselves.

FEATURES: HANDY FOR: Earl's Court, Olympia

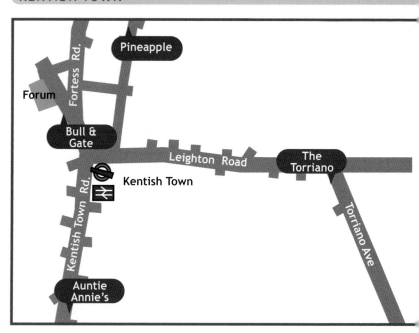

Forum

Pineapple

Fortess Rd.

Bull & Gate

Leighton Road

The Torriano

Kentish Town

Kentish Town Rd.

Torriano Ave

Auntie Annie's

Auntie Annie's Porter House

RATING:

180 Kentish Town Road

NW5 2AE

020 7485 3237

Begorra! A pub more Irish than Oirish. Auntie Annie's garish exterior might lead one to expect theme-pub shenanigans, but the inside may surprise you. It's a smart, roomy place with candles on the tables and a good atmosphere, and, when we stopped in for a few jars, there was a good mix of people enjoying themselves. The music was a contemporary blend thankfully free of the Saw Doctors and so on, and Auntie Annie's also hosts regular live music nights. In case you need a break from the black stuff, an excellent range of whiskies await behind the bar.

FEATURES: 　　　　　　　　**HANDY FOR:** The Forum

Bull & Gate

389 Kentish Town Road
NW5 2TJ
020 7485 5358

RATING:

A traditional Irish boozer with no pretensions, no knick-knacks, no gastro fare – it's just an honest boozer that is a fine old Victorian pub. Lovely interior, friendly staff and tolerant locals, and a nice drop of the black stuff – what more could you ask for? A refreshing place in these times and we're glad it hasn't changed in years.

FEATURES: 　　HANDY FOR: The Forum

Pineapple

RATING:

51 Leverton Street
NW5 2NX
020 7284 4631

A comfy place that was saved from closure a while ago through the actions of its patrons. As a result, any criticism of the place could sound a little churlish. It's certainly one of the more charming pubs in the area, the coal fire and red curtains giving the place a warm feel, and the upright piano in the corner being almost a provocation to a singsong. There's a touch of the lifestyle supplements to the place, but it's a fine pub if you can put up with some David Gray on the CD player. A renovation since it reopened has seen a patio and outdoor area added on to the back of the pub. Added to the smaller rooms off from the bar, this results in a TARDIS-like effect. And the bar food is not too bad, either. A decent effort, even though it's definitely a locals' pub. At least it's one that's not gone fully down the gastro route like some of the others in the area.

FEATURES: 　　HANDY FOR: The Forum

The Torriano

RATING:

71–73 Torriano Avenue

NW5 2SG

020 7267 4305

Take a stroll around this residential patch of NW5 and what first strikes you are the friendly names of the local shops: Maria's Travel and Tours, Rita's Hair and Design and Susan's Mini-Market. As The Torriano is situated amid such neighbourliness, expectations of a jolly local pub are raised high. And, after our most recent visit to the area, we're glad to say we encountered it. It's a stripped-out pub, which can look rather bare, but when it fills up it's fine. A decent range of drinks to enjoy here, with things helped along by the friendly staff and punters. The secluded sunken garden at the back looks a cracking place for the summer, and a real fire means winter times are adequately covered too. A neighbourly little boozer, then – worth the wander from Kentish Town to track down.

FEATURES:

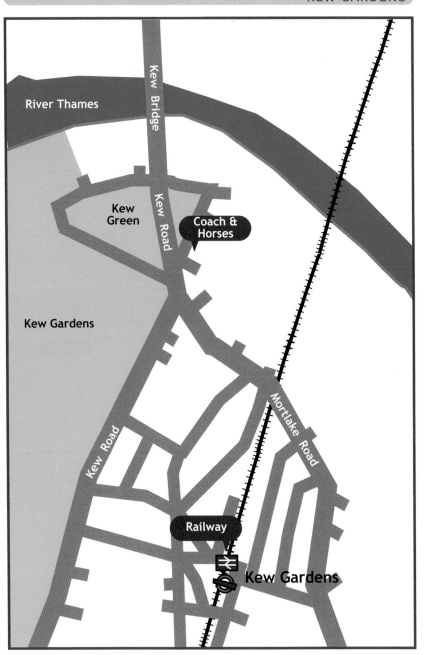

Coach & Horses Hotel

8 Kew Green

TW9 3BH

020 8940 1208

A large hotel pub close to Kew Gardens, this is a genial watering hole. Sport was on the TV when we were there on a Saturday afternoon sitting in a quiet corner reading the paper and doing the crossword. The genial staff and pleasantly rambunctious locals made it an amiable place to go after a Gardens visit (or before in this case), with an open fire for chilly winters. It serves a nice pint (sometimes including Kew Brew) and has pleasant surroundings – there even seems to be a kids' section, which made it for us.

FEATURES:    **HANDY FOR:** Kew Gardens

The Railway

Kew Gardens Station Parade

TW9 3PZ

020 8332 1162

Another old Firkin reborn as new Firkin under a different shade of paint. With its lofty, stripped-out interior and prominent use of glass, it's well placed to capture visitors en route to Kew Gardens. However, the large tables and L-shaped design result in a rather more cramped pub than you'd expect from the exterior and, as a result, it doesn't always feel too relaxing. There's Pride and Bombardier on the hand pumps, and a reasonable wine list to accompany the food. Expect meal deals and two-for-one drink offers during the week, and big-screen sport come Saturday and Sunday.

FEATURES: **HANDY FOR:** Kew Gardens

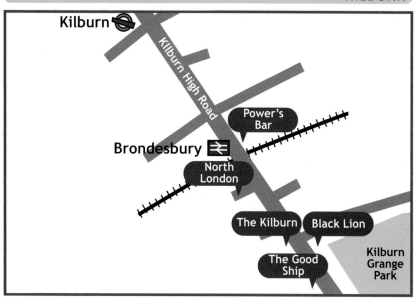

The Black Lion

RATING:

274 Kilburn High Road
NW6 2BY
020 7624 1424

When last orders were called for the final time and the former Irish regulars wended their way over the road to the Kingdom, what they left behind was a spectacular Victorian interior, which had simply been ignored for years. During its transition into an upmarket gastropub, it was thankfully refurbished sympathetically, maintaining the interior (notably the very ornate ceiling) and a glorious separate dining room. Despite their commitment to attract the young, trendy crowd (who are only now discovering the delights of Kilburn), the main room still feels and looks like a pub rather than a lounger's paradise. On the drinks front, after it initially didn't serve ale, we're pleased to see that a token pump (Adnams Broadside) has now made a belated appearance. We can't vouch for the quality of the food, and it was pricey, but the surroundings ought to numb the pain. Previously one of the roughest pubs in Kilburn, it's now worth a look if you're in the area; and, while you're there, try the Tricycle Cinema across the road – apparently London's best.

FEATURES:

The Good Ship

RATING:

289 Kilburn High Road
NW6 7JR
020 7372 2544

OK, maybe trendy DJ bars aren't actually aimed at anyone over the age of 25, so it's no surprise that we (well, some of us) often find them disappointing. Overpriced bottled beers and spirits, the young beautiful people full of disdain, nowhere to dance – but too loud to chat (OK, so now we really are sounding old). Well, the Good Ship is a trendy DJ bar on Kilburn High Road that seems to get it just right. It has a fair range of drinks, including London Pride on tap, Sky TV for your sports, a 100-CD jukebox that will astonish and amaze in its eclecticism, and best of all a separate, stage/dance floor area. As you look through the listings of recent and upcoming events, it's clear that they're going out of their way to provide a range of entertainment with bands and quizzes as well as DJs. You'll have to pay for entry after 10.30, but three quid isn't going to break the bank. So, grab yourself a bottle of Asahi or a pint of Pride, relax and enjoy.

FEATURES:

The Kilburn

RATING:

307–311 Kilburn High Road
NW6 7JR
020 7372 8668

What was once one large daunting Irish pub (McGovern's) has been cleverly divided into two separate ventures. The locals' pub has been squeezed into the right-hand side of the building and the rest has become the latest addition to the Kilburn trendy-bar scene. What we encountered was some fairly standard décor and, due possibly to our poor timing, loud DJs with no apparent talent for judging the correct ambience, volume or style of music to please the customers. The beer was overpriced, too. Music, beer and luck aside, it's a comfortable enough place for a couple of pints, and a staging post for many on their way to a gig next door at the Luminaire. However, there already are enough good pubs nearby (six at the last count), all of whom currently do a better job than the Kilburn.

FEATURES:

North London Tavern

RATING:

375 Kilburn High Road

NW6 7QB

020 7625 6634

Formerly as dependable as Jeeves in terms of Kilburn drinking, the North London Tavern has reopened under new management. The Irish flavour is gone, replaced by a more cosmopolitan air. The facelift keeps the pub's nice original features (ceiling, pillars, stained-glass canopy) but replaces the furniture with new tables and lots of comfy chairs. The atmosphere has changed, too, with jazz and Nancy Sinatra hits playing while you gaze at the gastro menu (typically £5 for snacks, £10 for mains) and sup your choice of Belgian draught beer. It is an agreeable place for a drink, clearly aiming to draw in younger locals who didn't fancy its previous incarnation. Devotees of the auld tavern will mourn its passing but should give the new model a chance. It is one of the better places to meet up the area.

FEATURES:

Power's Bar

RATING:

332 Kilburn High Road

NW6 2QN

020 7624 6026

Established by Vince Power of Mean Fiddler fame, Powers Bar is a dark and atmospheric 'proper' Irish pub. Unlike some other nearby scary Irish pubs, however, this one makes everyone welcome. Inside, there are two real fires, an abundance of candles and arty murals all over the walls. Predictably for a place owned by Vince, the jukebox is excellent, with a leaning towards early-nineties indie music, and, best of all, it's free. There's also (variable) live music and DJs at weekends, but it's not too obtrusive for you to carry on your conversation in peace. When you add the fantastic Guinness, the huge range of whiskeys and the good chance to strike up random conversations (as we often have), it gets hard to fault the place. Thankfully, the trendification of Kilburn hasn't diluted the atmosphere here and it remains a genuinely friendly pub as well as the cream of the crop on Kilburn High Road.

FEATURES:

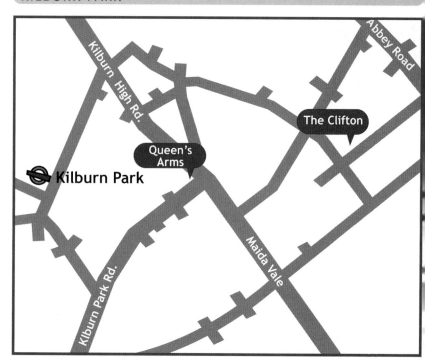

The Clifton

RATING:

96 Clifton Hill
NW8 0JT
020 7372 3427

An altogether charming villa establishment at which the then future Edward VII was reputed to engage in trysts with Lillie Langtry. Located in a suitably elegant, peaceful and tree-lined backstreet, the best part of a century later the pub remains exquisitely charming, combining two wood-lined rooms with a conservatory-like area, and for good measure a few seats outside. The welcome is warm, a good selection of beers and board games are available at the bar (anyone for a lengthy session of Risk?), and food is also on offer. The Clifton is a very fine place indeed, and well worth the long walk from either Maida Vale or Kilburn Park station.

FEATURES:

Queen's Arms

1 Kilburn High Road
NW6 5SE

The Queen's Arms is a large two-roomed locals' pub, with well-kept Young's beers on tap (a rarity on Kilburn High Road), real fireplaces and a genuinely mixed clientele. On our last visit, the youngest customer was barely eighteen and the oldest well over eighty. There's friendly service and a good atmosphere – it's the sort of pub where random people might come and chat to you about politics or football. Some may find it a rather dingy affair here, but others will infinitely prefer its down-to-earth nature compared with the anonymous stripped-pine sort of pub. It certainly serves the locals well enough, and for that you can't complain.

FEATURES:

KING'S CROSS ST PANCRAS

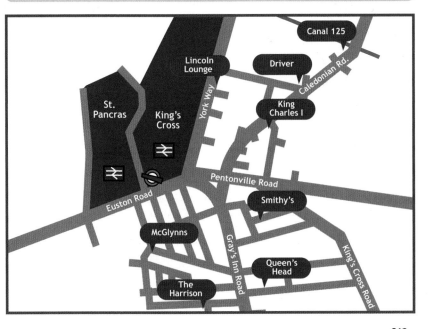

Canal 125

RATING:

125 Caledonian Road
N1 9RG
020 7837 1924

Set amid the mind-boggling 'rejuvenation' (ahem) that is taking place north of King's Cross at a phenomenal rate, Canal 125 may be trying to be all things to all people, and not really pulling it off. Inside, it's a great space: a separate dining area sits at the top of a long bar, leading to a spacious balcony over the canal. We didn't spot any supermarket trolleys sailing past, so maybe things are indeed being spruced up. Good range of beers and an extensive wine list are on offer and service at the bar is friendly, attentive and a real asset to the place. We tried the food and it was fabulous – not cheap, but well proportioned and beautifully presented with top-notch ingredients. However, the place is somewhat schizophrenic in reality. It is usually packed, and it's not exactly conducive to a good night out if someone's backside is constantly banging off the back of your head (there's a time and place for that sort of thing). And, if you're unable to hear what the person sitting next to you is saying due to the intestine-rattling soundtrack supplied by the DJ, you won't want to hang around. Canal 125 seems to think that it can offer something new to the crowded market: a gastroclub. We're not sure it's going to work. It just doesn't fit in such a small place. Our advice? Hang the DJ and give the speakers a rest.

FEATURES:

Driver

RATING:

2–4 Wharfdale Road
N1 9RV
020 7278 8827

Once the General Picton, Driver is a little pub marooned on a corner and recently reopened. At the moment, it doesn't seem too crowded, a miracle for a (rare) clean and pleasant pub around King's Cross. But – curses – it will fill up rapidly once its name starts getting around properly, because it's smart-looking and comfortable, cosy even, and does excellent bar food. The new guvnor is chatty and his personable demeanour has rubbed off on his staff. When we went, it was like having a gorgeous little soirée in one's comfortable home.

FEATURES:

The Harrison

RATING:

28 Harrison Street
WC1H 8JF
020 7278 3966

This backstreet pub has had a lick of paint and a change of furnishings. Nothing too dramatic, though. It helps that, even though the obligatory leather sofas have been installed, the period windows (with Watney's lettering) have been kept in place. The bad news first: there's not the widest choice of drinks you would hope for here (the basics up to Staropramen, but no ales apart from bottles). What this one does have in its favour is the eagerness of the staff and an amiable atmosphere. Best of all, even with the excellent food, this one isn't a food-led gastro conversion: it's still a pub. And one where the CD player works its way through Curtis Mayfield's back catalogue always goes down well with us. Plenty of pubs have been remodelled in the area around King's Cross but this one's arguably the most compact and friendly. A beer or two on tap wouldn't go amiss though.

FEATURES:

King Charles I

RATING:

55–57 Northdown Street
N1 9BL
020 7837 7758

Ponder a while the backstreets of King's Cross and you probably aren't thinking pubs. This place does its best to change that. A one-roomed affair, it's all rather basic, but it does the job well enough. For example, it doesn't offer food but you can order your lunch at the café over the road and they'll bring it across to you. This one's rather hidden away, and more convivial than you might expect given the location, but it's not a pub you feel the regulars want to keep to themselves. Its laid-back atmosphere means it's probably your best bet on this side of Pentonville Road.

FEATURES:

Lincoln Lounge

RATING:

52 York Way, King's Cross
....
N1 9AB
....
020 7837 9339
....

From the exterior, this wasn't too promising. Stuck on the barren York Way, it looked like a mercilessly renovated pub, reminiscent of a rundown eighties wine bar. Thankfully, then, inside was a pleasant surprise. The 'lounge' in the name is accurate, as armchairs and settees were the order of the day, even if it limited the seating. Walls were covered with cow-parsley patterns, and, with a huge mural on the back wall and a giant world map behind the DJ, it made for an eclectic and bohemian atmosphere. It's the kind of pub you could've found in Hoxton some fifteen years ago – tatty but vibrant, unpretentious and friendly. Regular live music, art exhibitions and even a book exchange all add to an impression that this is more than your usual bar. It's understandably popular (for those 'in the know', at least) and in a pattern reminiscent of Shoreditch, another sign that King's Cross is becoming the place to be.

FEATURES:

McGlynn's

RATING:

1–5 Whidborne St
....
WC1H 8ET
....
020 7916 9816
....

It's often the way that the more pleasant the exterior of the pub, the more attractive the interior. That's certainly the case here, where a colourfully painted frontage gives way to a well-cared-for boozer that has all the charms you'd expect of a hidden-away backstreet pub. Food at lunchtime for the experienced locals comes from a country-kitchen-style café at the back of the pub (china plates, Welsh dresser – the works), while at night the workers and a few media types settle in for a pint or two, perhaps as a respite from the nearby Clerkenwell bars. It's the sort of place where you'd expect to find Neil Diamond and Chas and Dave on the jukebox (all present and correct) as well as some choice Irish balladeers (the work of Sean Wilson is especially favoured here). The south side of King's Cross isn't the most salubrious area of London to be walking around in but a few drinks here will see you right.

FEATURES:

Queen's Head

RATING:

66 Acton Street
WC1X 9NB
020 77113 5772

An excellent, solid local. Good beers are on tap and they're well kept, too, with a decent mixed clientele but none too crowded. The piped music was loud, but it was decent stuff (again, a good mix) so it added to the atmosphere. The menu is extensive and cheap, the portions huge and the service excellent. While you wouldn't make a detour to admire the architecture, the pub is basically a hollowed-out Victorian place with some of its original splendour still intact. The façade is still in good nick, and jolly handsome it is, too; and there is excellent tile work on the bits of the original pub that remain inside. Good show.

FEATURES:

Smithy's

RATING:

15-17 Leeke Street
WC1X 9HZ
020 7278 5949

A former blacksmith's, Smithy's calls itself a wine bar, but it's a bit more than that. The food on offer is fabulous: you can fill your boots from the extensive bar menu offering spring rolls, huge sarnies and chips, or a full bistro menu. Everything we tried was expertly presented and tasted great, with generous portions the order of the day. Brunch is available on weekends, with fine roasts served on Sundays. An extensive wine list is a given, with plenty of fizz, too. But the beers don't fall short of the mark either, with a great selection on tap, including Ruddles and Brakspear. Staff are friendly and attentive, which is unusual in an area where a recent boom has seen a burst of new venues opening, many of which are really a triumph of style over substance. But then Smithy's is different, and you're as welcome to come in for a pint and crisps as you are for a bottle of vintage champagne and a three-course meal.

FEATURES:

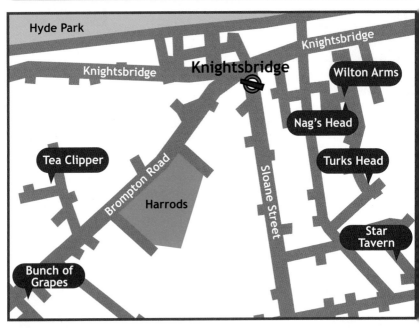

Hyde Park

Knightsbridge

Knightsbridge

Knightsbridge

Wilton Arms

Nag's Head

Tea Clipper

Brompton Road

Sloane Street

Turks Head

Harrods

Star Tavern

Bunch of Grapes

Bunch of Grapes

RATING:

207 Brompton Road
SW3 1LA
020 7589 4944

This pub is excellent, architecturally. Most of the features are nineteenth-century and the pub retains vestiges of the public bar and snug. Nice. Upstairs restaurant, decent drink, bar food and unobtrusive music. The only thing wrong with it is that it's located in a heavily touristy area, resulting in a very transient clientele. Still, worth chancing a look at.

HANDY FOR: Victoria & Albert Museum, Natural History Museum, Science Museum

Nag's Head

RATING:

53 Kinnerton Street
SW1X 8ED
020 7235 1135

Hidden away in a quiet Knightsbridge street, this is one well worth searching out. Wood-panelled, low-ceilinged and full of old penny-arcade games, this pub has a character all of its own and is ideal for a leisurely afternoon of drinking. Unsurprisingly, there's not a TV or a jukebox in sight (but there is a 'What the Butler Saw' machine in the corner). In such a carefully realised environment, playing CDs can seem a tad incongruous, but the choices from the bar are usually spot on (Nina Simone when we last looked in). The pub's independent nature comes from its landlord, who, when not insisting that customers hang up their coats, is improvising quality pub food with whatever comes to hand (the shepherd's pie is especially recommended). We've even seen him kick out punters who ignore the 'no mobile phones' signs. Top bloke, top pub.

Visitors' Award Winner 2005

The Star Tavern

RATING:

6 Belgrave Mews West
SW1X 8HT
020 7235 3019

Some would have you think (wrongly, we believe) that the Great Train Robbers supped here while pondering their scheme, but the Star Tavern doesn't need any hackneyed gangster chic to attract the punters. Being quite small, it's not the place for a rowdy night out, but you get a good selection of Fuller's ales and traditional pub food, served up by attentive staff who seem genuinely chuffed that you're frequenting their pub. Also, the clientele is a bit more mixed than other boozers in the area. It can be a bit of a trek finding this place, and it can fill up rapidly, but it's definitely worth a look. Lovely upstairs bar as well as the smallest gents' toilets in London.

FEATURES:

Tea Clipper

RATING:

19 Montpelier Street
SW7 1HF
020 7589 5251

From the outside it promises a good, cosy, English pub experience. Inside, it's a little short of the mark. It still has some Victorian stuff (mainly the windows) but most of it has been restored or faked. The nautical theme is there, but a little understated. With its recent relaunch, the beer is pretty good, particularly the TEA beer; the food's improved with a new menu; and the service is pretty prompt, even when it's busy. It's easy to see why it's popular with the locals – particularly on a warm evening – as it's a nice place to sit outside and enjoy a little sun.

FEATURES:

Turks Head

RATING:

10 Motcomb Street
SW1X 8LA
020 7245 0131

This place tries to attract a youngish clientele (that would explain the blary MTV) but doesn't always manage this. It may be the area (sedate Knightsbridge) or it may be the competition (the pub is midway between the more established Nag's Head and Star Tavern) but this pub always seems a bit lacking in numbers. But, if its more illustrious neighbours are too full, give it a look.

FEATURES:

Wilton Arms

RATING:

71 Kinnerton Street

SW1X 8ED

020 7235 4854

Given a spit and polish since being taken over by Shepherd Neame, this one has lost none of its attributes (though the sharp glare from the large number of lamps around the place did feel a tad intrusive). Good beer and a TV that's handy but doesn't dominate the pub. One point, though – the food's overpriced. Apart from that, it's a decent enough pub. Its local competitors may attract a lot of punters, but there's usually more chance of a seat in this one.

FEATURES:

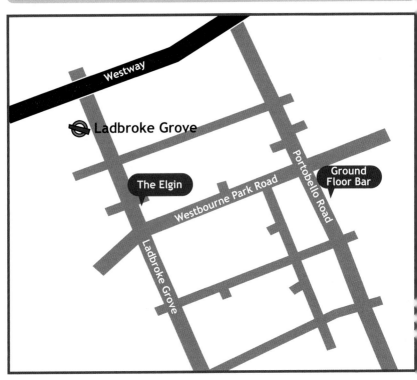

The Elgin

RATING:

96 Ladbroke Grove
W11 1PY
020 7229 5663

An old Firkin pub that's been reborn in an agreeable fashion. Butcher's-block tables and menus on clipboards are sops to gastropub culture, but the rest of the place is more traditional in feel. It's a fair size, with some remaining glass and tile work from its Victorian heyday. There's a reasonable selection of ales on tap and an even better range of bottled Belgian beers. The pub grub is decently priced for this part of town and the overall impression is of a fine pub, whether for passing punters just after one or locals settling in for a longer session.

FEATURES:

Ground Floor Bar

RATING:

186 Portobello Road

W11 1LA

020 7243 8701

Handy for the Electric, this place was one of the earlier pubs round here to get the bar treatment. The beer is mostly lager – although there's a Weißbier, which is available only in halves, probably to disguise the £5 per pint price tag (it's only 5.5 ABV). The Ground Floor is typical of the genre – with it's squashy settees, laid-back tunes and smug clientele, so, if that's your scene, you'll be happy here. If you're into beer, you'll need an alternative.

FEATURES:

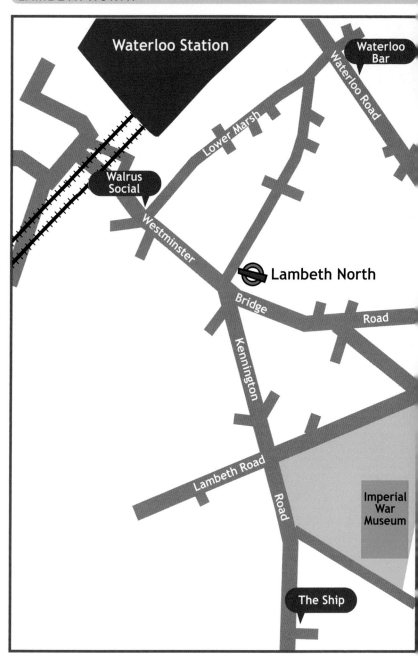

The Ship

RATING:

171 Kennington Road

SE11 6SF

020 7735 1371

A lick of paint has smartened up the exterior of this one, but thankfully not a lot has changed on the inside. The healthy mix of local residents and workers and the friendly staff make for arguably the best pub in the area. Food served only at lunchtimes, but it's fairly cheap and there's plenty of it.

FEATURES:

Walrus Social

RATING:

172 Westminster Bridge Road

SE1 7RW

020 7928 4368

A Lower Marsh boozer that's been adapted for a bar clientele. Rather a tender transition, though, with much of the original décor and furnishings left *in situ*. As a result, there's still the air of a pub to the place, rendering this one a touch above your usual, pale-wood All Bar One clone. Drinks are more in the cocktail rather than pint range though – beer drinkers may be forced into ordering a pint of John Smith's. Food isn't precious or expensive – lunchtime here looks a safe bet to us, especially with the main competition nearby being a greasy spoon and a bakery.

FEATURES: HANDY FOR: London Eye

Waterloo Bar and Kitchen

RATING:

131 Waterloo Road

SE1 8UR

020 7928 5086

A gastropub, for sure, but one that is straightforwardly classy, rather than pretentious. The Waterloo Bar and Kitchen is popular in the early evenings with those en route to the nearby Old Vic, and the food is excellent. As far as the drinks go, there's a reasonable range of Continental beers, including a German wheat beer that puts the stuff they sell in Sam Smith's pubs to shame. In many ways this is much more of a place to eat in, rather than just to drink, but we hear that those only popping in for liquid refreshment are made to feel at home by the welcoming staff. All in all, the Waterloo Bar and Kitchen is a reassuringly civilised and enjoyable place to spend some time.

FEATURES:

LANCASTER GATE

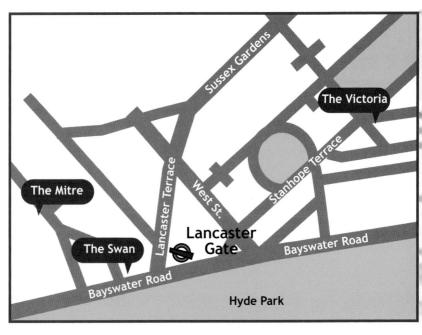

The Mitre

RATING:

24 Craven Terrace

W2 3QH

020 7262 5240

A large Victorian pub with lots of its original interior still intact, a good range of beers and reasonable pub grub. Not very many people on a weekday lunchtime, but it fills up in the evening. There aren't many decent pubs in this area and this one does have a pretty interesting interior, so, if you're hungry or thirsty and around Lancaster Gate, this one is definitely worth a visit.

FEATURES:

The Swan

RATING:

66 Bayswater Road

W2 3PH

020 7262 5204

A quintessential tourist pub – an old building, charmlessly updated, opposite Hyde Park. Most punters head for the beer garden to escape the jukebox; but unfortunately any chances of a peaceful drink are shattered by the traffic of the Bayswater Road thundering past. It's of note only if you're meeting up with mates, as there's plenty of room inside and it's close to the tube. If you're actually after a real boozer, though, head elsewhere.

FEATURES:

LANCASTER GATE

The Victoria

RATING:

10a Strathearn Place

W2 2NH

020 7724 1191

A fine old-fashioned corner pub, a bit smaller than it looks from the outside, but with a stunning Victorian interior – all etched mirrors, intricate tile work and two fires. Thankfully, the fare matches the setting – well-kept Fuller's ales, a large menu and friendly service. Also of note are the rooms upstairs, a function room that resembles the library of a gentlemen's club and a bar built from the décor of the demolished Gaiety Theatre's bar (allegedly). Sure, it's plush and opulent but there's still a local-pub feel to the place. One of the best in the area.

FEATURES:

LEICESTER SQUARE

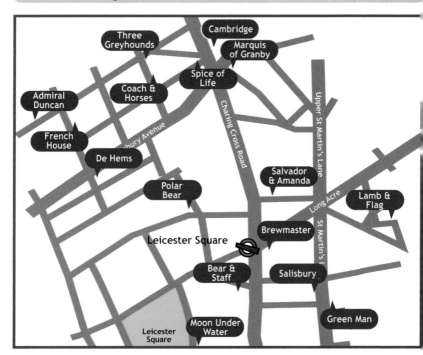

Admiral Duncan

RATING:

54 Old Compton Street
W1D 4UD
020 7437 5300

The Admiral has changed beyond recognition since the bomb in April 1999 that ripped through the old pub and killed three people. It's now cleaner, camp and trendy, and extremely popular in the evenings. Still, it does reasonable beer, good dance music on the box, and friendly staff and clientele. It's pretty tolerant most of the time, but there are bouncers on the door most nights with an understandable case of paranoia.

FEATURES:

Bear & Staff

RATING:

11 Bear Street
WC2H 7AS
020 7930 5260

A friendly enough pub on Charing Cross Road, which, given its proximity to Leicester Square, is seldom quiet. It fits the image for many visitors to London of what a pub is – real ales, traditional pub grub – yet also has a fair number of more regular punters. It's a touch above your usual West End pub – but just a touch.

FEATURES:

229

The Brewmaster

RATING:

37 Cranbourn Street

WC2H 7AD

020 7836 1038

Usually overcrowded, the ground-floor bar in this pub is rarely worth the effort. But the first-floor room is a welcome exception – when it's open. We've been in it when it's been practically deserted and the ground floor has had lager louts spilling into Charing Cross Road. When it's open, it can be a welcome refuge from the insane crowds around Leicester Square. Still a prime place to meet someone, with its close proximity to Leicester Square tube, but not a place to linger if you can't get into the upper bar.

FEATURES:

Cambridge

RATING:

93 Charing Cross Road

WC2H oDP

020 7494 0338

Another easy-to-find pub in the West End, and another one recently refitted under the Nicholson's brand. These pubs make a play for the tourist market, with prominent signs for 'traditional fish and chips' and notices making as much mention as they can of the pubs' history. The overall effect is not unlike that of the Sam Smith's pubs in London: the chains sharing a lack of TVs and an attachment to recreating 'traditional' pub interiors. Whereas the Sam pubs offer a variety of interiors, the West End Nicholson's are rather more of a type, with their similar furnishings and no-smoking rooms upstairs. On our most recent visit, the Cambridge was certainly pulling in a crowd of overseas visitors, though not too many seemed willing to try the four different ales on tap (and available on 'try before you buy'). This one fits the bill as a pub to meet up in but just wasn't comfortable enough for a longer session.

FEATURES:

Coach & Horses

RATING:

29 Greek Street
W1D 5DH
020 7437 5920

Even though its long-standing landlord has retired, this one hasn't changed (yet). It's a dump, really. A famous dump, but still a dump. Famous for its clientele, you'll find the Coach crowded of an evening with punters looking for famous people and regaling each other with (often) secondhand stories of past times. If you need a pint and you're in the area, there are other, more accommodating places not far away - although we quite like it here weekday afternoons, when it's quiet and the sarnies, unlike the beer, are cheap.

De Hems

RATING:

11 Macclesfield Street
W1D 5BW
020 7437 2494

This old Soho stalwart now comes under the ownership of Mitchells & Butlers and is part of their enlarging of the Nicholson's brand. If anything, this change has resulted in a better selection of Continental beers than the old pub had. However, this improvement on the drink side of things has come with a dilution of the pub's unique Dutchness. Most noticeably, the special Low Countries menu (Bitterballen etc.) has been replaced by a standard pub-grub choice. No surprise, either, to see the Dennis Bergkamp shirt disappear from the wall (such modern accoutrements don't fit with a heritage pub, you see). This one still packs them in but for us it's one that's had its individuality ever so slightly reined in. And, given that the original pubs in the Nicholson's chain were all about difference and unique identities, that's all rather sad. The sign outside puts things best: 'Dutch Café Bar', it announces; 'Traditional Fish & Chips', it adds below.

FEATURES:

The French House

RATING:

49 Dean Street
W1D 5BE
020 7437 2799

This place hasn't really changed in decades (except for the landlord's retirement). Famous for being famous, small, crowded and serving only halves. It's got a strong history, Leffe on tap, and staff who cope well with the crowds of customers. It is, however, a pub we've never really warmed to. That's due in no small part to an atmosphere that's not far off that of the most inward-looking of local pubs (for local people) and a clientele that could provide the dictionary definition of 'arrogant'. So, if you don't mind standing about in a crushed bar while fedora'd 'gents' eye you dismissively and reminisce about Gaston, Jeff and Francis, by all means pop in. It's just a bit too forced and precious for us.

FEATURES:

Green Man & French Horn

RATING:

54 St Martin's Lane
WC2N 4EA
020 7836 7644

This small pub has quietly been going about its business for years. It is refreshingly ordinary, in an area where most pubs are either trying hard to be different or are just mobbed with tourists.

FEATURES: 　　　　HANDY FOR: Trafalgar Square

Lamb & Flag

RATING:

33 Rose Street
WC2E 9EB
020 7497 9504

This pub is pretty famous and doesn't need too much of an introduction. It's old (and looks it) and it's just the sort of Olde Englishe Pubbe the tourists expect and love. It serves decent beer and food and, as a result of all the above, is usually pretty packed. If you can fight your way upstairs you might find a quieter spot or even a seat. If it looks quiet, do go in and have a nosey round, and, if you like cheery, crowded pubs, then you usually won't be disappointed here.

Marquis of Granby

RATING:

142 Shaftesbury Avenue
WC2H 8HJ
020 7836 8609

Fit and working again after a recent refurb, the Marquis has been smartened up, its new décor evoking theatrical times past (drapes, old opera programmes). With an interior not too dissimilar to that of many a gastropub, you might expect the menu to be upgraded too. On our visit, though, the bar menu merely consisted of a list of quality sandwiches. Beer selection was decent enough and things are governed over by a landlord of the old school. Worth noting as well that this one fills up for the football – may not be what the tourists are after, but it makes a change for the area. All in all, the pick of the pubs around Cambridge Circus.

FEATURES:

Moon Under Water

RATING:

28 Leicester Square
WC2H 7LE
020 7839 2837

Nowadays, this is one of the smaller Wetherspoon pubs, which is especially surprising given the location. As ever, it's a Wetherspoon pub, therefore cheap booze and food are on offer, without the distractions of music, pool and TV. However, its claustrophobic interior (low ceilings) means it is a very, very noisy place to inhabit. The service is incredibly prompt and attentive and it's easy for your out-of-town mates to find – you could do far worse in the immediate vicinity.

FEATURES:

Polar Bear

RATING:

30 Lisle Street
WC2H 7BA
020 7479 7981

This one's a handy place to meet before venturing into Chinatown and, when we last checked, the ales on tap were the standard Adnams and London Pride double act. It does cheap bar food, pulls in a crowd when the footy's on and plays host to DJ nights in the room downstairs. Some of the former regulars from the defunct King's Head around the corner took up residence here a while ago and another major change was the introduction of a no-smoking policy, a rule that has been recently and intriguingly overturned – so have a puff here while you still can.

FEATURES:    **HANDY FOR:** National Gallery, Trafalgar Square

Salisbury

RATING:

90 St Martin's Lane
WC2N 4AP
020 7836 5863

A big, ornate, well-preserved Victorian gin palace. This place packs in the tourists because of where it is and what it looks like – the tourist idea of a city pub. A pretty standard range of drink and food is on offer at Covent Garden prices. It's less gay than it used to be and nowadays it's pretty much another unatmospheric tourist pub, typical for the area. Do come here to have a look at the fixtures and fittings, but don't expect too much else in the way of a great pub experience.

Salvador & Amanda

RATING:

8 Great Newport Street
WC2H 7JA
020 7240 1551

Not a pub, but, given that this area isn't really overrun with great pubs, we don't feel any problems recommending a decent bar to you. Taking its name from Señor Dali and his muse of the 1960s, this basement bar doubles as a tapas venue, though it's hardly the sort of place that you'll stand out in if you just stick to the drink. This place prides itself on its sangria and its cocktails, though a decent range of spirits and bottled beers are also available. It's a fair-sized space, darkly lit and with an array of different-sized tables, so it's able to cope with small or larger groups. Heartening, too, that they haven't gone overboard on the Dali theme – just a few black-and-white photos on the wall of the man and his muse. That sort of subtlety works in this one's favour and, although it's got some of the bar features that we're not keen on (your change on a tray, for example), it doesn't go too far down that route (e.g. no sign on our visit of somebody pushing down the taps for you in the toilet). A cut above your average West End bar, then, but this one manages to evade the exclusive nature of London's swankier drinking holes. Stylish, yes; pretentious, no. And in case you're after a late night, this one's open till 2 a.m. Monday to Thursday and 3 a.m. at weekends (though you'll have to pay to get in after 9 p.m.).

FEATURES:

The Spice of Life

RATING:

37–39 Romilly Street

W1D 5AN

020 7437 7013

This a large pub in a in a prime location, which, of course, is what brings it down – it's in the heart of the theatre district and there's a constant tide of people flowing in and out as they make their way to and from the shows. Especially in the evenings, when all the regulars have gone home to suburbia. It being a McMullen pub, the choice of beers is not your usual West End selection. This pub's OK, but it's not really one you would go out of your way for. And there's live music in the basement every night of the week.

FEATURES:

Three Greyhounds

RATING:

25 Greek Street

W1D 5DD

020 7494 0902

This mock-Tudor extravaganza has been lovingly restored by its owners to its former glory. There's a good range of well-kept beers on the hand pumps and an extensive food menu, which is heavily promoted. We'd like to give it a higher rating, but the size of the pub works against it – you need little more than a handful of people to make the place feel pretty crowded, and, given where it is, that's easily achieved. Nevertheless, it's a Nicholson's and, with the excellent beers on offer, this place is a pretty good pub.

FEATURES:

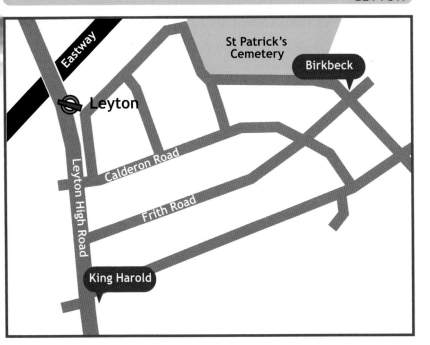

Birkbeck

45 Langthorne Rd

E11 4HL

020 8539 2584

This imposing locals' pub hasn't really changed much since we started going here almost a decade ago, which is no bad thing. Made up of a large public bar and a smaller room at the front with a pool table, it's a decent pub. It still sells 'Rita's Special', a bitter named after a previous landlady, as well as a rotating line-up of excellent guest beers which don't stick around very long. The local darts team meets here, as evidenced by the trophies in the cabinet over the door to the front bar. One of the dartboards is placed near the doorway to the large beer garden and requires good timing to get outside if there's a game on. Populated by friendly locals and genial bar staff, it's got a lot going for it. Now, if they only did Sunday lunch ...

FEATURES:

King Harold

RATING:

116 High Road

E15 2BX

020 8558 3635

This large, lively, friendly local shows how it should be done. OK, the beer won't have CAMRA members creaming their jeans, but there's enough of a range to keep all but the most fussy drinkers happy and the service is friendly, prompt and attentive. The locals are more than fine with outsiders being in their pub and there are loads of activities to keep people happy (even a large beer garden in case we get something resembling a summer). Any time of day it seems to have a buzzing clientele. Long may it last. Cheers!

FEATURES:

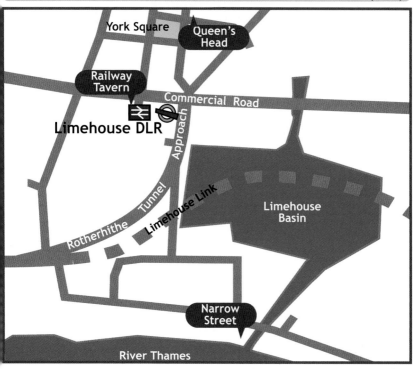

York Square

Queen's Head

Railway Tavern

Commercial Road

Limehouse DLR

Approach

Rotherhithe Tunnel

Limehouse Link

Limehouse Basin

Narrow Street

River Thames

The Narrow Street

RATING:

Narrow Street
E14 8DP
020 7265 8931

This old Limehouse Basin building was given another makeover a while ago: the first had been to rescue it from dereliction, the second to turn it from pub to gastropub. In the same way as the first repurposing didn't make this place into a genuine pub, this time around the place feels like a bar in a middle-market hotel than a genuine pub – it lacks conviction. The prices here are pretty close to hotel rates too. The drink is not particularly special: there are a couple of Belgians on draft, and there are no real ales. But you'll come here, along with almost everyone else, to sit on the terrace with its unique and, often bracing, view of Limehouse Reach.

FEATURES:

239

Queen's Head

RATING:

8 Flamborough Street

E14 7LS

020 7791 2504

Ever been in a Young's pub and wondered where that photo of the Queen Mum pulling a pint comes from? Well, it was here that Her Maj looked the East End in the face (well, midriff) from behind the bar. Have to say, the old dear chose a pretty decent pub for the shoot. Situated in a well-preserved square, it's a traditional two-bar affair, with a space for darts at the back and a food counter at the front. Can be quiet, and so a decent one for watching the world go by and sorting the wheat from the chaff on the jukebox (naturally, it fills up when the sport is on). And, even if *our* pints weren't pulled by a Windsor, they were up to the usual Young's standards.

FEATURES:

Railway Tavern

RATING:

576 Commercial Road

E14 7JD

020 7790 2360

Being both on the busy Commercial Road and underneath a railway bridge, this pub does have a rather offputting air to it. Our visit found it to be a fairly decent locals' haunt, appealing to both a gay and straight clientele. Although the sort of place where the bar staff greet their regulars as soon as they walk in the door, it doesn't have too much to offer the passing pub goer.

FEATURES:

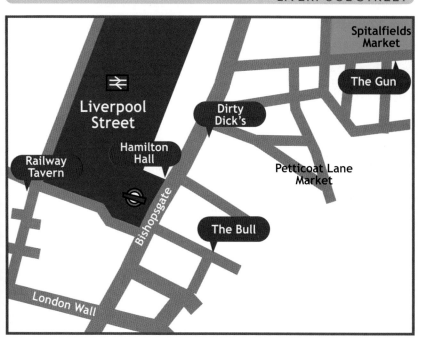

Spitalfields Market

The Gun

Liverpool Street

Dirty Dick's

Hamilton Hall

Railway Tavern

Petticoat Lane Market

Bishopsgate

The Bull

London Wall

The Bull

RATING:

2 Devonshire Row
EC2M 4RH
020 7247 6792

A decent, traditional pub just far enough off Bishopsgate to prevent it from getting overcrowded with the homeward-bound Essex commuters. It's a T&J Bernard pub, so there's a reasonable range of decent beer on the hand pumps, and, unlike some of their pubs in other, more touristy areas, this one doesn't feel too contrived.

FEATURES:

Dirty Dick's

RATING:

202 Bishopsgate
EC2M 4NR
020 7283 5888

This notorious City pub and tourist attraction underwent a facelift a few years ago, unfortunately eradicating all traces of the interesting dive it once was. Its proximity to Liverpool Street station makes it a popular last stop before getting the train home for many office workers. They serve vast amounts of lager, but can also pour a pint of Guinness and have the usual range of Young's excellent beers on tap. It tends to be very busy around lunch and immediately after work, but quietens down later. The downstairs bar, where all the interesting stuff used to be, can be hired.

FEATURES:

The Gun

RATING:

54 Brushfield Street
E1 6AG
020 7247 7988

Many pubs in the Spitalfields area are reinventing themselves as 'Bohemian' bars with crappy furniture, louder-than-usual music, candles, foreign-sounding menus, Smirnoff Ice and all that. Thankfully, this pub has stuck to its guns and presents itself as that increasingly hard-to-find venue – the traditional boozer. It's a regulars' pub, with blokes (mostly) from the offices nearby being ably catered for with decent beer – Broadside, Bombardier, Best and Young's Bitter on the hand pumps – food and service, with the occasional sporting event on the telly.

FEATURES:

Hamilton Hall

RATING:

Liverpool Street Station
EC2M 7PY
020 7247 3579

Since this pub seems to have it all – a dazzlingly ornate interior (part of the old Great Eastern Hotel – some say banqueting hall, some say ballroom, depends whom you ask), a large range of decent, well-priced beer (especially for the City) and cheap pub grub – you'd be forgiven for thinking it's well worth making an effort to visit here. Sadly, you'd be wrong. If ever proof of the 'the closer to the station, the worse the pub' theory was needed, then this is it. Relentlessly packed – with braying City commuters, bewildered travellers and usually both – this place is not a pleasant drinking experience. Add the Friday-night crowd and/or a bunch of footy supporters and you'll have a pretty close approximation of some people's idea of hell.

FEATURES:

Railway Tavern

RATING:

15 Liverpool Street
EC2M 7NX
020 7283 3598

Not many pubs in the Square Mile have an ivy-clad exterior; even fewer display the crests of the old railway companies. But, then, given this pub's name, that shouldn't come as a surprise. Shame, then, that this one hasn't many other touches of originality to it. As it's bang opposite the station, it's busy when you'd expect it to be with City commuters and other disparate transients. The beer selection's not bad and there's Sky Sport on the TV, should one feel so inclined. One plus point: it's open at weekends, and so offers an alternative to the nearby Wetherspoon for the weary traveller (safe and sound pub grub, too). It does a job, but not quite enough to disprove the old dictum: the closer you get to a mainline train station, the worse the pub. At least it's not as close as Hamilton Hall, though.

FEATURES:

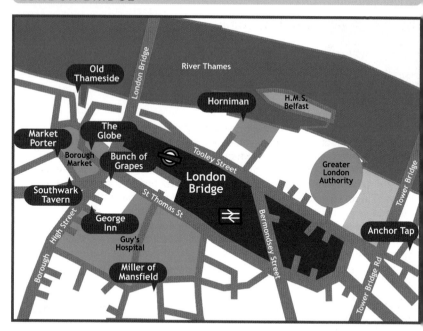

Old Thameside

London Bridge

River Thames

Horniman

H.M.S. Belfast

Market Porter

The Globe

Borough Market

Bunch of Grapes

Tooley Street

London Bridge

Greater London Authority

Tower Bridge

Southwark Tavern

St Thomas St

Anchor Tap

Bermondsey Street

George Inn

Guy's Hospital

Borough High Street

Miller of Mansfield

Tower Bridge Rd

Anchor Tap

28 Horselydown Lane

SE1 2LN

020 7403 4637

RATING:

An old pub right in the middle of Conran land (Butler's Wharf), but don't get the idea it's a trendy designer pub – it's not. It looks all right from the outside, but inside it's a bit pokey, with numerous small rooms. That said, some of these rooms can be quite cosy and it would be a shame to knock it all together, as is the trend when pubs get refurbished. Things get more cheery in the summer when the beer garden is open. The usual standard of drink you would expect from a Sam's pub and cheapish pub grub mean that, if you like Sam's fare (and we know not everybody does), it's not bad here and considerably better than some nearby places.

FEATURES: HANDY FOR: Tower Bridge, Design Museum

Bunch of Grapes

RATING:

2 St Thomas Street

SE1 9RS

020 7403 2070

This handsome pub (a Grade II listed building) offers the decent selection of beer and food that you would expect from Young's. It also has a pleasant split-level garden to the rear, which is ideal for a relaxing drink, and is particularly convenient for meeting people near London Bridge station. Being situated on a busy junction, and in the path of many commuters, means it can get pretty noisy in here, so you're unlikely to linger. (Don't come here on Sunday: it's closed.)

FEATURES: **HANDY FOR:** London Dungeon

George Inn

RATING:

77 Borough High Street

SE1 1NH

020 7407 2056

This well-preserved coaching house (owned by the National Trust) off Borough High Street serves a loyal following as well as the innumerable walking/coach tours that visit it. It serves a number of excellent guest beers, including its own George Ale (brewed by Adnams). All the usual suspects and some drinkable wines are here too. When the weather's good, the outdoor area's one of the best attractions of this pub, as it's a great place to sunbathe and people-watch while having an excellent pint. Seems to tolerate children, has a large no-smoking room, and the function room on the first floor is available for hire. These are all plus points, of course, but, in terms of a drinking experience, the George can be disappointing. The bars are often very crowded and it can take an age to get served, let alone find a seat; the George seems to be a victim of its own high profile. The cosy room to the far right, with a fire in winter, retains an antique atmosphere, but the other bar areas have been modernised in a rather anonymous way. The historical significance of the George notwithstanding, there are several other pubs that we prefer in this area.

FEATURES:

The Globe

RATING:

8 Bedale Street
SE1 9AL
020 7407 0043

Built in 1872 in an excellent location near Southwark Cathedral and the Thames path, this place has plenty in its favour. Yet, despite the attractive exterior, the Globe disappoints somewhat. The interior looks and feels as though it has been refurbished recently, outlined by a high rail stocked with jars, bottles and pots. The pub is curiously short of seats. There are also no surprises behind the bar to distract your taste buds as trains rumble overhead. Recently made famous in *Bridget Jones* films, the Globe is a place to drop into rather than somewhere for an evening, and it appears to give up completely at weekends, when it's seldom open. Disappointing.

FEATURES: HANDY FOR: Globe Theatre

Horniman at Hay's

RATING:

Hay's Galleria, Counter Street
SE1 2BA
020 7407 1991

Hornimans is a huge pub built in a refurbished wharf renamed Hay's Galleria. It's quite picturesque in an olde-worlde industrial way and consequently captures a lot of the tourists passing on the way to Tower Bridge or the Globe. The pub is large and sprawls over the ground floor of one side of the wharf on the riverside. It's all been done up in the style of a tiled Victoriana Turkish bath, which doesn't quite convince you that it's for real (which it isn't). However, the pub and its surrounding area manage to accommodate the crowds without feeling too stretched, so it doesn't get too uncomfortable, although Fridays are pretty manic. It has two nonsmoking areas, the downstairs Wharfside Cellar Bar and the upstairs Mezzanine, which can both be hired. Service can be slow at busy times, resulting in a thirsty wait. If it's not mobbed, it's worth popping into when you're passing it on the way to the tourist sites in the area.

FEATURES:

The Market Porter

RATING:

9 Stoney Street

SE1 9AA

020 7407 2495

This is a gem of a pub – it's got something for everyone, no matter what time or day of the week you choose to visit. It's a lively place on Friday and Saturday nights with a mixed crowd and a real pub atmosphere. The food is OK, there's a restaurant upstairs and the drink is excellent. There's an interesting and very well-kept range of beers on the hand pumps – the regular is Harvey's and some unusual beers and old favourites make up the rest, changing pretty often. A great pub that's worth going out of your way for and, what with the recent relatively sensitive refurbishment to the backroom, there's now more chance of getting a seat. It does get busy when Borough market is on (Fridays and Saturdays), with traders and visitors alike piling in.

FEATURES: *Reviewers' Award Winner 2005*

Miller of Mansfield

RATING:

96 Snowsfields

SE1 3SS

020 7407 2690

Nestling behind Guy's Hospital, the Miller of Mansfield is a welcome change from London's 'wine and pine' makeover circuit. A sizable place, the Miller offers local drinkers a great space to park themselves and their pints after a hard week's work. No surprises on the beer front, with a typical selection on tap, the Miller also has an ample and affordable wine list, it's home to a wide range of groups of hospital staff, King's students and workers from the local environs. Food is on offer; the menus espouse the philosophy '… we cook food we like to eat'. Judging by the punters chowing down, they agree. It's reasonably priced, well presented and filling. What makes this place is the staff. On our last visit, on a packed-to-the-gills Friday evening, the staff knew exactly what to do and when to do it. They were welcoming and charming, getting through the thirsty hordes in front of the bar, and keeping everything else ticking over nicely. There's a good-sized function room upstairs, with regular comedy nights. Plenty of outdoor seating awaits when the weather is warm.

FEATURES:

Old Thameside Inn

RATING:

Pickfords Wharf, Clink Street
SE1 9DG
020 7403 4243

Well established on the tourist trail, this once-overlooked Nicholson's pub is now a hive of activity. And why not? With fine views of the City from the riverside terrace (if you can get on to it) and a decent range of drink and food on offer, it's certainly a place you'd give a try if you came across it on holiday. But its very popularity is what lets it down: when there's a crowd in – which is more often the case nowadays – it can be a thirsty wait.

FEATURES: HANDY FOR: Tate Modern, Globe Theatre

Southwark Tavern

RATING:

22 Southwark Street
SE1 1TU
020 7403 0257

A splendid building, recently refurbished, giving it a slight change of character. Previously it had a predominantly 1930s interior, but now furniture, fixtures and fittings from later decades have been added to the mix, creating a more trendy, loungey atmosphere, and the Debtors Bar downstairs has all sorts of nooks and crannies where you can hide away for those more intimate moments. There are real ales on the hand pumps – Pride, Black Sheep, Greene King IPA – and a good few Continentals (e.g. Leffe, Hoegaarden, Fruli) on tap. The food is pretty standard for this type of pub and there's often something musical on (e.g. DJ) in the evenings. During the day you'll find a good few tourists in here and lunching office workers, but in the evening it's much more of a young locals' thing.

FEATURES:

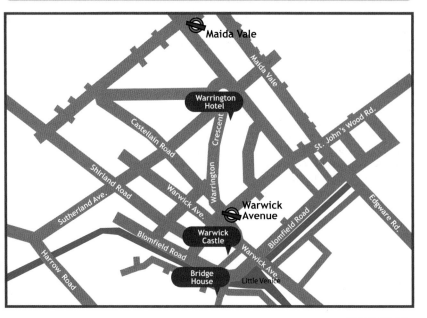

Maida Vale

Warrington Hotel

Castellain Road

Warrington Crescent

Maida Vale

St. John's Wood Rd.

Shirland Road

Warwick Ave.

Sutherland Ave.

Warwick Avenue

Blomfield Road

Edgware Rd.

Blomfield Road

Warwick Castle

Harrow Road

Bridge House

Warwick Ave.

Little Venice

The Bridge House

RATING:

13 Westbourne Terrace Road

W2 6NG

020 7432 1361

This place is just great, it must have one of the nicest canalside settings in London, but when you're in here all thoughts of narrowboating and other navigational pursuits are quickly forgotten. It's set in a grand neoclassical terrace, and you'll easily recognise its twenty-first-century gastropub aspirations from the interior décor. This is a place where you come to enjoy good drink, food and company. There's an excellent range of booze on offer, Adnams and Broadside, for example, on the hand pumps, and de Konninck, Leffe and Hoegaarden on tap, and more. There's a damned decent wine list and a choice of champagnes (including a vintage), cocktails and liqueur coffees. All alcoholic preferences seemed to be taken care of here. The food is decent and reasonably priced, and the service is good and the atmosphere relaxed. In case that's not enough for you, there's *NewsRevue* in the Canal Café Theatre upstairs.

FEATURES:

The Warrington Hotel

RATING:

93 Warrington Crescent
W9 1EH
020 7286 2929

On entering the Warrington Hotel, you are greeted by a stunning Art Nouveau interior of stained glass, orange lanterns and painted-wood furnishings. There's a special atmosphere about the place, too, with the handsome semicircular bar setting the tone for the spacious downstairs area, which retains the air of its previous incarnation as a grand hotel lobby. Happily, there is also an excellent range of ales on draught such as Fuller's ESB, Deuchars, Special and Greene King IPA. Ben's Thai restaurant is located upstairs in case you're hungry. What more could you ask for?

FEATURES:

Warwick Castle

RATING:

6 Warwick Place
W9 2PX
020 7432 1331

A nice little pub in a posh, leafy suburb on the Maida Vale–Paddington border. It does decent beer, with Pride, Bombardier and Young's on the hand pumps and there's food (pub grub) up until 9 o'clock, which is when they stop serving and you can bring your dog in. The service is friendly, as is the mood of the clientele, though it can get a little crowded at times, but it's all good-humoured. With a few seats and tables outside, it's nice for that out-of-the-way quiet pint with the paper.

FEATURES:

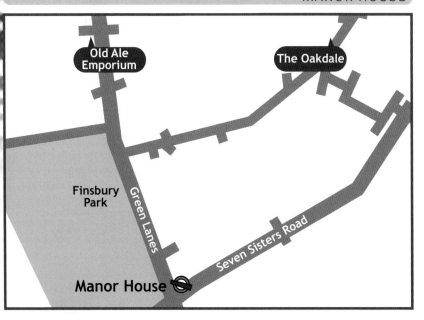

The Oakdale

RATING:

283 Hermitage Road

N4 1NP

020 8800 2013

The Oakdale is a large suburban local, certain to appeal to real-ale fans. At any one time, up to a dozen ales are on offer, mainly from the Milton Brewery, along with 'real' ciders, Belgian beers and a selection of single malts. A decent cross-section of locals popped in on our visit, all looking relieved that they have a decent pub in an otherwise barren area for drinking. A quiz night, pool table and a simple food menu add to the attractions, along with periodic beer, cider and perry festivals, offering up to fifty ales. The lighting is pretty harsh and it's a pain to get to unless you live in the area, but it's certainly worth the occasional visit. The pub was rescued from closure when originally taken over a few years ago, and an application to demolish it to turn it into (ubiquitous) luxury flats was rejected in 2005. Sadly, it seems an appeal by the building firm has been lodged and the sword of Damocles is once again hanging over the Oakdale. Hopefully the town planners will see sense and leave it alone.

FEATURES:

MANOR HOUSE

The Old Ale Emporium

RATING:

405 Green Lanes

N4 1EU

020 8348 6200

Outside, the Old Ale Emporium looks a bit unloved. The paint on the sign has faded and is starting to peel. Inside is not much better – ramshackle and dark. From its descriptive name to all the ornamental wooden ale casks dotted about, you'd think there might be some real ale about. Well, you'd be wrong – just the normal fizzy lagers. Never mind, though, since what could have been a grubby old-man's pub was actually a lively place, with a varied mix of people and friendly service. The jukebox was playing some pretty decent tunes, but we were probably lucky to have escaped one of the numerous *Now!* pop compilations on it. Although it's not a pub to everyone's taste, its atmosphere made this one work for us.

FEATURES:

MANSION HOUSE – *see Cannon Street, pg 77*

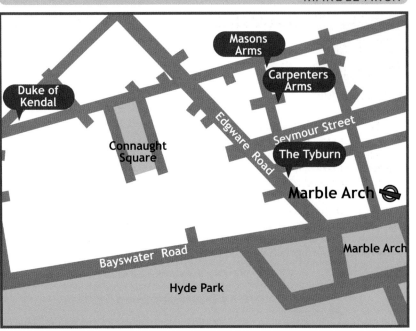

Masons Arms

Carpenters Arms

Duke of Kendal

Edgware Road

Seymour Street

Connaught Square

The Tyburn

Marble Arch 🚇

Marble Arch

Bayswater Road

Hyde Park

Carpenters Arms

RATING:

12 Seymour Place
W1H 7NE
020 7723 1050

This is a pleasant old, traditional-looking boozer a little off the beaten track in a heavily touristy area. Dark and cosy with lots of stuff on the walls (including some nice Victorian tile work) and an excellent, varied and ever-changing range of beers on the hand pumps. Service is good and the grub looks decent and cheap, although we still haven't tried it. Saturday afternoons are great for those who want to while away an hour or two with the sport on the TVs.

FEATURES:

Visitors' Award Winner 2005

253

Duke of Kendal

RATING:

38 Connaught Street

W2 2AF

020 7723 8478

This is one of the closest real locals' pubs to Oxford Street, but it's possible to get a decent seat, even at busy times such as Friday teatime. Considering its size and location, though, this is quite an achievement. The beer ranges from Directors to Adnams but also proving popular on our visit was the Thai food in the back bar (there's also a takeaway service for locals). Note, too, the upright piano in the front bar – if you're after a singalong of a Sunday evening, then be sure to pop by. This one's also close to the property recently bought by Tony Blair, but whether he'll be found propping up the bar after he moves on from Downing Street can't be guaranteed. Though there's always the Thai takeaway if Cherie fancies a night off from the cooking.

FEATURES:

The Masons Arms

RATING:

51 Upper Berkeley Street

W1H 7QW

020 7723 2131

A small pub with great beer – Tanglefoot, Badger and Sussex. With its open (albeit gas) fires and tongue-and-groove boarding up to the ceiling, it's a very comfortable and cosy boozer. This pub is definitely worth a visit for any pub aficionado; it does traditional grub and has friendly locals and prompt and friendly service. However, a word of warning: it does fill up with tourists in the summer.

FEATURES:

The Tyburn

RATING:

18 Edgware Rd
W2 2EN
020 7723 4731

As with most Wetherspoon pubs, the one great strength of this one is cheap booze. The allure is added to by the fact that this is one that serves cheap booze *just off Oxford Street*, which is something of an attraction come the 29th of the month. The atmosphere is rather lacking, but that's no great surprise in the heart of tourist land. The décor is a bit odd, but we think it's trying to be American diner *circa* 1960. It has a nice picture window from which one can watch the world go by up Oxford Street during a summer's evening or watch the new York Building complex take shape. Apart from that, there's not much to say: it's a bog-standard Wetherspoon.

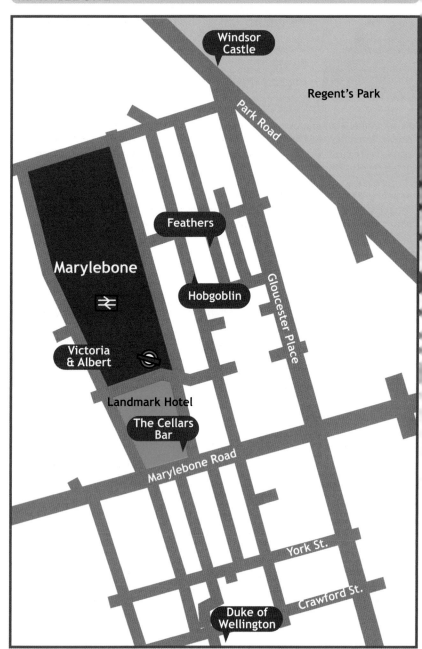

The Cellars Bar at the Landmark   RATING:

222 Marylebone Road
NW1 6JQ
020 7631 8000

Every so often at Fancyapint? we have a desire for grander surroundings than those offered by the average boozer and the Landmark's Cellar Bar fits the bill perfectly. Because it's a grand hotel of the old school, possessing one of the finest lobbies of any, anywhere, you might feel that a pint here would prove to be a wallet-busting experience, but it isn't. The wine, spirits and cocktails certainly do carry a premium price but the beer is only a tad more expensive than that of many of the pubs in the area. Couple this with five-star table service, spicy nuts and excellent air con, and you've got a comfy place to while away a relaxing hour or two before the commute home. Cheers!

Duke of Wellington   RATING:

94a Crawford Street
W1H 2HQ
020 7224 9435

Although Marylebone High Street is fast becoming the home of clothes shops and trendy eateries, a swift walk westwards past Baker Street finds you a world away in the company of some of the most characterful pubs in London. On a par with the gewgaw-filled Windsor Castle is the Duke of Wellington, a pub devoted to all things Arthur Wellesley-related. Busts, portraits, signposts – if it's of the Duke, it's in here. Odd thing is, clear away all the memorabilia and you still have a locals' boozer with a relaxed air and lived-in feel (which isn't always the case with pubs packed with antiques). Not a large pub by any means, though definitely one to look out for if the more popular ones nearby are full. Decent drink and simple food (toasties and the like). All visitors welcome, though perhaps those of a Gallic hue may find the atmosphere slightly intimidating.

FEATURES:

The Feathers

RATING:

43 Linhope Street
NW1 6HL
020 7402 1327

If you wanted to define a backstreet boozer – look no further. This is quite possibly the smallest pub in London, and coming here feels like stepping into someone's living room. The area around Marylebone station has an air of forgotten London, and that's certainly the feel you get here. Staff chat away to customers old and new alike, and an easygoing atmosphere permeates. If the landlord's on form, you'll hear the whole, tragic story of his life and the pub. The jukebox might seem a tad incongruous, but there's some space outside if you need to escape the music. Flowers Original and London Pride are on tap. The sort of pub you wished was at the bottom of your street.

FEATURES:

Hobgoblin

RATING:

21 Balcombe Street
NW1 6HB
020 7723 0352

Appropriately for the name and a Wychwood pub, this pub looks a tad dark and foreboding from outside. Step inside and you'll find a jolly traditional pub – and one that houses a happy mix all round. It sits on a quiet corner of this delightful area, just two minutes from Marylebone station and the unstoppable A40. It's on a road that mixes Georgian charm with the calling card of the Luftwaffe, the latter the nemesis of the pub's earlier building. The pub caters equally well for a good mix of locals and suits, and offers Thai food and real ale from Wychwood. For those in party mood, there are jugs of Vodka Red Bull or Pimm's, and you can even hire the cellar bar. The staff are friendly and helpful and encourage you to sample the beers before you decide, and, though pretty full on our visit, it's usually quieter than a pub like this deserves to be.

FEATURES:    HANDY FOR: Madame Tussaud's

Victoria & Albert

RATING:

Marylebone Station

Melcombe Place

NW1 6JJ

020 7402 0676

Hardly the most desirable accolade you can bestow, but this one is probably London's best mainline railway station pub. Given the relatively small size of Marylebone station – and the quality of the competition – that's probably not a surprise, but judged on its merits this one pretty much does the business. Sure, it's mostly chaps in suits delaying their evening journey back home, but not too many station pubs have two pool tables available or a range of six beers on tap. Best of all – just like the station that houses it – a slightly wistful air can dominate. What with its sepia photographs of steam trains or the hat stand and (disused) fireplace in the side bar, this one harks back to times past and feels slightly out of kilter with your average pub – although, unless you're departing to locations such as Amersham or Banbury, it's doubtful that you'll be beating a path to this one's door. However, if you do find your way here, you'll find it to be a decent enough spot and one that might even suggest attempting a London stations pub crawl. Don't bother, though – just stick with this one.

FEATURES:

Windsor Castle

RATING:

98 Park Road

NW1 4SH

020 7723 9262

This is located on the edge of Regent's Park, and a recent refit has gone to its head – or maybe the clientele has moved upmarket. It's gone a bit gastro, and the prices reflect that accordingly both for food and the beer. They do have a nice selection of guest ales and some Belgian beers and the food looked very nice. It's got comfy sofas upstairs – and you can reserve this area – and it seems pretty relaxed overall. As it's located near the London School of Business, it does get staff and students visiting on a regular basis (a group from the LSB had reserved the space upstairs last time we were in). And, if you've gone for a walk in the park, it's a good place for a sit-down.

FEATURES:

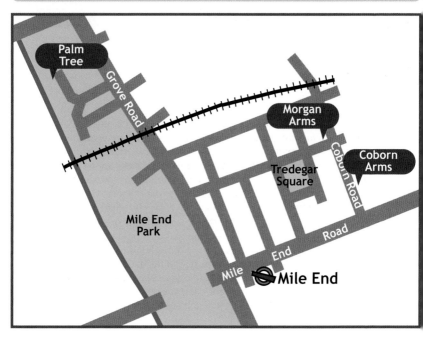

Coborn Arms

RATING:

8 Coborn Road

E3 2DA

020 8980 3793

A decent Young's pub serving reasonable drink and food. A favourite with the locals, it's a pretty large pub with a dedicated darts room (resplendent with trophies) and beer garden. If you're in the area, it's definitely worth popping in. Serves food – proper pub food – lunchtimes and evenings on weekdays and Sunday lunch.

FEATURES:

The Morgan Arms

RATING:

Morgan Street

E3 5AA

020 8980 6389

The relentless gentrification of parts east continues and the Morgan Arms is among the latest to receive the treatment. Having had a bit of an up-and-down career in recent years (mostly down), the Morgan Arms has been turned into a gastropub. We're a little surprised it took so long for this to happen in this area: there are some pretty posh houses nearby, many of the original inhabitants having taken the money and run, and every bit of available land around is having some sort of dwelling squeezed on it. So what's the pub like? It's OK, especially for the area, and there's Adnams and Landlord on the hand pumps (excellent!), and the service is good. Friday and Saturday nights will see it filled with the bright young things of Bow. Its recent elevation to stardom – *Evening Standard* Pub of the Year – has been accompanied by an elevation in tariff, so you won't see many drinks under £3 here. We suppose it keeps out the riffraff.

FEATURES:

Palm Tree

RATING:

Haverfield Road

E3 5BH

A great East End pub, with live music Friday, Saturday and Sunday nights. At first glance, it's not so different from many pubs in the East End, but the people who play and sing here do it with gusto, and there's some real talent, too. It's a great night out. The pub is hidden away in the Mile End Park, so it's not terribly easy to find, although it is one of the few surviving buildings in the area and it has been on telly quite a few times. There's usually a guest beer on the pumps and the food really only amounts to sausage rolls and sarnies for the darts teams, but that's not why you'd come here. It's got atmosphere – everybody knows everyone else in the pub, but that doesn't mean strangers aren't welcome. It's especially lively at weekends, when everyone goes for a singsong. It's not changed much over the years. We sincerely hope it stays that way.

FEATURES:

MOORGATE

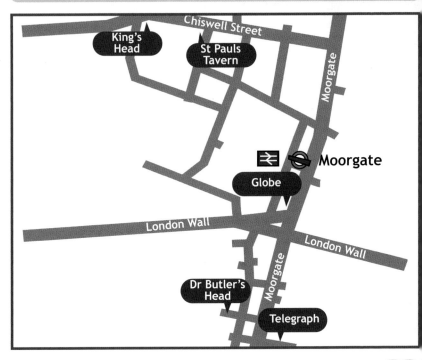

The Globe

RATING:

199 Moorgate
EC2M 6SA
020 7780 9241

This previously two-part pub (Globe/John Keats at Moorgate) has been unified under the Globe banner – the Keats moniker being relegated to 'Keats Bar' status, there are some claims that Keats was actually born on the site, but other sources are pretty vague. However, back to the pub. It's a pretty standard City hostelry, with decent hand-pulled beers and a reasonable and unpretentious menu, and it can get crowded at the usual lunch and/or commuting times. An easy pub to find, but not one to get worked up about, if truth be told.

FEATURES:

King's Head

49 Chiswell Street
EC1Y 4SA
020 7606 9158

A large City pub located 'but the throw of a stone' from the Barbican Centre. This pub is full of City types, students and musicians at peak times. Taken over by Greene King not long ago, it's got the usual selection of bottled beers and alcopops available alongside the more usual IPA and Abbots. Not a great place for that quiet chat – it's usually too lively and the music can be overpowering. The food available usually consists of standard pub grub. Not a bad pub at all, and one of the few in the City open at weekends.

FEATURES: HANDY FOR: Barbican Centre, Museum of London

The Old Doctor Butler's Head

RATING:

2 Masons Avenue
EC2V 5BT
020 7606 3504

Oscar Wilde had it spot on: 'Other people are quite dreadful.' What right has the heaving mob to invade this glorious, Traditional (with a capital T), olde-worlde (with a couple of 'e's tacked on), beautiful pub? It's hidden down a tiny alley and easy to miss for first-timers. But the suits track it down lunchtimes and early evenings. Yes, there are those who claim it quietens down in the evening – but then it closes early most nights and what good is a seat as last orders ring out? Through the throng you can see you're in a true, classy Victorian pub complete with genuine gas lighting. The hand pumps feature a good range of beers, including on occasion the moreish and potent porter. The doorstep sandwiches are reputed to be excellent – but how do you find the space to eat anything bigger than a cocktail sausage? The biggest available free space was probably the horse-trough-like handbasin in the gents'. Get there early, or get there late, or if needs be just get there and adopt a Churchillian 'they shall not pass' stance on whatever square foot you manage to colonise. But get there. It's worth it.

FEATURES:

St Pauls Tavern

RATING:

56 Chiswell Street
EC1Y 4SA
020 7606 3828

It's got a bit more of a genteel air than some of the other City watering holes. The décor is traditional – stripped floorboards and pine – and it's a long, thin pub, stretching along Chiswell Street, so it feels like a number of smaller pubs in very close proximity. If you find you're getting crowded in one area, you just hop to the next, something you might need to do, since it is a pretty popular place. It gets packed lunchtimes and early evenings, particularly towards the end of the week, getting even more crowded when some of the end rooms are roped off for private parties. As it's now a Cask Marque pub, the beer's pretty reliable and the service is prompt and polite.

FEATURES: **HANDY FOR:** Barbican Centre, Museum of London

The Telegraph

RATING:

11 Telegraph Street
EC2R 7LL
020 7920 9090

Installed in one of a bunch of buildings, arranged according to a medieval street plan, this 'modern' bar is where Fuller's take on All Bar One, head to head. The ales, beers, wines, staff and clientele are slightly more upmarket than those of its rivals and, it must be said, so are the prices. The atmosphere is correspondingly more refined, but not overly appealing. If you're looking for a modern take on the City wine bars of old, this might be for you, and, as to who's winning the bar wars, only time will tell.

FEATURES:

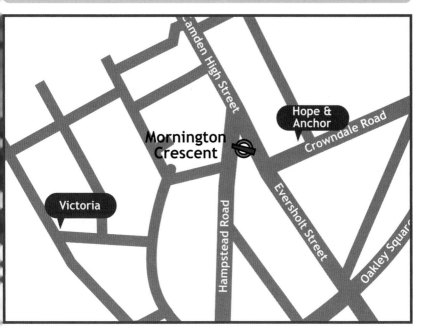

Hope & Anchor

74 Crowndale Road
NW1 1TP
020 7387 9506

The Hope & Anchor sports a splendid tiled exterior, while internally there's a no less charming engraved mirror behind the bar. The wood flooring is also rather old school and the front part of the pub, in particular, serves, at least for part of the time, as a real local haunt, a public house worthy of the name. (There was quite a crowd in celebrating a baby's christening when we visited late on a Saturday afternoon.) The area above and behind the bar, a little hidden away from this front room, has a pool table and a jukebox and is a little more spacious and less traditional in appearance. We reckon it would fill up pretty quickly on evenings ahead of gigs at Koko (formerly the Camden Palace) just down the road. But at other times it's an unpretentious, almost timeless, local. A decent enough place for a drink, to be sure.

FEATURES:

The Victoria

RATING:

2 Mornington Terrace
NW1 7RR
020 7387 3804

Midway between Camden and Euston, in its way this is as good a pub as any in these areas. It's a smart redevelopment of an old pub, but in this instance it's been done with care and a bit of style. It's a foodie pub too, but, even with the words 'pine nuts' and 'jus' on the lunchtime menu, there's not as much pretension about the place as you'd imagine. The interior gives off the air of a room in a smart country house, and the beer garden has a pleasant feel to it, too. It's the atmosphere that wins you over here – even at night there's a relaxing air. Maybe the punters enjoy it so much they don't want to let everyone else in on the secret. The one downside is their beer: you'll find only Pride on tap and even that often seems to run out. A shame, as that's the only drawback to this one.

FEATURES:

MUDCHUTE – *see Island Gardens, pg 195*

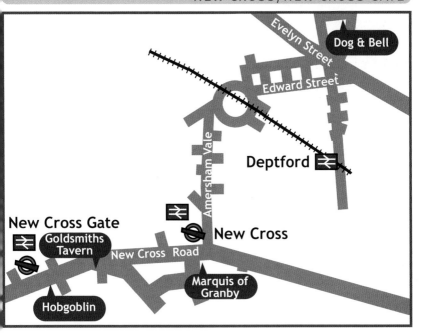

Dog & Bell

Evelyn Street

Edward Street

Deptford

Amersham Vale

New Cross Gate

Goldsmiths Tavern

New Cross Road

New Cross

Marquis of Granby

Hobgoblin

Dog & Bell

RATING:

116 Prince Street
SE8 3JD
020 8692 5664

Should you find yourself thirsty in Deptford, this place is indubitably your best bet. Unlike many pubs in the area, the Dog & Bell is neither grubby nor intimidating. It's a well-kept establishment with a range of unusual real ale on tap, plus a variety of exotic bottled beers in the fridge. Friendly service and a relaxed atmosphere among the locals are the order of the day. A bar billiards table adds to the charm and there's a rear terrace for sunny days. Look out for the plates daubed with TV chefs, too. The pub has recently changed hands, but, thankfully, all seems well. A new expanded menu is offered, and some odd slogan-led wax-based art (we prefer Delia and co.) is for sale in the side room. Fans of industrial architecture may want to see Borthwick Wharf before its imminent possible demolition.

FEATURES:

Reviewers' Award Winner 2004

fancyapint?

Goldsmiths Tavern

316 New Cross Road
SE14 6AF
020 8692 7381

Is this the new face of New Cross? The Goldsmiths is a spare, modern place with colourful décor and lots of natural light. It serves a decent range of beer (no real ale on tap but Spitfire and Bishops Finger in bottles). With tasty burgers and pizzas for under a fiver, this is one of the best New Cross pubs for food. The pub's diary is full too: salsa on Thursdays, R & B Fridays and DJs on Saturday nights. The large dance floor at the back makes all this possible, and the big-screen video jukebox is worth a punt, too.

FEATURES:

Hobgoblin

272 New Cross Road
SE14 6AA
020 8692 3193

This place seems to do things on a big scale. There's a sizable beer garden at the back for summer weather, which draws locals and students for sunshine and four-pint jugs of lager. The service is excellent – and honest, too: when we pondered getting food, the barman told us it could be ages in coming. Hobgoblin, Bombardier and IPA are on tap and there's a 20 per cent student discount on offer. In a pretty mixed area for drinking, this place seems to keep everyone happy.

FEATURES:

Marquis of Granby

RATING:

322 New Cross Road

SE14 6AG

020 8692 3140

This pub is also known as Kelly's Bar, which makes more sense given its Irish identity. Giant photos of the auld country, harp signs and a fittingly sentimental jukebox complete the picture. Greene King IPA and London Pride are on offer at the bar. It's a typical example of the dimly lit, cavernous Irish pubs you find all over London, but a good mix of older locals and Goldsmiths students keep it lively.

FEATURES:

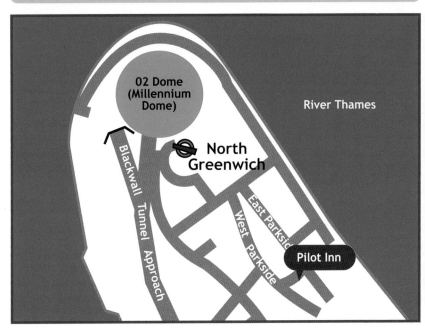

Pilot Inn

RATING:

68 River Way
SE10 0BE
020 8858 5910

A lovely old pub that only narrowly missed being demolished to make way for the Greenwich Peninsula revitalisation. It's got something for everybody: good beer, an enormous range of food, a bit of history (the pub and the terrace it sits in are just about the only old bits left in these parts), beer garden, TV – the lot. Cheerful, well kept and very pleasant.

FEATURES: HANDY FOR: O2 Dome

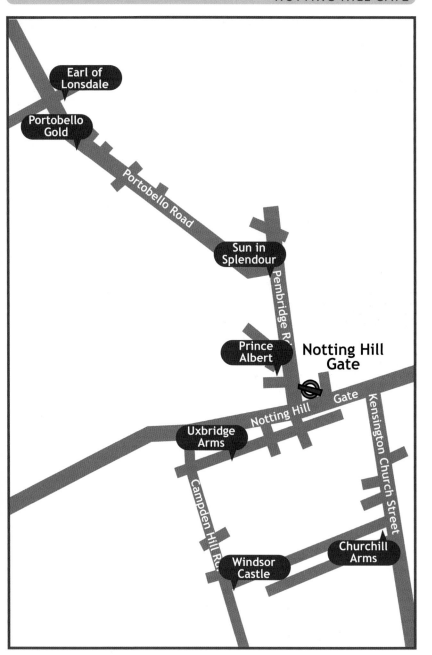

Churchill Arms

RATING:

119 Kensington Church Street
W8 7LN
020 7727 4242

One of the greats, and it's been consistently great for a long, long time. Good pint of Fuller's, one of the best pints of Guinness around town, traditional food and one of the first (if not the first) pubs to serve Thai food. Eclectic decoration, a mixed clientele and a genial landlord go together to make one of the best pubs in London. If they're open, what are you hanging around for?

FEATURES:

Earl of Lonsdale

RATING:

277–281 Westbourne Grove
W11 2QA
020 7727 6335

Nowadays, when most pubs get around to doing a refit, you know the 'stripped-out' look isn't far away. Sam Smith's, not being ones to follow fashion (it's Yorkshire, after all), have tried something different. Having found the original Victorian plans, they've turned back the clock in the Earl of Lonsdale. Now, where the large open bar once was is a succession of snug compartments, with tiny interconnecting gates – definitely not for the elderly or infirm. Even more etched glass can be found than before and it seems as if the dark wood has been given a needed revarnish. The cynical would say it was all for the benefit of attracting tourists looking for a 'Ye Olde Pubbe' experience; after all, they already feel the need to provide beer menus on all the tables, for those who might struggle ordering from the exclusively Sam Smith's range. Nevertheless, the place looks more cared for and feels considerably more cosy than before. For those who find the whole thing a little too claustrophobic or twee, the large backroom is still open-plan, with plenty of couches and two open fires, and the beer garden has been greatly improved, albeit by sacrificing the conservatory. In an area where pubs are going the way of the dodo, this place is a welcome relief, especially as on the Saturday afternoon we visited it wasn't as heaving as other places in the area.

FEATURES:

Portobello Gold

RATING:

95 Portobello Road
W11 2QB
020 7460 4910

Fit and working again after a fire a while back, this place packs a lot in –
Internet access, guest rooms, conservatory and a roof garden. Oh, and a bar
and restaurant. Somehow, despite the intriguing décor, we've never quite
warmed to this one. It's a handy stop on a Portobello Road crawl, but it just
seems more café-bar than bar-pub. Unduly cruel, perhaps? Give it a go and see
what you make of it.

FEATURES:

Prince Albert

RATING:

11 Pembridge Road
W11 3HQ
020 7313 9331

An old theatre pub that's probably not far off its next lick of paint. The formula
is certainly not new – large island bar of which half is a grill/kitchen to show
where your chosen dish was assembled. You could call the pub a compromise:
old and new styles; an attempt to be gastro without scaring drinkers away; the
music and art touch on reggae (but not exclusively); the décor invites loungers;
and candles, well, burn. The bar offers a mix of beers to suit the Notting Hill set
– De Konninck, two varieties of Staropramen, Budweiser, Hoegaarden and Leffe,
alongside Pride and Adnams ales. Though it's quiet, the service was a little too
laid back, though we finally got a fine Bloody Mary, and even on a more recent
visit – when the pub was a lot busier – the service was still very much on the
slow side. We'll stick to the pubs just south of Notting Hill Gate.

FEATURES: HANDY FOR: Portobello Road

273

Sun in Splendour

RATING:

7 Portobello Road
W11 3DA
020 7727 6345

Another one of Mitchells & Butlers loungey refits, this one with the added feature of being no-smoking. You'll find a decent range of beers from both the UK and the Continent, and a reasonable menu of modern British pub grub, priced for the area. And that is the problem. Anyone going to Portobello Road from Notting Hill tube will pass this attractive-looking pub and as a result it suffers the consequences. Weekday evenings aren't too bad, though. Should be a three-pinter, but the crowds of tourists force us to downgrade it. Sorry. However, if you do follow the crowds in, do sneak a peek at the secret garden (which is where you'll find the smokers).

FEATURES:

Uxbridge Arms

RATING:

13 Uxbridge Street
W8 7TQ
020 7727 7326

A jolly decent local tucked away from Notting Hill Gate. It has a good range of beers, an unostentatious, welcoming atmosphere and on the right side of Notting Hill Gate – away from the hordes of tourists and quixotic bargain-hunters on Portobello Road. It does seem that there are quite a few little gems in this area, away from the main drags and largely neglected by the tourists. Interesting.

FEATURES: HANDY FOR: Portobello Road

Windsor Castle

RATING:

114 Campden Hill Road
W8 7AR
020 7243 9551

A fine old pub that wouldn't be out of place in a much more rural setting, the Windsor Castle has been a favourite with Fancyapint? for years. It's a rambling, higgledy-piggledy place, with the sort of pub interior you'd expect to find in *Treasure Island*. The beer is pretty good, with well-kept real ales on the hand pumps, and so is the food, but it is pricey – hardly a surprise, considering where it is. There's a nice enclosed beer garden, but it's unlikely you'll find a seat on a warm summer's evening. It's a very pleasant place when it's not crowded, and, when it is, it's often a jolly crowd.

FEATURES:

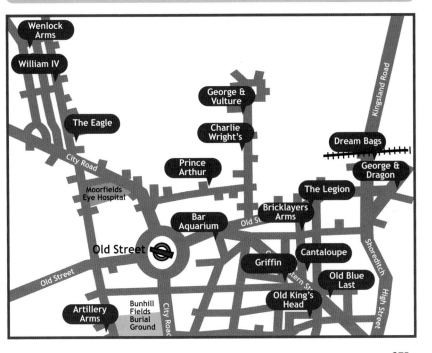

Artillery Arms

RATING:

102 Bunhill Row
EC1Y 8ND
020 7253 4683

The Artillery is one of the real pubs in the Square Mile. It's old, small and has served Fuller's beer for ever, as well as decent plain old pub grub. It's had a bit of a tidy-up and a lick of paint, but it hasn't lost its appeal. It's still an oasis on the fringes of the City.

FEATURES:

Bar Aquarium

RATING:

262–264 Old Street
EC1V 9DD
020 7253 3558

What with the people behind the Aquarium club next door taking on the old Lord Nelson, we thought Bar Aquarium would be a pure pre-club hangout, all expensive sofas and loungey trimmings. However, despite a new dining room and redecorated interior, there's still a pub feel – with the dartboard and Sky Sports remaining in place. It's not a small pub, either: you should be able to find a bit of space in the main bar, or, failing that, there's another bar – and a roof terrace – upstairs. Catering as much for those winding down after work as for those gearing up for a big night out, Bar Aquarium attracts a mixed crowd and manages to stand out in an area brimming with pubs and bars.

FEATURES:

Bricklayer's Arms

RATING:

63 Charlotte Road

EC2A 3PE

020 7739 5245

A long, long time ago (or so it seems), this pub was a traditional boozer, frequented by a smattering of locals and a few people out for a quiet pint. It served a decent pint, had an interesting range of beers and the interior had been unchanged for years. Then the Hoxton/Spitalfields revival got going and that was to the detriment of this pretty decent pub. Now it is often crowded with people who think the world is a better place thanks to their presence. But, if you manage to avoid this crowd, you'll appreciate this pub.

FEATURES:

Cantaloupe Bar and Restaurant

RATING:

35 Charlotte Road

EC2A 3PD

020 7613 4411

The strident, heady days of the dotcom boom are well behind the locale now, but the whole area is still trendy-bar city. Cantaloupe can lay fair claim to being one of the bars (if not *the* bar) that established the area as the capital's capital of cool. Things are somewhat more tranquil than they used to be – although the weekend evenings are still pretty busy – and it is a decent place to relax on a weekend afternoon. There aren't any real beers on tap – it's not that sort of place – but there are plenty of Continentals (including the original Bud) and not a bad pint of Guinness. Wine and spirit drinkers have far more choice, which after all is the main thrust of the place. The restaurant's OK too. If you can bag the squashy settees in the backroom, you can have a pretty chilled afternoon – and that's what we tend to do here.

FEATURES:

Charlie Wright's International Bar RATING:

45 Pitfield Street

N1 6DA

020 7490 8345

A pub that puts together a combination of Belgian beers and Thai food doesn't sound original, yet this one manages to stand out, even in a part of town overloaded with bars. The décor is Spartan to say the least – one room divided up into spaces for diners and drinkers (and dancers). It all clicks into place though: the aforementioned Mr. Wright keeps a cheery eye on proceedings and DJs keep things lively till the small hours. You'll have to part with a couple of quid to get in after 10 p.m. at weekends (but it is open until 4 a.m.), but that sounds fair enough to us. The pub–club hybrid isn't always a winner, but this one does it as well as any other.

FEATURES:

Dream Bags Jaguar Shoes RATING:

34–36 Kingsland Road

E2 8DA

020 7739 9550

The owners had a great concept. Whether it was to cut expense, or a flash of inspiration, the place looks as if almost no renovation was done to turn it into a bar. Even the original signs from when it was two separate wholesalers' shops (hence the name) are present. Inside, it's stripped back to bare brickwork and concrete, with only a few pieces of artwork and old leather sofas in place. In the basement a brick fireplace is the only decoration and the only thing hinting at the building's Victorian past. Its smoky, dark ambience makes it feel like a beatnik hangout, only with philosophical discussions about Sartre replaced by conversations about haircuts. Ultimately it's a great place, erring on the right side of pretension and one of the better bars in Hoxton – we just couldn't work out whether the DJ's choice of eighties power ballads was ironic or not.

FEATURES:

The Eagle

RATING:

2 Shepherdess Walk

N1 7LB

020 7553 7681

'Up and down the City Road / In and out the Eagle / That's the way the money goes / Pop! goes the weasel.' For those who like a bit of history, not many pubs can lay claim to being mentioned in a nursery rhyme – an old cautionary tale of spending all your money on booze. Times have changed (perhaps) and, although the Eagle was Islington-ised a while back, at heart it's still a pub. The staff are friendly and there's a fine choice of beer – real ales plus guests on the hand pumps and plenty of fine Continental beers on tap. In addition, the ivy-covered garden is pretty and there are barbecues in summer. Although often eerily quiet on Saturdays, its location off Old Street roundabout means during the week its full with an oil-and-water mix of local office workers, flat sharers, council estate dwellers and Hoxtonites. Overall, not bad at all.

FEATURES:

George & Dragon

RATING:

2–4 Hackney Road

E2 7NS

020 7012 1100

Hoxton bohemia meets the East End in this pub. It was rescued from near-dereliction a couple of years ago, and the new owners have kept what they could of the old place (after all, it was falling to bits) and added a dash of the early twenty-first century (i.e. seventies and eighties retro). The décor all works very nicely and it creates a relaxed ambience. There's a CD jukebox, playing pretty decent tunes earlier in the day, and a couple of decks come to life in the evenings, knocking out an eclectic, often retro mix. It's a small place and it takes only an average-sized party to pack it out, but even so the atmosphere is relaxed and genial, even when people are dancing around and it's always a shame when the evening has to end. The beer no longer includes anything on hand pumps and the Double Diamond has gone – we guess there wasn't a huge demand for it – but the rest of the stuff is still there, including San Miguel on tap. A great, fun pub.

FEATURES:

George & Vulture

RATING:

63 Pitfield Street
N1 6BU
020 7253 3988

A solid Fuller's pub dispensing their produce to the high standards you'd expect from this brewer. It has a friendly local atmosphere (a little surprising for the insalubrious surroundings) and a wide mix of clientele. With such decent beer, pool table, big-screen sport and a real fire in winter, what more could you ask of a local?

FEATURES:

The Griffin

RATING:

93 Leonard Street
EC2A 4RD
020 7739 6719

Some people might feel sorry for this pub because it looks so run down, standing on the corner of a largely barren plot in an otherwise built-up area. We love it for this – nearby almost all the other pubs are being refurbished and sanitised, formularising the heart and soul out of the pub-going experience. For us, it's eccentric places like the Griffin that make going to the pub worthwhile. We hope it stays that way for all our sakes and, given its popularity last time we were here, we can't see any good reason to change it. The range on offer includes a few ales on the hand pumps and usual lagers, and the service is excellent. Decent jukebox, too (when there isn't a DJ on).

FEATURES:

The Legion

RATING:

348 Old Street,
EC1V 9NQ
020 7729 4441

Proving that the words 'DJ Bar' and 'Shoreditch' won't always have us running for the hills, here's the Old Street offering from the people behind The Social. All present and correct are the ingredients from their bars in Little Portland Street and Arlington Square – the excellent jukebox, DJ nights, pies and fish-finger sandwiches. Here, though, there's even enough space for some live bands every so often. Lots of the bars in the area go overboard on stylish interiors; this one keeps it simple with some benches and tables. This one has arguably the most idiosyncratic music policy in town, but, even on the few occasions there aren't any DJs on, it's a lively one.

FEATURES:

The Old Blue Last

RATING:

39 Great Eastern Street
EC2A 3ES
020 7739 5793

An average boozer in a prime site on Great Eastern Street? It couldn't last. One of the few remaining old-school drinking dens in Hoxton has been taken over and the Hoxtonites are beginning to descend. But fear not. For, despite a fair few new-wave and new-romantic wannabes, the atmosphere heavy with hair-care products and (rather good) obscure electro-punk/rock nights on the first-floor bar, it seems devoid of much of the annoying judgemental preening clientele who permeate other nearby venues. Be who you wanna be seems to be the mantra. Perhaps it's this slapdash approach that has kept them away. The pub looks pretty untouched from the outside since its olden days – rough and a little sleazy – and inside all they've done is swap the chairs for sofas and remove the carpet. It looks like a student flat from 1991. The only criticism is that the beer, including the lager, tastes poorly kept – but hopefully that'll improve. A cool pub in Hoxton that isn't annoying? It can't last.

FEATURES:

Old King's Head

RATING:

28 Holywell Row
EC2A 4JB
020 7247 1363

Despite the fact it's surrounded by designers and other trendy types, this is very much a locals' pub. If you fancy a pint without the crowds and don't mind a few stares, it does the job. Pretty average when it comes to the victuals, though the big screen and the dartboard keep the regulars happy.

FEATURES:

Prince Arthur

RATING:

49 Brunswick Place
N1 6EB
020 7253 3187

There are not too many pubs left with an old-style visible hot grill for lunchtime bar food, nor one that gives so much of its limited floor space over to dart players, but this place proves there's still a market for all that. Add Shepherd Neame's fine ales to the equation and you've got a thoroughly old-school pub, enjoyed by one and all. We've seen this one packed with office staff and with locals from the flats next door – though rarely both at the same time. An 'andsome, busy little boozer.

FEATURES:

Wenlock Arms

RATING:

26 Wenlock Road

N1 7TA

020 7608 3406

On paper, this pub should be awful: it's in the middle of a less than salubrious council estate, the décor hasn't been updated since England last won the World Cup, it's smoky and it's full of locals who know each other's name. However, once you've found it, you'll see that it's a gem: some of the best (and cheapest) real ale in London, jazz music or quizzes in the evening and a genuinely friendly atmosphere. Recommended. Just don't flash your £2,000 laptop around on the way there.

FEATURES:

William IV

RATING:

7 Shepherdess Walk

N1 7QE

020 3119 3011

A piano in one corner, a real fire in the other and the pub cat meowing contentedly in the background – is this an untouched backstreet boozer we've discovered? Well, not quite, as this one's had the decorators in and relaunched as a gastropub. On first impressions, the makeover appears a bit different from your usual pub redesigns, though you quickly realise that they've just painted the wooden furnishings off-white. Admittedly, though, the British flag and imposing portrait of William IV do catch the eye, although we're a bit mystified about the stuffed birds. Off peak, its rather quiet and we're intrigued to know if the upstairs restaurant will entice some of the foodies who flock to Jamie Oliver's nearby Fifteen. However, either by luck or judgement, the new owners have apparently made this pub the new place to be seen, as only a few weeks after opening our Friday-night visit found the place filled with trendy hipsters and us. With well-kept beers (Black Sheep and Flowers IPA – served in traditional glass tankards) and friendly service, the new-look William IV comes recommended.

FEATURES:

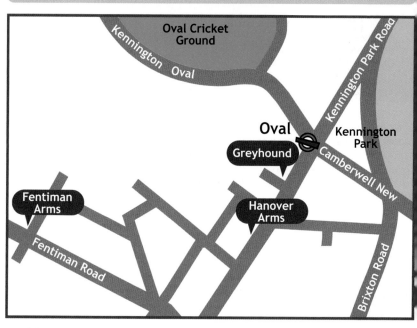

Fentiman Arms

RATING: 🍺🍺🍺

64 Fentiman Road
SW8 1LA
020 7793 9796

Stepping out from Vauxhall station into the grim urban chaos that greets you, you'd never think you were only ten minutes' or so walk from a smart gastropub, though once you start passing the large Victorian houses of Fentiman Street you realise Geronimo Inns did their homework and that there are enough local takers for their brand of loungey pub-bars. Even the most hard-bitten fan of the traditional pub experience has to admit that this place does what it does effectively (you sense there's as much thought been put into the décor as into the food and drink). A few ales on tap (Deuchars and Greene King IPA), though most of the clientele were opting for wine to accompany their modern pub-grub choices. The split-level beer garden is a handy feature for warmer days, even if the use of decking makes you wonder if Titchmarsh and Dimmock have just passed by. It's all very nice, very tidy – very Geronimo Inns.

FEATURES:

The Greyhound

RATING:

336 Kennington Park Road
SE11 4PP
020 7735 2594

Another old-school pub that's escaped the gastropubification of many such places. There's a good choice of beers and Irish whiskies in stock and the staff seem to take care to keep their wares in good condition. For this reason (and the live racing) we would give it a slight edge over its neighbour. But they are both agreeable places and much of an unfashionable muchness.

FEATURES: 　　　　　HANDY FOR: The Oval

Hanover Arms

RATING:

326 Kennington Park Road
SE11 4PP
020 7735 1576

A big, noisy, uncomplicated place this. Perfectly well suited for a Saturday afternoon reading the *Sun* and watching the big screen over a pint. The devotion to sport extended to showing non-League football, even though no one appeared to be watching. There would appear to be one or two characters among the clientele, including one fellow at the table next to us with a stock of Shane McGowan anecdotes.

FEATURES: 　　　　　HANDY FOR: The Oval

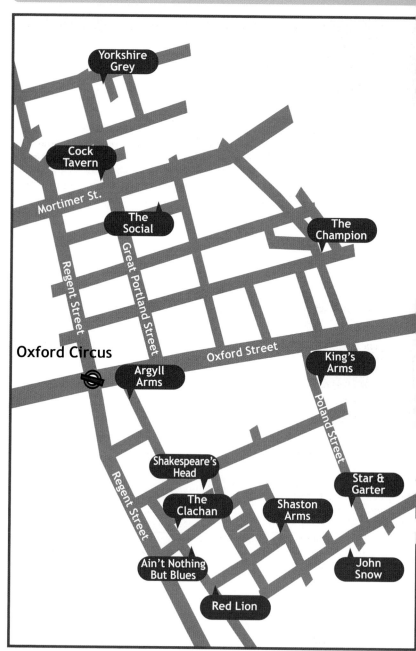

Ain't Nothin' But Blues Bar

RATING:

20 Kingly Street
W1B 5PZ
020 7287 0514

Something a bit different for these parts – a dedicated blues bar. There's live music most nights of the week (with the add-on of a late licence), but, if the blues isn't your thing, it's still a handy one to meet up in before a night out in Soho, because before the musicians start up you can usually get a seat, a bit of grub and a fine pint of Adnams. If you're after something a bit different from the more run-of-the-mill drinking dens of the area, give it a look.

FEATURES:

Argyll Arms

RATING:

18 Argyll Street
W1F 7TP
020 7734 6117

The Campbells are coming, the Campbells are coming, right after they've visited the shops, the theatre and Carnaby Street. Any place this close to Oxford Circus is bound to have the trappings of a tourist, er, trap. It naturally gets incredibly busy because it's in this location. After a much-needed refurbishment not too long ago, the place is still very much the Olde Englishe Pubbe in appearance, albeit one with a transitory feel – this pub doesn't have much in the way of regulars. Still, it's not that bad, with a good range of ales, solid pub grub, some nice old prints on the walls and friendly staff. It can be a useful place to meet, if nothing else – if you can get in.

FEATURES:

The Champion

RATING:

12–13 Wells Street
W1T 3PA
020 7323 1228

If you're worn out by the shopping hordes of Oxford Street and need a drink, the Champion is the place to go. It's a beautifully appointed pub with a lovely exterior and fantastic champion-themed stained-glass windows. It seems that Sam Smith's is annexing the West End for Yorkshire and taking the best-looking pubs to boot. The service is excellent, even when it's busy, and on a warm evening towards the end of the week it can get very, very busy. During shopping hours, however, it's a fairly relaxed place and, if it's crowded downstairs, there's always the upstairs bar.

FEATURES:

The Clachan

RATING:

34 Kingly Street
W1B 5QH
020 7494 0934

If you go into a Nicholson's pub and don't find an opulent Victorian interior, you should be disappointed. But don't worry, you definitely won't be disappointed here: the fixtures and fittings are everything you would expect of the brand and, if that's all you're looking for, you'll be happy here. Owing to its prime location, the clientele can be unpredictable: it can be crowded with tourists and drinkers – usually Friday nights – or occupied by a few regulars and shoppers. The food's decent, with service both downstairs and in the upstairs, no-smoking Liberty Bar (which is often empty, and a better place for a conversation). The fare is Nicholson's, so expect a good range of beers on the five hand pumps, well kept and well served. You can even try the beer before you buy in their 'Sup before you Tup' promotion – very nice.

FEATURES:

The Cock Tavern

RATING:

27 Great Portland Street
W1W 8QG
020 7631 5002

This terrific-looking pub has large glass lanterns outside and a wonderfully ornate interior. It has plenty of seating and serves the usual range of Samuel Smith beers. Like all the other pubs in this area, it can at times (usually Friday evenings) be packed, but is certainly worthy of your patronage.

FEATURES:

John Snow

RATING:

39 Broadwick Street
W1F 9QJ
020 7437 1344

Rather than celebrating the life of the newsreader (Jon), famed for his garish ties, this Victorian pub in the heart of Soho is named after the doctor who established that cholera was a water-borne disease. The site of the original water pump, which was key to his discovery, is marked by a pink slab outside the pub. It serves decent cheap pub grub and all the standard Sam Smith's fare. What Snow, who was said to be teetotal, would make of this, we don't know. The larger upstairs bar, often crowded with media types, all fully paid-up members of the John Snow Society, is the most welcoming, though there are a number of seats on the ground floor. Drinkers often spill outside on a summer's evening, but if it's crowded downstairs try the upstairs bar.

King's Arms

RATING:

23 Poland Street

W1F 8QJ

020 7734 5907

This gay pub in Soho isn't bad at all, being more trad pub than trendy bar. The selection of beer is nothing to shout about, but what they do have is well kept. Guess it gets busy at weekends, but can be a good place to go for a quiet drink during the day. It has some interesting attributes left, which may or may not be original, but the quote on the wall is quite interesting: 'In this Old Kings Arms tavern was the Ancient Order of druids revived 28th November 1781'.

FEATURES:

Red Lion

RATING:

14 Kingly Street

W1B 5PR

020 7734 4985

A fine old oak-panelled place with two bars downstairs and one upstairs. It serves the usual Sam Smith's range of fare, not to everyone's taste, we know, but it's OK here if you like it. Towards the end of the week, the pub (upstairs in particular) fills with large groups of people meeting up for an after-work pint and getting a few jars inside, before getting down to the real business of the evening, so there's a jolly atmosphere all round. (If you're not tall you'll love the bar: it's so low down you feel like a giant.)

FEATURES:

Shakespeare's Head

RATING:

29 Great Marlborough Street
W1F 7HZ
020 7734 2911

Any pub called the Shakespeare's Head in an area as touristy as Carnaby Street would just *have* to be an olde-worlde building with leaded glass and a large open fire – and, true to form, this is. It hasn't changed at all in recent years. The only critical recent addition is probably the chairs and tables on the pavement outside, just in case the weather turns nice (it does occasionally). The pub gets chock-full at weekends and in the evenings, with a mixture of local workers and tourists. There is an upstairs restaurant serving pub food, and it seems to do it well enough, as it's always busy. It's not a bad place and well placed for Carnaby Street – it can be a great place to meet when it's not full, but that doesn't seem to happen very often.

FEATURES: HANDY FOR: Carnaby Street

The Shaston Arms

RATING:

4 Ganton Street
W1F 7QN
020 7287 2631

A fairly new pub for Soho, this is another fine Hall & Woodhouse refit. Here they've taken a wine bar and done their best to make it look like a pub with a bit of history. So, expect a few mirrors, wooden floors and dividers in the décor. It's a reasonable effort, especially as it's not the biggest space, but there still feels room enough to hide away in. Decent Hall & Woodhouse beers – Badger, Tanglefoot – and a good atmosphere. A welcome pub for the area.

FEATURES:

The Social

5 Little Portland Street
W1W 7JD
020 7636 4992

Running since 1999, the Social is owned by the Heavenly record company, and as a result music has a big part to play in the place. The Social offers drinks, music and food to a self-consciously fash-tastic crowd sporting ridiculous haircuts, obscure trainers and, God love them, studded belts. There are two levels to the place: a larger basement area, where there are a range of music events on the programme; and the smaller ground-floor area. There are a limited number of brews on tap, but this is balanced by a wide range of bottled beers from around the globe and an extensive range of spirits. There are a number of things going for this place: its central London location makes it a handy place to meet up; the food, including tasty fare from the Square Pie company, is reasonably priced (but why you'd want to eat spaghetti hoops on toast in a bar is beyond us). The jukebox is amazing, doesn't bleed you dry and offers an excellent mix of classics and new music (so new, in fact, that two of the albums weren't even out in the shops on our last visit), and it's not played at ear-splitting levels, so you can actually carry on a conversation. The place is relatively quiet and sociable (excuse the pun) during the week, but it does get absolutely ram-jammed towards the end of the week (it's closed on Sundays), and it can feel very impersonal, especially given the preponderance of loathsome asymmetric hairdos trying to outdo each other in the style stakes. However, if you like beats to complement your beer, this could be the place for you. A word of warning: careful you don't get spaghetti hoops all down your Stussy sweatshirt – unless you're trying to make a statement, of course.

FEATURES:

Star & Garter

RATING:

62 Poland Street
W1F 7NX

Decent little boozer that's ideal for a quick drink or a longer session. Sporting not much more than a jukebox and a small TV, the pub has a lot more character than many of the more renowned Soho pubs. The Star & Garter offers a welcome respite from the area's trendsetting stylistas.

FEATURES:

Yorkshire Grey

RATING:

46 Langham Street
W1W 7AX
020 7636 4788

This is a nice-looking Victorian pub, in the eating and drinking area centred on the junction of Great Titchfield Street and Langham Street. It serves the usual Sam Smith's fare (a bonus for some, a bane for others) and basically just gets on with the job. The walls are decorated with BBC-related memorabilia (it's just round the corner from Broadcasting House). The whole area tends to get mobbed on Friday nights with workers from the local offices (mostly rag-trade and publishing types), so it's not an area for a quiet drink. But, for the rest of the time, it's a pretty peaceful place.

FEATURES:

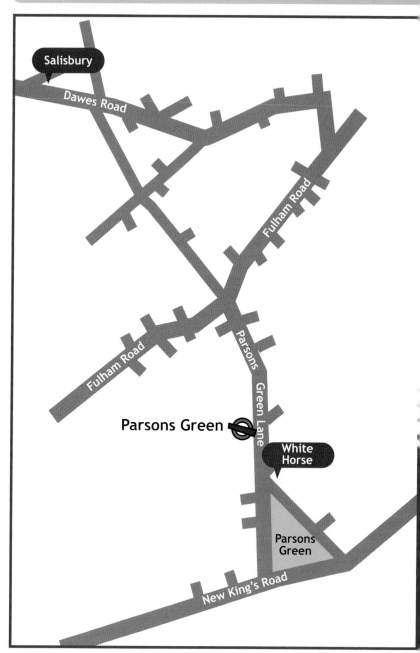

The Salisbury

RATING:

21 Sherbrooke Road
SW6 7HX
020 7381 4005

Your take on this pub will depend entirely on your take on Fulham: the pub encapsulates the area and, if you like that as a concept, you'll like it here. Like a lot of things in SW6, it's difficult to find; but, unlike a lot of Fulham, the area looks a little grotty around here and, at first glance, so does the pub. However, inside, it's a completely different story with pleasing hardwood boarding up to the dado rail and the rest of the pub decorated in clean, modern, designery colours and none of the grubby mix-and-match second-hand furniture we've become used to. It's all quite tasteful, perhaps even a little avant-garde. To complement the décor the menu is also somewhat *outré*, with the likes of quails' eggs and pumpkin risotto as bar snacks. Which makes the drinks side of things rather underwhelming – nothing remarkable in the beer department and a pretty typical range of wines, spirits and cocktails. The clientele round off the Fulham microcosm, and if you're at all familiar with the area you'll know what to expect. OK?

FEATURES:

The White Horse

RATING:

1–3 Parson's Green
SW6 4UL
020 7736 2115

This pub makes a lot of noise in its considerable promotional bumf about its lengthy history – it was one of the last staging posts on the route out of London, etc., etc. On entering, you realise that actually the place lives up to its 'Sloaney Pony' nickname as the innocent punter is assailed by the almost deafening noise of the braying bright young things of Fulham. They're a nice enough crowd, but don't come here if you want a quiet drink and a sit-down. Given the local clientele, it's not a surprise that the establishment has been pushed down the gastropub path with associated high prices for both food and drink. A shame, really, as there's a CAMRA prizewinning range of beers on offer, which would be just the thing to while away a Sunday afternoon.

FEATURES:

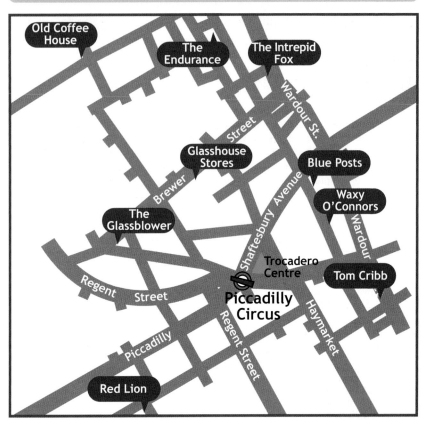

Blue Posts

RATING:

28 Rupert Street

W1D 6DJ

020 7437 1415

For a pub so close to the tackfest that is the Trocadero Centre, this one makes a fair go at being a normal boozer. That a decent drop of Timothy Taylor Landlord can be had helps, as does the rather lived-in feel of the pub (you sense there've been some good nights celebrated here over the years). Not a stone-cold classic but, given the area, a pub with a welcome bit of atmosphere.

FEATURES:

The Endurance

RATING:

90 Berwick Street
W1F 0QB
020 7437 2944

Replacing the King of Corsica – a rather rough-and-ready boozer in Berwick Street market – is this modern take on the pub experience. Even though it was a bit of a rough house, the old pub had a certain something. It's probable that the old clientele will be looking for a new regular now, as this one is clearly aimed at a younger and trendier crowd. Smart and plush inside, it's worth noting that food is served only until 6 p.m. Once the plates get cleared away, attention shifts to the excellent jukebox (arguably the best in Soho). An above-average venue for this neck of the woods, it's just slightly odd that this self-styled 'traditional fish and game pub restaurant' is sited so close to most of Soho's strip joints – are they due for a *Wallpaper*-style makeover, too?

FEATURES:

The Glassblower

RATING:

40–42 Glasshouse Street
W1B 5DL
020 7734 8547

Busy, bustling, noisy – why will these places crank up the music volume any time the conversation falls short of shouting? But handy for much of the West End, friendly staff, the feel of a local rather than a tourist rip-off. The smaller upstairs bar is often hired out to private functions and the main (but still smallish) downstairs bar does get crowded – but so does any pub round here. Blackboards promise pies of the day, specialist sausages and seventeen wines by the glass. A good place to meet, we agreed – an hour after finding ourselves comfortable and settled, with our plans for moving on forgotten.

FEATURES:

Glasshouse Stores

RATING:

55 Brewer Street
W1F 9UN
020 7287 5278

A quirky Sam Smith's pub in the heart of the touristy bit of Soho. Some nice old features remain and give the pub an olde-worlde atmosphere. The service is friendly and there's usually a regular or two in the front part of the pub – it's that kind of place. It's better than a lot of the tourist traps in the area, made even better by Sam Smith's (cheap) pricing. It's a good place to meet on a Saturday to get a pint or two in if you enjoy Sam Smith's fare before going to the more packed of the Soho pubs, bars and clubs.

FEATURES:

The Intrepid Fox

RATING:

97–99 Wardour Street
W1F 0UD
020 7494 0827

Soho's a lot safer place than it used to be, with Westminster Council cleaning everything up in pursuit of the tourist dollar, and it seems as if the Intrepid Fox has joined in the effort. The edge has been blunted somewhat: you no longer feel challenged if you're out of uniform and the music, clientele and ambience feel a little too 'clean' nowadays. A pity, really: we used to like to alarm our unsuspecting mates by arranging to meet in here. The booze was never particularly remarkable – that was never the point of the place – but it's the one thing that hasn't changed. If you're looking for a grittier experience you'll be better off in Camden or consulting your knowledgeable metal-headed friends. Incidentally, until a recent visit, we didn't realise the pub operated a dress code – they won't serve you if you wear a tie. Does that mean Angus wouldn't get a pint? Anyway, it's a pity, because operating a dress code loses a pub a pint in our ratings – we don't like any form of discrimination.

FEATURES:

Old Coffee House

RATING:

49 Beak Street
W1F 9SF
020 7437 2197

A traditional-looking pub, with loads of knick-knacks hanging from the ceiling and pictures on the wall to impress the tourists, but it doesn't have that faked olde-worlde look that some places do, because it's looked this way for years. After work, it's packed with local workers. Some stay and some go. There's a steady turnover of people, but the atmosphere somehow manages to remain relaxed. Every so often you will get a bunch of tourists wandering into the place, but this pub takes them in its stride. Directors, Young's and Pedigree are on draft and, with prompt, attentive service, this pub would be a pretty decent local anywhere, especially remarkable in Soho.

The Red Lion (Duke of York St)

RATING:

2 Duke of York St
SW1Y 6JP
020 7321 0782

The Red Lion is an old-style traditional pub. It's small, has great beers and a stunning interior. This is a great pub to come to when you are out and about in the West End and fancy a quiet pub – unfortunately, the world and his mother has had the same idea, so it's seldom you'll get a bit of peace. However, if you time your visit with precision, you'll be suitably rewarded. Lethal stairs to the toilets, though.

FEATURES:

Tom Cribb

RATING:

36 Panton Street
SW1Y 4EA
020 7747 9951

A small pub with a lovely tiled exterior, this one is far enough off the beaten track that you should be able to enjoy a reasonable drink most of the time. It can fill up after the Prince of Wales Theatre empties out, but it's a friendly enough place and a nice pint, too. Worth visiting if you're in the area on a Saturday afternoon.

Waxy O'Connors

RATING:

14–16 Rupert Street
W1D 6DF
020 7287 0255

More theme park than pub, this cavernous, never-ending hostelry is truly enormous. A full-grown tree in the middle of the pub adds to the Tolkien-esque air of the place. Still, it does serve a mean pint of (rather rare nowadays) Beamish and a decent enough pint of the other dark stuff. Overall, though, it's about as authentically Irish as an inflatable leprechaun.

FEATURES:

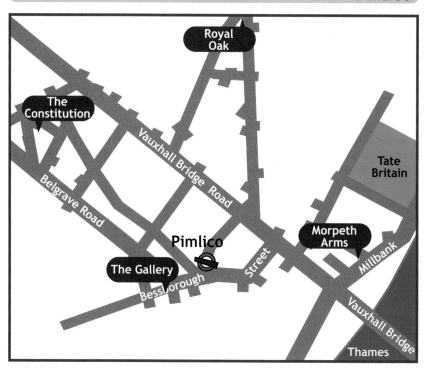

The Constitution

RATING:

42 Churton Street

SW1V 2LP

020 7834 3651

Nestled in the more charming villagey part of Pimlico, the Constitution is a butterfly of a pub. On the weekend afternoon we went there, the clientele were resolutely of the local-old-men variety, all there to watch the football. The place seemed a little shabby, though the staff were efficient, the food was cheap and great, if the company was less so. However, by the evening, a metamorphosis began to occur, and, as the lone men began to wend their way home, they were replaced by younger, friendlier couples and groups all out for a quiet evening of socialising. As a result, the place had magically become warmer and more inviting.

FEATURES:

The Gallery

RATING:

1 Lupus Street
SW1V 3AS
020 7821 7573

We remember this some time ago as a rather down-at-heel boozer, but this one's now a safe enough option for a drink and some food. There's nothing too out of the ordinary here, just a decent – if very upholstered – boozer. Within staggering distance of Pimlico tube, which is also handy.

FEATURES: HANDY FOR: Tate Britain

Morpeth Arms

RATING:

58 Millbank
SW1P 4RW
020 7834 6442

It's an odd one, this pub. We've known it for a good while but it's seldom the sum of its parts. All the ingredients are here – decent Young's ales, a mix of punters, decent staff – but it's never quite clicked for us. Worth a look either before or after a visit to Tate Britain, but not really one we'd go out of our way to visit. Shame, really, as there are the makings of a decent pub here.

FEATURES: HANDY FOR: Tate Britain

The Royal Oak

RATING:

2 Regency Street
SW1P 4BZ
020 7834 7046

The Royal Oak is one of the more decent pubs in this area. The beer and food are good, bar staff friendly and the atmosphere is relaxed. It is busiest at the usual lunchtimes and few hours after work, but there appear to be enough locals to keep it pleasantly ticking over at other times. Worth a visit if you're in the area.

FEATURES: HANDY FOR: Tate Britain, Westminster Cathedral

PUTNEY BRIDGE

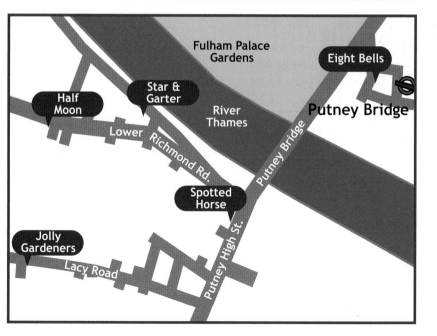

The Eight Bells

RATING:

88 Fulham High Street
SW6 3JS
020 7736 6307

When it's not packed with weekenders – footy, Boat Race, similar stuff – this pub is a real locals' place. A few decent beers on the hand pumps, ordinary pub grub for the lunchtime locals and friendly service. Handy to meet in, as it's so near the station, and is a place many people start Putney pub crawls from.

FEATURES:

Half Moon

RATING:

93 Lower Richmond Road
SW15 1EU
020 8780 9383

A pub that makes a lot of its musical heritage (U2 and the Stones both played here in their early days) with nods in that direction in the rota of covers bands that play here (Limehouse Lizzy, Achtung Baby – no sign of Half-Sister Sledge, though). Still, the stage is removed enough from the pub if you're not here for a gig, and out of hours it's a relaxed sort of place. It's competent and nonthreatening – a bit like their musical bill.

FEATURES:

Jolly Gardeners

RATING:

61–63 Lacey Road

SW15 1NT

020 8780 8921

Situated in the quiet suburban road of Lacey Street, SW15, the Jolly Gardeners is a rather good gastropub. In keeping with other such establishments, this one's all dim lighting, comfy leather seats, blackboards and coffee-table mix tapes on the stereo. Still, a nice, roomy, welcoming place, and not a bad selection of beers: when we visited, Hopback Summer Lightning and Adnams were on and well kept. We can't speak for the food, unfortunately, as we were too lazy to get out of our leather sofas and order any. Still, it looked pretty much par for the course with mozzarella, olives, ciabattas and the like in abundance. Probably not much chance of a beanburger and chips, though. If you're in the area and fancy that kind of thing, you could do far worse.

FEATURES:

Star & Garter

RATING:

4 Lower Richmond Road

SW15 1JN

020 8788 0345

We remember this place from way back when it used to be packed on hot summer nights with the young and trendy from the area and hordes of SW rugger buggers. Saturday nights were always a bit lively and the area in front of it teemed with happy drunkards, trying not to get their feet wet. And we always stayed away on Boat Race day. Now this huge place has been given the dreaded 'bar' treatment. Upstairs it looks like an All Bar One with carpets and serves a very similar offering, but without the panache. We're not sure about downstairs, as it was closed. But, judging from the purple paint outside and the 'Bar M' moniker, we feel it's all a bit un-needed. Not one for the beer drinkers any more, then.

FEATURES:

Ye Olde Spotted Horse

RATING:

122 Putney High Street
SW15 1JN
020 8788 0246

The tiny frontage of this famous old place (the starting point of many a good Putney pub crawl) is deceptive: this place is pretty large, but can still get pretty full. Young's serve up all their range here (after all, they're only round the corner) and complement it with a pretty extensive food offering. The service is prompt and friendly and it's a good venue to watch big sports on the TV. Tourists love it – it looks just like an Olde English Pubbe; beer drinkers like it for the well-kept Young's range; and everyone likes it in summer for the air con.

FEATURES:

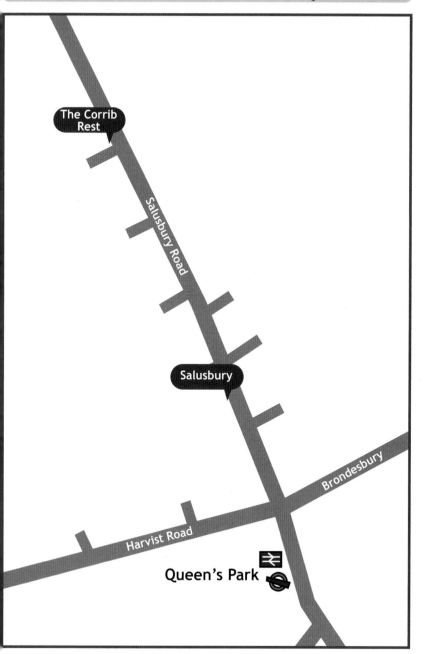

The Corrib Rest

RATING:

76–82 Salusbury Road

NW6 6PA

020 7625 9585

When you're drinking in this pub, it's quite easy to believe you are in Ireland (especially as there are few windows to see London through). The pub is huge and wood-panelled with plenty of knick-knacks on the walls, but this is no theme pub: it has a traditional two-room bar/lounge design; you have to wait the proper length of time for your Guinness; and the emphasis is definitely on drinking. Most tellingly, virtually all of the staff and customers during our visit were Irish. There's live music at the weekends and the food's decent, too.

FEATURES:

Salusbury Pub & Dining Room

RATING:

50–52 Salusbury Road

NW6 6NN

020 7328 3286

Is this a gastropub or just a pub with a restaurant attached? However you describe it, the separation of pub from dining area here means you're not getting in the way of the diners and vice versa. Whereas most pubs limit the reggae they play to having Bob Marley's *Legend* on the jukebox, it's nice to find a place rather more in thrall to lesser-known Jamaican artists. Covers of classic reggae albums adorn the walls, and on our visit some ska and rock-steady sounds were being aired. It certainly adds to the relaxed air of the place. There was a wide selection of lagers – Bitburger, Grolsch, Stella, Hoegaarden and others – and it was also nice to see two Adnams beers on tap (and tasting fine). We still can't vouch for the dining room (or the Salusbury's organic-food shop down the road), but the pub part of the equation works well.

FEATURES:

QUEENSWAY – *see Bayswater, pg 35*

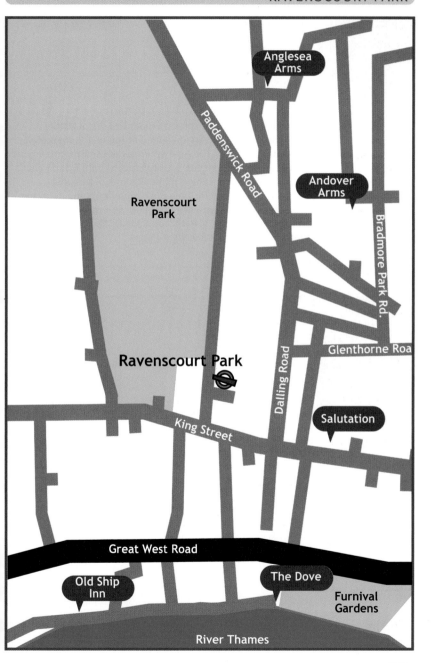

Andover Arms

RATING:

57 Aldensley Road
W6 oDL
020 8741 9794

Visit a pub between Hammersmith and Shepherd's Bush and it's probably a boozer bordering on scuzzdom, or a conversion aimed at the gastro market. If you're really unlucky, an Australian bar. The Andover Arms doesn't fit into any of those categories (thankfully), being a decent, well-run locals' pub. Good Fuller's beer, friendly staff and a pleasant atmosphere make this one of the best drinking holes in W6. It's the sort of comfortable pub where 'popping in for one' may stretch to an afternoon session. If you like your pubs in London to be hidden away with a 'village' air to them, give this one a look. Good Thai food and a pub cat are added bonuses in this excellent boozer.

Anglesea Arms

RATING:

35 Wingate Road
W6 oUR
020 8749 1291

Very popular gastropub that caters for the well-spoken trendsetters of W6. A pleasant little place when quiet, it can get horribly busy when it's feeding time at the zoo. Although furnished in the archetypal gastropub style of stripped floors and wooden chairs, this is still a more comfortable place to drink in than most of the dives on the nearby Goldhawk Road. Word of warning if you are after food here: it's first come, first served, so you may have to wait an age for a table.

FEATURES:

The Dove

RATING:

19 Upper Mall
W6 9TA
020 8748 9474

A pleasant old pub on the river close to Hammersmith Bridge. It looks like a good British pub should – situated in a narrow alleyway, a low door opening into a dingy interior with nooks and crannies furnished with old wooden chairs, stools and benches. The pub opens at the back into a riverside terrace, which has had a couple of extra ad hoc extensions, and that gives a clue as to why we don't rate this pub any higher than a three – quite simply it's almost always packed. If you like jostling shoulder to shoulder with people and doing the furtive vacant-table search as you chat to your mates, then this is the pub for you – but it's not for us. The beer is well kept (it doesn't exactly have far to travel), but the food is no better than average.

FEATURES:

Old Ship Inn

RATING:

25 Upper Mall
W6 9TD
020 8748 2593

A huge pub on the north bank of the river, just down from Hammersmith Bridge. It has a large range of beers and food, which look pretty well presented. It does breakfast from 10 a.m. in the week and 9 a.m. at weekends, has a reasonable lunch menu, an unsurprising nautically themed décor and a video player with TVs all over the place. And therein lies the rub: it's not really a pub, more a large catering establishment stuffed into a pub. If we had to describe this pub in two words, they would be 'borderline Harvester'. If you're taking the kids out you'll be happy here: there's a large terrace, a kiddies' playground and even a nappy-changing room. If you're after a pub, though, you're best off looking elsewhere.

FEATURES:

Salutation

RATING:

154 King Street
W6 oQU
020 8748 3668

A pleasant enough pub, with a rather nice Victorian façade, serving excellent Fuller's beers and basic pub grub. It has an airy feel, helped by the sizable beer garden at the back of the pub. A big screen for the football too. Nothing remarkable, just a good pub in an area lacking in them.

FEATURES:

REGENT'S PARK – see Gt Portland Street, pg 146

RICHMOND

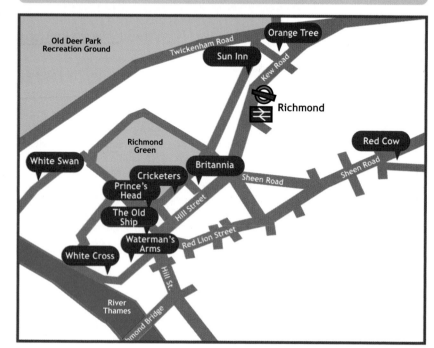

The Britannia

RATING:

5 Brewers Lane

TW9 1HH

020 8940 1071

Promisingly situated down a side street called Brewers Lane, this is possibly the best of the cluster of pubs just off Richmond's George Street. All bases seem to be covered: decent food, fair drink and an atmosphere conducive to enjoying them in. The TVs for the sport don't seem to get in the way of nattering locals, and, when the weather allows, there's a garden and roof terrace at the back to sample. As an optional extra, there's also a comedy club upstairs on a Sunday night. Back to the drink, the wine list seemed well chosen, while ales offered were Speckled Hen, Bombardier and Courage Best. In showing there's more to the Massive pub brand than Identikit Tup pubs, this one has a rather singular air to it – which is probably why photos of Sean Connery (as Bond with his Aston, naturally) and hirsute rakes Charles Rennie Mackintosh and Graham Hill fit in nicely on the wall.

FEATURES:

The Cricketers

RATING:

The Green

TW9 1LX

020 8940 4372

A handsome pub in a picturesque setting – the tourist ideal of an English pub, especially in summer with cricket on the green. It's a Greene King pub so the drink and food are well up to scratch and the service polite and efficient. And when the British weather behaves as you expect you can go indoors and watch sport on the TV. A popular place and rightly so.

FEATURES:

The Old Ship

3 King Street

TW9 1ND

020 8940 3461

Some pubs just work. This is one. Clean, stylish wood panelling and beams give an appropriate ship-like feel to a place that has been serving ale since at least 1735, when it was a major coaching stop. And a newly introduced beer-and-skittles night on the second Monday of the month sounds like a fun nod to tradition. Other Monday nights feature quizzes. But the twenty-first century is represented by two substantial and quality plasma screens complete with surround sound for the big sports events. There are two bars served by the central island and, with simple common sense, one is smoking, the other tobacco-free. The upstairs bar can be hired out. Good food, drink and ambience for all. There are a thousand or more London publicans who should call in to take a look at how you do the basic things properly.

FEATURES:

Orange Tree

45 Kew Road

TW9 2NQ

020 8940 0944

One of the more famous pubs in the area, the stylish nineteenth-century exterior leads you to believe the interior is of a similar age. Alas, it appears as though the All Bar One people have sneaked in and redesigned it when Young's weren't looking. So it's another one of those bare-floorboard-and-sofa venues, designed to appeal to the same punters you'll get down at the Pitcher & Piano on Richmond's riverfront. As a result, perhaps, this one gets pretty busy when the rugby is on. Expect to pay Richmond prices for the usual Young's food and drink.

FEATURES:

Prince's Head

RATING:

28 The Green
TW9 1LX
020 8940 1572

A fine, old-fashioned, darkly lit pub that befits its setting on the village green. It looks small when you first go in, but there are plenty more tables at the rear of the bar. You won't be wondering about indoor seating in the summer, though: if there's no cricket on, then the adjoining Green becomes a full-scale beer garden.

FEATURES:

The Red Cow

RATING:

59 Sheen Road, Richmond
TW9 1YJ
020 8940 2511

The Red Cow has been serving beer to the locals of Richmond for over 200 years and continues to do a fine job today. On our last visit it was relatively quiet on a Sunday afternoon, though it is more likely to pull in the crowds when there is sport on TV or a live band in the bar. The pub also hosts a quiz every Tuesday. Being a Young's pub, it has an excellent range of ales, which can help you wash down home-cooked food from a menu that changes daily. If you really want to build up an appetite, why not put your pads on and play for the pub's own cricket team?

FEATURES:

Sun Inn

RATING:

17 Parkshot
TW9 2RG
020 8940 1019

No surprise to find a pub with such strong rugby ties here, but there is such a proliferation of Union photos, drawings, shirts and even boots that the ceiling has been pressed into action to accommodate it all. Of course, it can get rammed on the usual match days, and has a big screen and small screens throughout to show them, but somehow, with the handful of outside tables, a big back seating area and determined service, it seems to cope quite well. Despite this, outside the rugby calendar it functions competently as a decent side-street local. They offer pub grub, and seem to play easy-listening, which was, well, easy to listen too. The small central bar had hand pumps offering Pride et al. and a standard range of lagers etc. Oh, and there's a baby-footy table, presumably to make visiting French rugby fans feel more at home.

FEATURES:

Waterman's Arms

RATING:

12 Water Lane
TW9 1TJ
020 8940 2893

Hidden away on the approach to the river, this Young's pub is slightly overshadowed by its bigger relation, the White Swan Hotel, just around the corner. On first impressions it seems like a solid little locals' pub, and entering it confirms those impressions. A friendly local, then, with a regular crowd, very possibly those of a river-faring nature. If you don't fancy nursing a pint of ordinary while you search for a corner that isn't already taken, you can pop upstairs and get a fine and reasonably priced Thai meal. If you don't feel up to the rough and tumble of crowded bars filled with thick-necked, collars-up rugger buggers, this could the sensible option.

FEATURES:

White Cross

RATING:

Riverside
TW9 1TJ
020 8940 6844

On a hot summer's night everyone wants to be by the river and this is where they come. Hordes of them, milling between the water's edge and the pub – a space that gets narrower as the tide comes in. The pub itself is a large old building, but it doesn't have the room you think it should have inside, although it is easy enough to get a seat when everyone else is outside. The fare is the usual Young's stuff, so there are no real surprises. Oh, and the staff are efficient and pleasant, even when the pub is mobbed.

FEATURES:

White Swan

RATING:

Old Palace Lane
TW9 1PG
020 8940 0959

Tucked away on a road between the green and the river, this pub is much more of a locals' place. Being just off the beaten track means that, on days when the rest of Richmond is bursting at the seams, this place is a welcome oasis of calm. The choice of beer available is a little more varied than most and is well kept. At first glance, the food looks a little bit on the pricey side until you try it – it's excellent. Service is good and the locals friendly. Try it, you'll like it.

FEATURES:

RUSSELL SQUARE

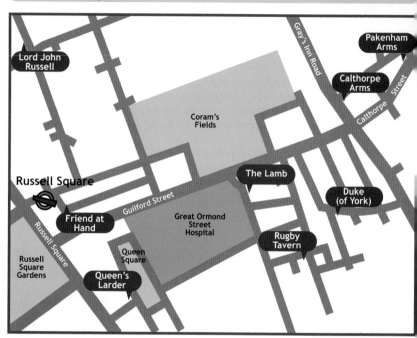

Lord John Russell

Pakenham Arms

Calthorpe Arms

Gray's Inn Road

Calthorpe Street

Coram's Fields

Russell Square

The Lamb

Duke (of York)

Friend at Hand

Guilford Street

Great Ormond Street Hospital

Rugby Tavern

Russell Square

Queen Square

Russell Square Gardens

Queen's Larder

Calthorpe Arms

RATING:

252 Grays Inn Road

WC1X 8JR

020 7278 4732

This is a fairly quiet and comfortable pub not far from King's Cross, with a local crowd enjoying its traditional atmosphere. A nice pint of Special is to be had and they do food all day, too – all the Young's range is usually on offer. When we were there last, the telly was on for sport, but few people took any notice. There's also an upstairs bar and restaurant, which is available to hire. This is a fine pub and, if you're in the area, give it a go.

FEATURES:

Duke (of York)

RATING:

7 Roger Street
WC1N 2PB
020 7242 7230

Slightly off the beaten track, this gastropub has a local feel and caters for local workers. The pub forms part of a handsome Art Deco building. The striking bar area catches the imagination – Formica tables, bold red and black lino flooring – and the dining area is wood-panelled with private, dark-leather booths – the kind of place you can picture Percy Wyndham Lewis sneering at you over lunch. Full marks for the décor, then, though the beer selection of Continental lagers and the odd ale is less impressive. A visit to the Duke is recommended more for the architecture, less for the decent, but unremarkable, fare.

FEATURES:

Friend at Hand

RATING:

4 Herbrand Street
WC1N 1HX
020 7837 5524

We remember this pub when it used to have a bit of a seafaring theme (the pub sign was of a lifeboat rescue) and the interior was done up to look like the inside of a capsized sailing ship (or at least that's how it appeared to us). More recently, the interior was returned to a more sensible, Victorian-esque style of décor, more befitting the exterior, and the sign now depicts a Saint Bernard. Basically, it's back to what it should be, an honest boozer, in a very touristy location, serving decent drink (e.g. Directors and Best) and food (until 9 p.m. during the week) to a thirsty and hungry clientele – local workers at lunchtime and tourists the rest of the time. All this offered with a genial smile on its face and plenty of sport on the telly.

FEATURES:

The Lamb

RATING:

94 Lamb's Conduit Street
WC1N 3LZ
020 7405 0713

A genial old boozer, with lots of Victorian charm – and that's just the locals. This pub has been one of the better ones for a long, long time and continues to maintain its high standards. The beer's good, the food's pretty decent and it's got some quaint Victorian fixtures and fittings, without being too olde-worlde – it gets the balance just right. The clientele are the genial pub-going type and even the drunks are polite and apologetic (they seem to operate a shift system to make sure there's always one in!). The Lamb is in an easy-to-get-to location, but just far enough from the tourist trails to deter all but the determined and appreciative. Oh, and there's an upstairs function room for those who you need that kind of thing.

FEATURES:

Reviewers' Award (overall Winner) 2005

Lord John Russell

RATING:

Marchmont Street
WC1N 1AL
020 7388 0500

This is a nice little pub with no pretensions. It's quite small and bright with large picture windows on two sides. It has a couple of benches outside too. It can get very crowded, but it's a real pub in an area where most have had makeovers. There is a very extensive range of beers including Adnams and Bombardier from the cask, and, with the offices of Budweiser Budvar just nearby, they arguably pour the best pint of lager in town. Keep an eye out, too, for the rather rare Budvar Dark. The lunchtime food is of good quality and reasonably priced. Definitely one worth a look.

FEATURES:

HANDY FOR: British Library

Pakenham Arms

RATING:

1 Calthorpe Street
WC1X 0LA
020 7837 6933

This pub is a bit of all right, loads of well-kept, interesting beers on the hand pumps, loads of great, cheap pub grub, loads of screens to watch the sport and a matey atmosphere (and we don't mean bubble bath). Its proximity to the Mount Pleasant sorting office probably has something to do with this, especially as the pub does breakfasts 9–11.30 – but, whatever the reason for the way it is, we like it.

FEATURES:

Queen's Larder

RATING:

1 Queen Square
WC1N 3AR
020 7837 5627

A tiny, tiny pub that's been here a long time. Expect decent beer, quite nice olde-worlde décor, a dining room upstairs, and a huge throughput of clientele (who always seem to be on their way somewhere else). Not a bad place, though, being a cosy little spot in the depths of winter and a handy one for a seat outside in the summer. It shares a space on Cosmo Place with two restaurants and another pub and it's a bit of a touristy area, so, if you do chance an alfresco pint, be prepared to be serenaded by chancers with accordions. That aside, it's one of the best in the area.

FEATURES:

Rugby Tavern

RATING:

19 Great James Street
WC1N 3ES
020 7405 1384

What a fine pub! A jolly crowd, good drink and food (after all, it is a Shepherd Neame pub), in a quiet, leafy location with some outdoor seating, and it's right in the centre of London. It's recently-ish been sympathetically refurbished (not stripped out like many pubs today) and has a pretty nice atmosphere. Well done all round, we say. Just watch out for the nights when all the corporate sporty types are in.

FEATURES:

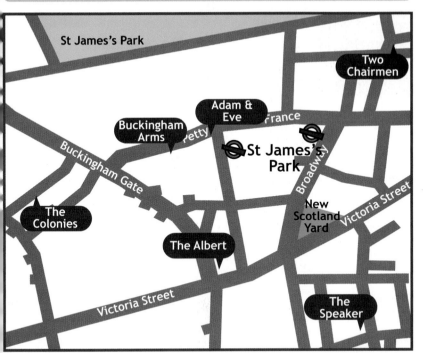

St James's Park

Two Chairmen

Adam & Eve

Buckingham Arms

etty France

St James's Park

Broadway

Buckingham Gate

The Colonies

New Scotland Yard

Victoria Street

The Albert

Victoria Street

The Speaker

Adam & Eve

81 Petty France
SW1H 9EX
020 7222 4575

This pub is fairly standard for the area around St James's Park. Pleasant enough, with standard refurbished wood décor, standard beers, standard food and standard prices, the Adam and Eve is busiest at lunchtimes and after work. As with all T&J pubs, the beer is well kept and there's a reasonable choice, but the downside to this is, like most T&J pubs, it lacks a convincing pub atmosphere. It's one of the two default pubs on the walk back to the tube station from the offices roundabout, so there are no prizes for guessing who comprises most of the clientele.

FEATURES:

The Albert

52 Victoria Street
SW1H 0NP
020 7222 5577

This huge Victorian pub is well placed for what it does – it's what all the tourists are expecting from an English pub, so it's popular with them (and Chelsea Pensioners, apparently). That said, it does its job well enough, with decent beer on tap and (fairly) traditional pub grub available both in the bar and in the separate restaurant. If you're looking for that undiscovered gem, this isn't it. It is a useful pub to know, however, if you're in the area, as it's pretty hard to miss.

FEATURES: HANDY FOR: Westminster Cathedral

Buckingham Arms

RATING:

62 Petty France
SW1H 9EU
020 7222 3386

Quite a handsome pub dating from the 1840s that draws in crowds from the nearby civil service offices and Buckingham Palace. It's very much a blokes' pub, and was entirely populated with them when we were in last. There's decent Young's beer on the hand pumps and decent food at reasonable prices. It's a good place to go for a natter in the afternoon or to read the paper over a late leisurely lunch. It can get busy at lunchtime and after 5 p.m. most days, getting absolutely rammed on Friday nights. Still, it's a lovely pub and worth a visit, with its excellent beer and genial atmosphere.

FEATURES:

The Colonies

RATING:

25 Wilfred Street
SW1E 6PR
020 7834 1407

The best pubs in this area all tend to be tucked away in side streets and the Colonies is no exception. It's a vibrant place that is tailor-made for the after-office jar, and consequently it fills up with local workers in the early evening. Directors, Best and Bombardier and guest beers (in the last instance, Jennings' excellent Cocker Hoop) are all on tap, accompanied by a standard range of beers and wines. It's also a fine place to go on a sunny day, as the beer garden out the back proves very popular with the local workers. Don't bother at weekends though: it's closed.

FEATURES:

The Speaker

RATING:

46 Great Peter Street
SW1P 2HA
020 7222 1749

Despite its proximity to Parliament and Channel 4's offices, this is a cosy little pub, ideal for a few jars on a dark night. It has the feel of a friendly local, mostly due to its cheery landlady, who treats everyone as if she's been serving them for years. One of the best in the area, and well worth hunting down.

FEATURES: HANDY FOR: Westminster Abbey, Houses of Parliament

Two Chairmen

RATING:

39 Dartmouth Street

SW1H 9BP

020 7222 8694

This was a hidden gem for many years before being 'discovered'. It does manage to retain a bit of the old local feel to it, as quite a few of the clientele are regulars and know the barmen (and vice versa). It's a reasonable place for a pint in the area if you get there early. It's busy at lunchtimes and by Friday it's a madhouse in the early evenings. It does have an upstairs bar, which can be quieter. All that said, they have a good selection of regular and guest beers on tap. Sadly, this pub isn't open at weekends, but that's hardly surprising for the area. We'd recommend this one if you're in the area, as it's still a good boozer despite the crowds.

FEATURES:

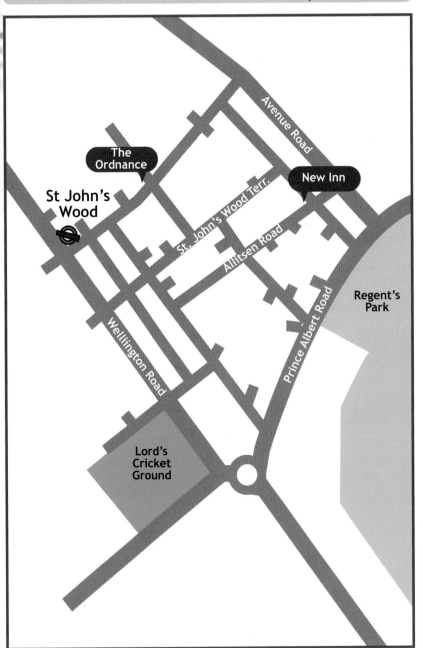

New Inn

2 Allisten Road, St John's Wood
NW8 6LA
020 7722 0726

The mental image conjured up by St John's Wood might well consist of elegant Georgian houses, upmarket boutiques and ladies who lunch. But, in a rare moment of light relief, only minutes away from this potential Richard Curtis film location lies the New Inn. Sitting anywhere other than at the edge of a perfectly nice council estate, this would be described as a stripped-out affair. Here, however, monikers aren't needed: it's simply a great pub. The predominantly older locals, all looking unusually dressed up, clearly didn't mind us interlopers in their pub. So, while we sat eating our rather good Sunday lunch, we listened to the live over-fifties blues band and looked around us: there was laughing, joking, chatting, smiling. It was friendly and genuine. Did we find the New Inn on an unusually good day? Maybe. But, on our first impression, we wish more pubs were like this.

FEATURES:

The Ordnance

29 Ordnance Hill
NW8 6PS
020 7722 0278

You'd be forgiven for imagining that if the Ordnance is as good on the inside as it is on the outside – sitting, as it does, on this quiet tree-lined road – a very nice pub indeed lies within. Rather upmarket and with St John's Wood prices to match, this is an unpretentious Sam Smith's pub, away from their usual W1 area. With a predominantly wooden interior, a couple of couches and interesting lighting, there is a warm, homely atmosphere, even in the conservatory. There is also a conscious effort on the food front and, although pricey, it's reasonable for the area and well made. Finally, as a bonus, a small leafy garden extends around two sides of the pub. It's never too crowded – presumably, the wealthy locals aren't pub fans. It's a shame the welcome from the staff is never exactly enthusiastic and the poorly chosen chain-wide 'no-music' policy somewhat kills the atmosphere. Still, small quibbles – this is still a solid three-pinter.

FEATURES:

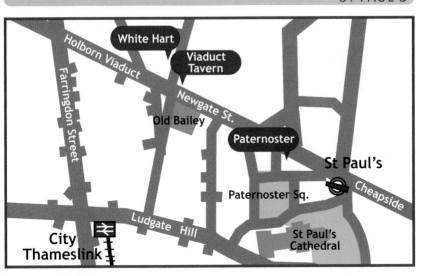

Paternoster

RATING:

2–4 Queen's Head Passage, Paternoster Square

EC4M 7DX

020 7248 4035

Settling in nicely as a replacement – but never a replica – of the genial old dump that was the Master Gunner, the Paternoster has found its feet as a modern, comfortable bar in keeping with the twenty-first-century recreation of the whole square. They were right not to keep the name and try to rival the excellent traditional pubs nearby. It's a businesslike place, serving businesslike people in a businesslike way. It's bigger than it looks from the outside and the raised central seating area helps break it into separate areas, which include comfortable armchairs or spacious tables for dining – or lining up the glasses. The food is of good quality and interesting, if a trifle pricey, and the Young's beer is well kept and served. A rather odd design flaw puts the solid wooden door to the kitchens just along from the door down to the lavatories. One day, one of these charming waitresses is going to swing that lump of timber straight into a passing punter and then baptise them *avec moules marinières*. Suits and City workers in abundance but it is also a place for dignified old coves in blazers and medals to gather and quietly remember after attending memorials at St Paul's. (Open weekends until 5 p.m. – food until 4 p.m.)

FEATURES: 　　　　　HANDY FOR: St Paul's Cathedral

Viaduct Tavern

126 Newgate Street
EC1A 7AA
020 7600 1863

RATING:

Another great Victorian pub interior – what else would you expect of Nicholson's? Trips round the cellars are available if that takes your fancy. However, the beer and food don't really live up to their opulent surroundings. But it's still worth popping in if you happen past. (Closed Sunday.)

HANDY FOR: St Paul's Cathedral, Old Bailey, St Bart's Hospital

White Hart

7 Giltspur Street
EC1A 9DE
020 7248 6572

RATING:

One thing we lost when all-day opening was introduced in the 1980s was the satisfaction of being able to be a member of some dive that would allow us the pleasure of nipping through an often unmarked door to pay over the odds for unremarkable booze at four o'clock in the afternoon. Utterly classless, bus drivers and bankers, tarts and vicars united in the anonymity and discretion of their private haven. Paint out the pub frontage here and the inside could be a vintage example of the old drinking clubs. It may be 50 feet deep but is probably little more than 15 wide. Stools at narrow shelves along the wall allow the committed solo drinker his privacy to knock back the needed 'livener' with only the wall as witness. Equally, business can be conducted surprisingly discreetly for such a small place or a (not too big) group can simply feel comfortable and at ease. It's handy for the Old Bailey and for Bart's Hospital and we would lay odds that as many cases have been settled out of court here as have clandestine affairs been pursued. None of the glamour of the centuries-old temples of London pub-land, but places like this are, just as much, what the capital is all about. Appears to be closed weekends, when signs say it is available for hire.

FEATURES: **HANDY FOR:** St Paul's Cathedral, Old Bailey, St Bart's Hospital

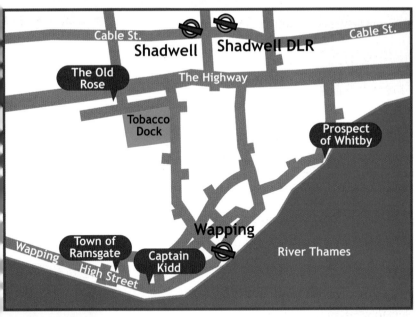

Captain Kidd

RATING: ▮▮▮

108 Wapping High Street

E1W 2NE

020 7480 5759

This is a pretty respectable pub in a good location. It's built in an old warehouse and you wouldn't believe it hadn't been there for a hundred years, but it really dates from the eighties (*nineteen* eighties, that is). It's a Sam Smith's pub, so there are no surprises with the drink – it's well kept and reasonably priced and the service is good. The bar food is good and there is a still untried (by us) restaurant on the top floor – we just never end up eating round here, but if the bar food is anything to go by it should be OK. There are usually two floors you can drink on (the restaurant is on the second), but sometimes the upstairs bar hosts private parties, as do other bits of the bar, and it's a good place for a party, too. All the rooms have splendid views of the river, with large windows that open up in summer to provide a cooling breeze, and there is a large terrace at the side of the pub.

FEATURES:

331

The Old Rose

RATING:

128 The Highway
E1W 2BX
020 7481 1737

A long, long time ago, there were dozens of pubs around here serving the dockworkers in Wapping. But, now that the docks have been filled in and planted with dozens of brick apartment blocks, there are precious few pubs left around here. It seems that the new inhabitants are not the big drinkers of old. Fortunately, among these few is the Old Rose – a decent, traditional local, serving good beer and cheap food with good service. We often find that, when you get these drinkers' deserts, as Wapping has now become, a lack of competition leads to complacency, but the Old Rose bucks this trend. Thanks.

FEATURES:

Prospect of Whitby

RATING:

57 Wapping Wall
E1W 3SP
020 7481 1095

This pub should be no stranger to any visitor to London. The coachloads of tourists are testament to its worldwide recognition. It bills itself as the 'oldest riverside pub in London', and there's no reason to disbelieve this. It's an attractive old place, with an unusual pewter bar, cute olde-worlde nooks and crannies and extensive riverside views, but its once-dominant presence on Wapping Wall has been diminished in recent years by the developments towering around it. The pub's only nods to the twenty-first century are a couple of squashy settees and an ATM, hardly affecting the historic atmosphere. There are decent beers on the hand pumps – Broadside, Speckled Hen and IPA – and the food is OK, but the pub's popularity means a premium price.

FEATURES:

Town of Ramsgate

62 Wapping High Street

E1W 2PN

020 7481 8000

Popular with the people who live round about, this old pub has had its ups and downs, but has settled down in the last few years to become a jolly decent boozer. While it is, by and large, a locals' pub, it's not at all unwelcoming. The pub is an old, narrow building next to one of the first warehouses to be converted into apartments (well before the eighties property boom) and backs on to the Thames, where it has a small terrace with a limited view of the river. It's well looked after and a relatively recent redecoration has done nothing to spoil the old-world (as opposed to olde-worlde) atmosphere. There are all sorts of historical claims made about the place (e.g. Judge Jeffreys was captured here attempting to flee to the Continent), so it often appears on the tourist map, but not many tourists manage to seek the pub out. Despite the fact that this area was the heart of the old London docks – and at one time there were 36 pubs on Wapping High Street alone – it is nowadays a pub desert and, of the few pubs that are left, this is certainly one of the better ones.

FEATURES:

SHEPHERD'S BUSH – see Goldhawk Rd, pg 139

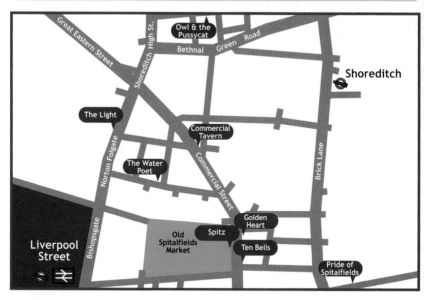

Commercial Tavern

RATING:

142 Commercial Street
E1 6NU
020 7247 1888

Well, guv, the old Commercial's been knocked on the 'ead and been replaced with a much artier affair. The exterior is much as it was, the most obvious clue to its new identity being the tinselled parasols outside. Inside, the Victorian interior has been repainted baby blue, as has the furniture. Motifs cut out of magazines have been pasted on to the furniture, chairs adorned with poetry, and the walls plastered with a collection of other ephemera – a panel of *Interview* covers and a collection of cuckoo clocks among them. Look up, and you will see no fewer than half a dozen chandeliers. The world of wackiness extends to candles on the table stuck in red and white (real) cabbages – bring your own mayo for a DIY coleslaw. On the drinks front, things look interesting, with Black Sheep and Scrumpy among others on the hand pumps, but repeated tastings have shown none to be particularly well kept. However, in these times when it's increasingly hard to distinguish the most independent of bars from each other, there are few places with such a unique and innovative flavour.

FEATURES:

The Golden Heart

RATING:

110 Commercial Street

E1 6LZ

020 7247 2158

The Golden Heart is in the right location to draw in punters walking between Brick Lane and Spitalfields market. The atmosphere was jovial too. There is a smaller wine bar section on the left-hand side, while the main bar area serves a decent range of beer. One of the first pubs in the area to be done up, the Golden Heart certainly packs them in.

FEATURES:

The Light

RATING:

233 Shoreditch High Street

E1 6PJ

020 7247 8989

Located between the City and Hoxton, here you have a besuited, but often clamorous and ill-mannered, clientele imbibing in an artfully rendered postindustrial zone (or an old substation if you're being honest) – a clientele that often queues for the privilege. We're in the territory of style over comfort here with tables at such a height that you can't properly sit or stand at them. The service at the equally lofty bar can be pretty slow too. Certainly plenty of takers for the (pricey) fare on offer on our visit, so the recession can't be with us just yet. If the thought of drinking in a mini-me version of Tate Modern (with a late licence) sounds appealing, give it a try.

FEATURES:    HANDY FOR: Spitalfields Market, Brick Lane

The Owl & The Pussycat

RATING:

34 Redchurch Street
E2 7DP
020 7613 3628

A pub between the City and Shoreditch conjures up images of suited gents haranguing Hoxton Fins, but there's none of that here. Just a fine pub. The well-kept interior has loads of space, and the inviting bar area glitters away at you in a welcoming fashion. There are good ales on tap and favourably priced pub food. Add on a garden for summer drinking and you've got all the ingredients of a fine pub. As an added bonus, there's a carvery upstairs on Sundays. Sure, it's a bit hidden away, but it's certainly as good as anything between Liverpool Street and Old Street. Give it a try. Unfortunately, its recent 'discovery' apparently by the occupants of the nearby Tea Building means that Thursday and Friday nights here are no longer the jaunty occasions they used to be.

FEATURES:

Pride of Spitalfields

RATING:

3 Heneage Street
E1 5LJ
020 7247 8933

A lovely old boozer just off Brick Lane. Formerly the Romford Arms, this place is warm and cosy with a pleasingly wooded interior, old pictures and hundreds of beer bottles lining the walls. The staff are friendly and offer up a good range of well-kept beers (Fuller's, usually, and guests). It can get pretty crowded at night with punters drawn from all shades of East End society – old Cockneys, Bangladeshi restaurant staff and artsy types – but it's all very friendly and harmonious. By day it's quieter but it's definitely worth a visit whenever you're passing. If only the real world were more like this.

FEATURES: HANDY FOR: Whitechapel Gallery

Spitz

RATING:

109 Commercial Street, Old Spitalfields Market
E1 6BG

020 7392 9032

The Spitz is another of those venues that sneak under Fancyapint?'s door, as you'd be hard pushed to describe it as a pub, or even a bar. Definitely one for the artier drinker, Spitz is an eclectic music venue, gallery and bistro, all wrapped into one. Still, drinkers are welcomed here and you can still easily have a pint, mainly towards the rear of the ground-floor bistro. Our preference is to get a seat outside at the back, where you can enjoy great views of Old Spitalfields Market (the original bit, rather than the tedious 'landmark office, retail and leisure scheme' bit). For those who fancy a drink in the upstairs music venue, there are occasional free live music nights, where you can listen to an interesting mix of artists who probably won't be appearing on *MTV* any time soon.

FEATURES:

Ten Bells

RATING:

Commercial Street
E1 6LY

020 7366 1721

This old boozer, formerly a stop-off on the Ripper tour, has been given the bohemian bar treatment. It's retained the ornate Victorian tile work on the walls, but now it's been filled with a load of old settees, low tables, candles etc. The atmosphere is pretty lively, but nowadays all Spitalfields is like that. There's nothing remarkable on the booze front – it's one for the bright young things, rather than hardened drinkers, who'll be in the murkier places round the corner.

FEATURES:

The Water Poet

RATING:

9–11 Folgate Street

E1 6BX

020 7426 0495

If you're looking for a smart boozer, you've come to the wrong place, this pub has thrown its heart and soul into the scruffy Bohemian trendy-bar look and more or less pulled it off. It's a huge place with rooms seemingly in all directions, where you'll find the games, screens, decks and settees necessary for an urban evening out in the early 21st century. The beer's pretty good and the usual bar type stuff you expect in a place like this. The clientele is very mixed, but they seem to get on nevertheless. Everybody's here for a good time and, by Jove, they get one. As we said of the old Pewter Platter tavern (its previous incarnation), you could do far worse in this neck of the woods.

FEATURES:

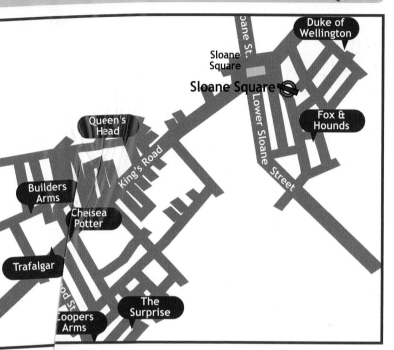

Duke of Wellington

Sloane St.

Sloane Square

Sloane Square

Lower Sloane Street

Fox & Hounds

Queen's Head

King's Road

Builders Arms

Chelsea Potter

Trafalgar

od St

Coopers Arms

The Surprise

Builders Arms

RATING: 🍺🍺

13 Britten Street
SW3 3TY
020 7349 9040

A trendy modern gastropub, with real ales, Continental-style cool lagers, wines and spi̶ A finalist in the *Evening Standard* Pub of the Year in 2000 – it had a reputa̶or excellent food, which, from more recent feedback, appears to be on the̶ne. Alas, we were not in the mood to test this on our last visit. It being ̶rm Friday evening, the pub and the pavement outside were packed with t̶aying, bright young things from the shire. But this seemed to be of little ̶̶rn to the punters, so we left them to it. At other times, things may well ̶re equable here, but there are plenty of similarly specified alter̶es in this area. It may be the victim of it's own success, but we do exp̶ore of an effort from Geronimo Inns.

FEP:

fancyapint?

SLOANE SQUARE

Chelsea Potter

RATING:

119 King's Road
SW3 4PL
020 7352 9479

The pop on the box in here can be a little loud, but this boozer hasn't changed in years (well, the carpet feels as if it's been soaking up beer since the sixties). Still, it's got reasonable beer, food during the day and a fairly usual Chelsea crowd. As it's the first pub on the King's Road coming down from Sloane Square, it's a good place for meeting people.

FEATURES:

Coopers Arms

...NG:

87 Flood Street
SW3 5TB
020 7376 3120

A spacious, well-kept place offering the usual excellent range of \g's ales. The large windows bring plenty of light into the pub, giving it a re¬ingly open feel. A relaxed atmosphere pervades the place and, with its le seating and fires for a winter's day, this is a great place to nurse a drink o¬ with the Sunday papers. Popular with locals, especially towards the end of weekend as a meeting place before going on to later things. The beer is You the food is excellent and, especially for the area, even the prices aren't bad. good show.

FEATURES:

340

The Duke of Wellington

RATING:

63 Eaton Terrace
SW1W 8TR
020 7730 1782

Small but perfectly formed, this busy little Shepherd Neame house offers a glimpse of how great pubs can be. With a good mix of punters and a warm atmosphere, it's just the sort of place made for a cosy drink on a dark winter's night. There are three good ales on tap and simple, old school pub grub on offer – the mentality here is that sandwiches come with crisps, rather than hand-cut wedges. Indeed, the price of food is equally old-school, in some cases half that of nearby Chelsea gastropubs. It's already a good pub, but, without hesitation, the first-class landlord merits this place an extra pint. Not only does he greet the amiable locals with a warm welcome, but also unfamiliar faces with that simple yet increasingly rare question, 'How are you?' Although it sports a Belgravia postcode, it's a lot more down to earth than its location suggests and is worth seeking out.

FEATURES:

Fox & Hounds

RATING:

29 Passmore Street
SW1W 8HR
020 7730 6367

The Fox & Hounds has an interesting past. Up until 1998 it was the last 'beer-only' pub in London and for a while afterwards the place had a rather bare feel to it, but thankfully things have improved. It's now a Young's house with a fair range of drinks and a lunch menu too. Tucked away on a backstreet, this tiny place, complete with a real (gas) fire and a profusion of wood, is warm and glowing. They've even managed to put a Chesterfield at the back without making it claustrophobic. That said, with the only windows being at the front, it's probably more of a pub for those cosy winter evenings. There's a good mix of customers, too: apart from the regulars at the bar, there were both young and old, meeting for a pint or three. When we last looked in, there was even a troupe of musicians, complete with instruments. Not only one of the best in the area but, given its proximity to the tube, a handy meeting-up spot as well.

FEATURES:

Queen's Head

RATING:

25 Tryon Street
SW3 3LG
020 7589 0262

An ordinary Victorian boozer, which makes a bit of a pun of its name. The Markham on King's Road used to be one of the main gay pubs in the area, but, since it stopped being a pub, the clientele have had to look elsewhere and the backroom at the Queen's Head seems to be where they have gravitated to. Not that this bothers us in the slightest, as it's a friendly enough place and the service is prompt and efficient. The range of fare on offer is nothing remarkable and the prices are what you would expect for the area. A handy place to get away from the hurly-burly of King's Road.

FEATURES:

The Surprise

RATING:

6 Christchurch Terrace
SW3 4AJ
020 7349 1821

This is a nice old pub, with a jolly atmosphere. Decent fare on offer and friendly, helpful staff serving it. Apparently, it features on tourist pub crawls (especially on Sundays), so expect the odd, periodic influx of gangs of tourists knocking back halves before hurrying on to the next. Still, it doesn't spoil the atmosphere. With the loss of the Phene Arms, this is one of the last old school pubs in Chelsea. Worth a look before the developers get their hands on it.

FEATURES:

Trafalgar

RATING:

200 King's Road
SW3 5XP
020 7349 1831

The designers have worked hard on this one. Not only a new duck-egg-blue exterior, but a mad interior – a mishmash of sofas and chairs, as if someone had made a collage out of back issues of *Wallpaper*. Oddly enough, it somehow works. Once you get it out of your head that you're trapped in some kind of lounge-furnishings version of *The Crystal Maze*, you can relax and enjoy some decent food and drink. Chelsea prices for sure, but the eager staff help add a friendly air to the place. This one's next door to the Chelsea Cinema, so don't be surprised to overhear earnest discussions of the latest art-house films.

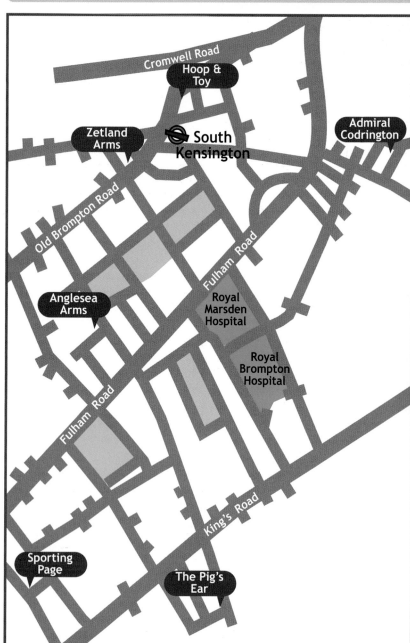

Cromwell Road

Hoop & Toy

Zetland Arms

South Kensington

Admiral Codrington

Old Brompton Road

Fulham Road

Anglesea Arms

Royal Marsden Hospital

Royal Brompton Hospital

Fulham Road

King's Road

Sporting Page

The Pig's Ear

Admiral Codrington

RATING:

17 Mossop Street
SW3 2LY
020 7581 0005

On the outside, this place looks rather like a pub you'd find on a council estate, but inside turns out to be a trendy pub/restaurant chock-a-block with people we used to describe as Sloanes. Apparently, Fergie used to enjoy a tipple in here, but these days, probably, Weight Watchers keeps her at bay. Unlucky for her, as you sense some of the clientele might be in her dating range. The pub has a light, airy feel to it, much aided by the adjoining restaurant, with a small patio-esque outdoor seating area to its side. Only a couple of beers on offer last time we were in, and, unsurprisingly, a wide selection of wines and lagers. It's also not cheap, with a pint coming in over £3.

FEATURES:

The Anglesea Arms

RATING:

15 Selwood Terrace
SW7 3QG
020 7373 7960

The sort of classy, slightly tweedy, pub you'd expect in this neck of the woods, it's still worth a look even if you don't have a flat in Chelsea Harbour or a nice mews house in Kensington. There's a cosy main bar for the dark nights of winter and a tree-lined beer garden for the summer. And, for those who're feeling especially swish, there's an elegant dining room at the back. The fine range of ales (there's usually Adnams, Pride and regular guests on call) and excellent bar meals are the focus of attention here: no jukebox or games machines in sight, and if the TV is on it's usually with the sound down. The pub can fill up rapidly with bright young things at the weekend, often spilling out on to the pavement, so it's maybe not ideal for large groups. Definitely one of those pubs that are worth nicking off from work to visit out of peak hours, though.

FEATURES:

Hoop & Toy

RATING:

34 Thurloe Place
SW7 2HQ
020 7589 8360

On paper this pub should be good – there's an excellent choice of beer on the hand pumps (Cask Marque), the bar staff know what they're doing and service is polite and friendly; there's also decent and (relatively) cheap pub grub and tea, coffee etc. for nominated drivers and abstainers. The trouble is, it's so very close to South Ken tube – it's a handy place to meet if you're in the area – and, as a result, it suffers. Unlike some places we can think of, this pub doesn't set out to be a tourist pub, but they do pile in and, as with every pub we know with such a transient clientele, it amounts to a rather synthetic (everyone seems to play at being in a pub) and soulless experience. Pity.

FEATURES: HANDY FOR: Victoria & Albert Museum

The Pig's Ear

RATING:

35 Old Church Street
SW3 5BS
020 7352 2908

Given what happened to the Phene Arms, the phrase 'revamped pub in Chelsea' is one we're still wary of. All that may change, given this redesign of the old Front Page pub, which has transformed it into something pleasing to both diners and drinkers alike. Out go the pale wood and butcher's-block slabs and in come dark paintwork and Formica-topped tables. There's a whiff of the Continent about the place – helped along by an adaptation of that old Toulouse-Lautrec poster of the chap in the hat and scarf – yet there's still a traditional pub at the heart of things (there's a queue in wintertime for the seats around the real open fire). The use of the Pig's Ear name on the food and drink side of things is a witty touch: you can nibble on deep-fried porcine lugs while trying a pint of Pig's Ear beer from the Uley Brewery in Gloucestershire. Although the bar menu is fairly priced, the £3 for a drop of Uley's finest reminds you you're in Chelsea. Oh, and there's a dining room upstairs which can be hired. This is one of the more impressive pub reworkings we've seen recently and one that (thankfully) doesn't live up to one interpretation of its new name.

FEATURES:    *Reviewers' Award - best pub renovation 2005*

The Sporting Page

RATING:

9 Camera Place
SW10 0BH
020 7349 0455

A small pub that tries to look as unassuming as possible from the outside, though the word 'Bollinger' on the awnings rather gives the game away. The limited space inside may prove uncomfortable if you're averse to Sloanes, though for the anthropologically curious the mating rituals of the upper classes are often on full display. Usual Front Page pubs' offerings of food and big-screen sports are also supplied.

FEATURES:

Zetland Arms

RATING:

2 Bute Street
SW7 3EX
020 7589 3813

Although this Victorian pub is in the heart of a very touristy area, it's also aimed at the sports fan. There are a few screens scattered around the place and the big events can draw the crowds. It still does a decent job of catering for tourists, with food available most of the time (part of the upstairs focuses on dining), and it offers a reasonable range of well-kept drink and food. Not a place for a cosy pint and the crossword, but handy to meet in and watch the big match.

FEATURES:

SOUTH QUAY – see Canary Wharf, pg 74

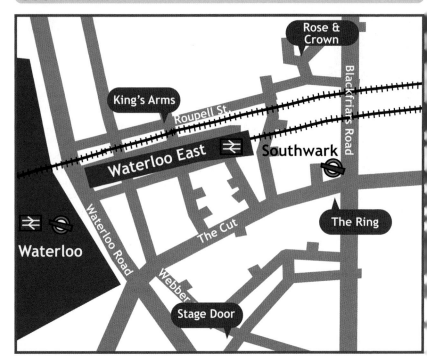

King's Arms

RATING:

25 Roupell Street
SE1 8TB
020 7207 0784

An excellent local in a quaintly picturesque (especially if you like industrial Victoriana) area just at the back of Waterloo East station. We're sure we've seen the blackened terrace houses in the nearby streets in many a period drama and the pub just fits right in. That's not to say it's an olde-worlde, touristy pub-going experience. It's not. The beer is good (decent selection), the service prompt and efficient (it has to be on busy Friday nights) and the food (Thai) is pretty reasonable, too. We like this place a lot – so much so we gave it an award.

FEATURES:

Visitors' Award Winner 2004

The Ring

RATING:

72 Blackfriars Road
SE1 8JZ
020 7928 2589

The Ring seems to have moved with the times, evolving from an old-fashioned boozer into something more palatable to modern tastes. Following a recent refit, it now attracts a smart young crowd of local workers who enjoy the laid-back music and relaxed atmosphere. A link with tradition is maintained in the hundreds of framed boxing photographs that adorn the walls, although their spotless condition feels a little antiseptic. On our visit, Greene King IPA was the lone ale among several lagers on tap. The only Claret you'll see spilled here nowadays comes out of a bottle.

FEATURES:

Rose & Crown

RATING:

47 Colombo Street
SE1 8DP
020 7928 4285

Lovely, well-kept old boozer frequented by locals and effusing a local atmosphere. It's just off the beaten track, so it means it doesn't get too crowded. It serves a pretty good pint of Shepherd Neame and decent, cheap pub grub. We're not sure about opening times, and we've yet to find it open at the weekend. But it's a very nice place to pop into during the week.

FEATURES:

Stage Door

RATING:

28–30 Webber Street

SE1 8QA

020 7928 8964

Stage Door is a lively, friendly backstreet pub, a stone's throw from Waterloo tube station and appropriately tucked around the back of the Old Vic theatre. The service is as good as you'd hope for and the overall relaxed atmosphere was helped considerably by the subtle lighting. There was a good-looking, late serving, un-gastro-esque menu and a couple of real ales on tap. Off to one side, they've managed to squeeze a pool table into the tightest possible space, which must've been tricky for those long shots, and a few TVs were dotted about, showing cricket on our visit (we hear it gets busy for the important matches). Add to this live music at the weekends and, if this were your local, you'd be happy to spend an evening here. Who knows, maybe local man Kevin Spacey does, too?

FEATURES: 　　HANDY FOR: Old Vic Theatre

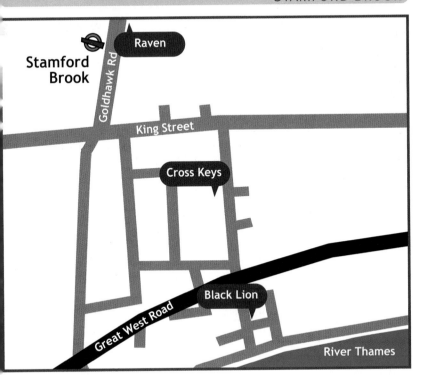

Stamford Brook

Goldhawk Rd

Raven

King Street

Cross Keys

Black Lion

Great West Road

River Thames

Black Lion

2 South Black Lion Lane
W6 9TJ
020 8748 2639

A decent pub near, but not on, the river near Chiswick. It has a standard range of ales on tap and the usual lagers and bottled beers. Despite being a fair size, this one can be a bit quieter than some of the other pubs nearby (no bad thing, really). The staff are friendly, the menu looked fine and there's a beer garden for the summer. And, after a recent change in ownership, this one now lays on music nights as well. The Black Lion may not be as famous as the Dove or as popular as the Old Ship, but arguably it's the pub along this stretch of the Thames that offers the most pleasant drinking experience.

FEATURES:

Cross Keys

RATING:

57 Black Lion Lane
W6 9BG
020 8748 3541

A Fuller's house that's ideal if you're finding the bright lights of the Chiswick High Road too much of a strain. The Cross Keys has always come across as the sort of sleepy-eyed locals' pub where time seems to move just that bit more slowly. It offers a decent pint, a rather homely layout and a large screen for the football. Too quiet for some, but handy if you need a drink and don't want to be disturbed.

FEATURES:

The Raven

RATING:

375 Goldhawk Road
W6 0SA
020 8748 6977

The Raven is a small, enveloping pub housed in an attractive Georgian building. It manages to be both modern and homely and there's a warming atmosphere even on Mondays and Tuesdays. The Raven is a good place for a meal and a chat as well as for drinking, and there is some semi-open-air seating in what looks like an old stable. It's probably rather more manic at weekends.

FEATURES:

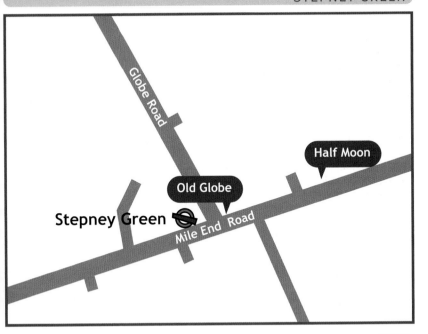

Globe Road

Half Moon

Old Globe

Stepney Green

Mile End Road

Half Moon

213–233 Mile End Road
E1 4AA
020 7790 6810

RATING:

This place starts off very well. An impressive conversion of one of the previous homes of the Half Moon Young People's Theatre, it's well designed, spacious, looks interesting and serves an enormous range of well-priced drink, including Cask Marque ales and cheap food. And, unfortunately, that's as good as it gets. The Wetherspoon pricing policy (we're talking provincial prices in the city centre here) makes this place very attractive to groups, who, while we would not consider them to be undesirable (and we won't name names), tend to be overenthusiastic about the booze (especially at these prices), and, as a result, end up bringing the tone of the place down. It's just unfortunate, we guess. Transplant this pub to a location with a classier catchment area and you'd be looking at a four-pint rating – alternatively raise the prices (but that would never do). A Catch-22 made manifest.

FEATURES:

Old Globe

RATING:

191 Mile End Road

E1 4AQ

Astronomical objects abound in this area, what with the New Globe at Mile End, just up the road, and Moon just up the way, but this one has precedence (the flashy exterior paint job is just there to fool you): it is the oldest of them all and so deserves the 'Old' prefix. It's a solidly *local* local, not unfriendly at all, offering all amenities you'd expect – Charles Wells beer on the hand pumps, lagers etc., darts, quizzes and Sky TV for the sport (and the music when there's nothing to watch). The promotions for shots hint at more hedonistic aspirations, but this pub is about as dependable as they come.

FEATURES:

STOCKWELL

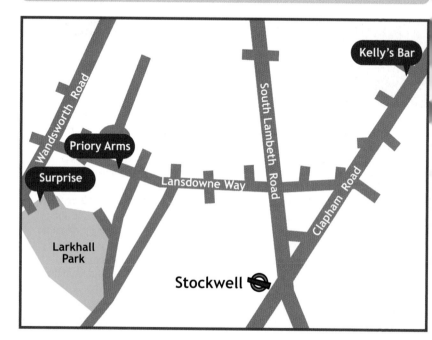

Kelly's Bar

RATING:

124 Clapham Road
SW9 0AL
020 7735 5657

From the outside it looks like a rather threatening south London council-estate pub. From the inside it turned out to be an uncomplicated and friendly enough Irish pub, although we could have done without all the shamrock, leprechaun and Irish-language sign clichés. We were amused to see a young lady drinking a pint through a straw at the bar, but rather less amused by the fact that all the proper beer had run out. Not that it matters if you like Guinness; and, if you don't, there's little point in your coming here.

FEATURES:

Priory Arms

RATING:

83 Lansdowne Way
SW8 2PB
020 7622 1884

Just as the Wenlock Arms is the real-ale Mecca in north London, here's the equivalent south of the river. Going by the beer mats plastered round the pub, they've had more ales guesting here than you'll probably taste in your life. You'll always be guaranteed an excellent pint – Adnams Broadside was our choice when we last looked in. As you've probably guessed, the food is of the traditional variety and the service is warm and friendly, if at times rather slow.

FEATURES:

fancyapint?

STOCKWELL

The Surprise

RATING:

16 Southville
SW8 2PP
020 7622 4623

Living up to its name, this place is not the sort of pub you'd expect to find off the busy Wandsworth Road. Being on the edge of Larkhall Park adds a certain rural touch, which the cosy size and amiable atmosphere of the pub build on. The usual Young's fare (and interior) is on offer, though no sign of their seasonal beers being on tap. The back bar is adorned by caricatures whom we take to be locals (we're sure we matched up the picture to the drinker for at least one customer). It's the sort of neighbourly pub where knocking out illustrations of your fellow drinkers doesn't seem out of the ordinary. A little charmer in an otherwise dour environment.

FEATURES:

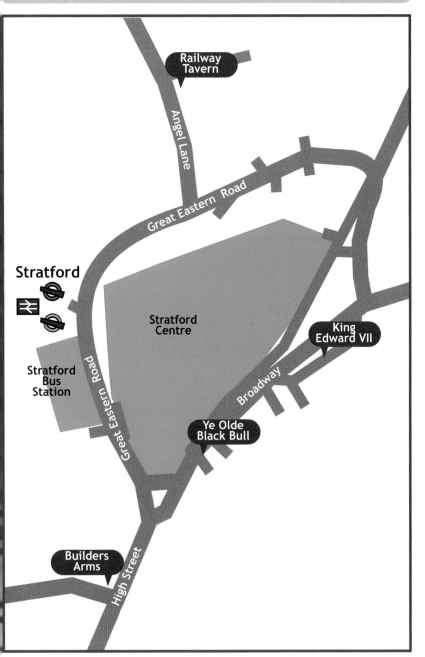

The Builders Arms

RATING:

302 High St

E15 1AJ

020 8534 1598

This large local got a makeover not long ago, which probably wasn't a bad thing. It's now a mix of traditional pub features and more trendy pub couture, which works somehow. Prints of old Stratford line the walls, comfy chairs and stripped floors, none of which detracts from the 'ambience'. It can get busy, particularly at weekends, as it's just over the main road from the Rex. With cheap beer on tap (if mostly lager, only one ale on tap), stalwart and friendly regulars and large tellies, it's a bit of a haven from the bars and clubs nearby. It's got seats outside to enjoy any good weather in the East End, if you don't mind being inches from the busy High Street. Still, it's a good place to have a few beers and watch the sport or play a little pool without any hassle.

FEATURES:

King Edward VII

RATING:

47 Broadway

E15 4BQ

020 8534 2313

This small-looking pub on the Broadway in Stratford is deceiving – the TARDIS-like interior just seems to go on for miles. It's kept a lot of the original Victorian features, including a lovely tiled hall, which is off to one side of the pub, and a massive bar in the backroom. With all the changes taking place in Stratford, it's not surprising that it's calling itself 'King Eddie' inside, and it's gone a bit gastro. It's got a good menu at not too unreasonable prices, both in the bar and the separate restaurant, which, combined with their commitment to finding the best ingredients, looks like a winner. It's still got a range of guest beers on the hand pumps and, judging by what the patrons were ordering, they go down well. On a nice afternoon, the garden out the back is inevitably crowded, so it's best to get there early. Still, a great pub. Give it a go if you're in Stratford.

FEATURES:

The Railway Tavern

RATING:

131 Angel Lane

E15 1DB

020 8534 3123

A grand old Victorian local in a pretty barren part of East London. There's not much left that's Victorian inside the pub, but that's OK. The place has been a family-run pub since the sixties and they know how to look after their clientele. It's a friendly, bustling place and there's lots of entertainment on offer. There are three ales on the hand pumps, but there's not really much else to remark about beerwise. The Channel Tunnel rail link will probably change the surrounding area when it's completed and we'll have to see how it affects this place. But for now it is an oasis of hospitality in an industrial desert. One thing to note: it's frequented by West Ham supporters and is correspondingly busy when the footy's on.

FEATURES:

Ye Olde Black Bull

RATING:

13 Broadway

E15 4BQ

020 8519 6720

This large and comfy Irish pub was called something else once (and we can't remember what that was), but ended up getting its original name reinstated and it has been Irish for as long as we can remember. It's a fab place to go if you like a drop of the black stuff or the whiskey in these parts. It does traditional pub lunches and a pretty standard beer range, too. It gets a little busy of an evening, although it's a lot better than the one across the road. There is a slightly seedy air about the place, but it doesn't stop it from being a decent pub.

FEATURES:

SWISS COTTAGE

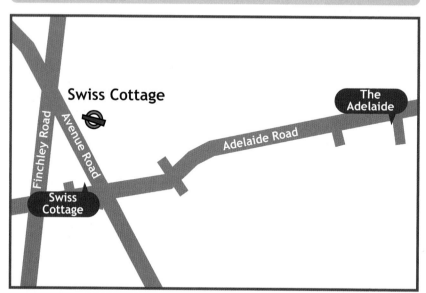

The Adelaide

RATING:

143 Adelaide Road
NW3 3NL
020 7722 3777

The Adelaide is a bright and breezy pub, which attracts a fair few Antipodeans, along with a smattering of the less down-to-earth preening types. It's a spacious pub, with high ceilings and plenty of seating, including a very nice Middle Eastern-style conservatory. The pub garden is also pretty big and the rusting barbecue in the corner alluded to possibilities of alfresco eating in the summer months. Until then, the Thai menu will have to suffice. Not a bad place at all and worth the trip down from Chalk Farm.

FEATURES:

Ye Olde Swiss Cottage

RATING:

98 Finchley Road

NW3 5EL

020 7722 3487

Externally, at least, this is one of the more eccentric pubs in London. Having taken its name literally, it consequently has the appearance of a Swiss chalet. A Swiss chalet, that is, on the edge of a multilane traffic island, with the back of a cinema looming in the background, like a metaphorical Matterhorn. Inside, it has a few large rooms, all of which are fairly comfortably laid out. The atmosphere is hotel lobby-ish, but that may be an unfortunate side effect of its size and shape. The food is fine and, it being a Sam Smith's pub, the beer is reasonably priced. Indeed, it's probably the cheapness of the beer and the absence of a nearby Wetherspoon that probably attracts a fair few local older gentlemen. It's still a lively place and since being taken over at the start of the year has got better. It also has a beer garden, which in most cases would be a bonus, but in this instance is a warning, due to its position on one of the busiest roads in north London.

FEATURES:

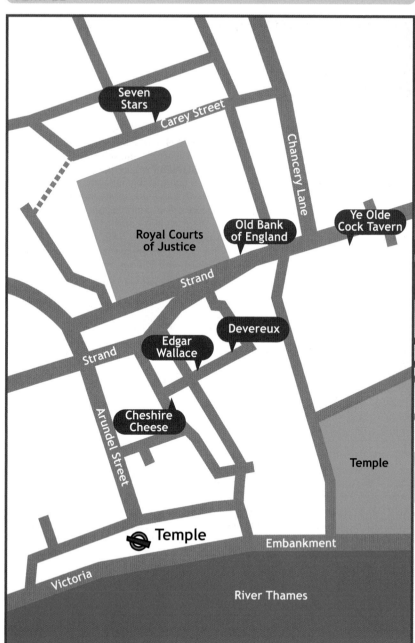

Cheshire Cheese

RATING:

5 Little Essex Street
WC2R 3LD
020 7836 2347

Not to be confused with the nearby, much more famous *Ye Olde* Cheshire Cheese, this pub quietly goes about the business of providing local workers in the surrounding legal establishments with sustenance and relaxation. It's a quiet pub, being hidden in the backstreets just off the Strand, almost villagey in feel, but without the territorial attitude that comes with some village pubs. It has several hand pumps with a couple of standard beers and a guest, and a decent enough wine list, and it also provides pub-grub lunches and evening meals. You won't find this place in the guides to great pubs, but if you want decent fare, with decent service at a decent price (especially for this area), you'll be OK here. Be warned: it can close early and isn't open at the weekends.

FEATURES:

Devereux

RATING:

20 Devereux Court (just off Essex St)
WC2R 3JJ
020 7583 4562

Well off the beaten track in one of the quiet, quaint alleyways that are a feature of the Inns of Court, the Devereux is an attractive pub enhanced by its interesting location. There are pretty decent beers on the hand pumps and the service is good, but it gets pretty crowded at lunch and pre-commute home times. However, outside of those times, the genteel, relaxed air of its surroundings is a pleasant relief from the hustle and bustle of the Strand and Embankment, between which this pub lies. There's an upstairs restaurant, but we've yet to sample the food there.

FEATURES:

Edgar Wallace

RATING:

40 Essex Street
WC2R 3JF
020 7353 3120

A handsome, but deceptively pokey pub once you get inside, which gets crowded pretty quickly at the usual after-office-hours times. Given the area, the number of suits was not a surprise, but it's not unbearable and they head off to their homes pretty quickly after work. There is an upstairs function room with bar, which can be hired, offering some breathing space, but expect this to be occupied on Friday evenings. The beer's decent and there's a pretty standard range of pub grub on the menu. Add to this table service (even when the pub is very busy) and you've got a very nice pub indeed.

FEATURES:

Old Bank of England

RATING:

194 Fleet Street
EC4A 2LT
020 7430 2255

The opulent interior of this pub is the best bit; the rest is just the ordinary Fuller's Ale and Pie offering. The crowds that frequent this place (very noisy suits) bring down our rating to a two-pinter, which is a pity. It could easily be a three otherwise. Pop in, if you're passing, for a quick half and a nosey around the interior.

The Seven Stars

RATING:

53 Carey Street
WC2A 7JB
020 7242 8521

An ancient, tiny little pub that's great when it's not packed (lunchtimes and early evenings). Very olde worlde and would be just the thing for the tourists if it weren't already packed with people from the surrounding law courts. Excellent Adnams beers on the hand pumps, well-made pub grub and friendly service make this one well worth a visit if you're in the area. Just watch out for the stairs to the toilets (especially when you've had a few).

Ye Olde Cock Tavern

RATING:

22 Fleet Street
EC4Y 1AA
020 7353 8570

Don't be misled by the name of this pub: following a refit, Ye Olde Cock Tavern has all the antique charm of a TV-advertised sofa. The narrow interior has a long pine bar with stools and tables to its right, and more seating to the back. This pub has nothing exceptional in terms of character, drinks or décor, but the local office crowd seem to like it. Bland.

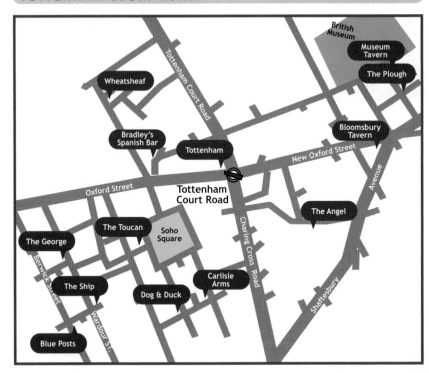

The Angel

RATING:

61–62 St Giles High St

WC2H 8LH

020 7240 2876

This is a lovely Victorian pub in the grey area between Covent Garden (Shaftesbury Avenue) and Tottenham Court Road. Because of its location, it can be a great place to meet/drink in town. It's got a lot of original Victorian features – including tile work – and has been refurbished with great care and attention. It does food, which is a bit basic, and not the best representation of a Sam Smith's pub. It serves the usual Sam Smith's fare and is very reasonably priced for central London. It's obviously had complaints from local residents, as the beer garden now closes promptly at 5.15 p.m. Don't let that put you off though – definitely worth a look.

FEATURES:

Bloomsbury Tavern

RATING:

236 Shaftesbury Avenue
WC2H 8EG
020 7379 9811

This pub is one that most shoppers and tourists in London will have spotted, being a distinctive, handsome, late-Victorian pub, in the busy area just to the north of theatreland and on many a bus route. The fare is Shepherd Neame's usual range of beers (a good thing in our view) and there's a decent wine list should you feel so inclined. The service is fast, polite and friendly and there's Shepherd Neame's pub grub, too. It's a rather small place but there is another room upstairs where you can usually find extra space. The TVs are usually showing some sporting event or another, but it's not very obtrusive. It's a handy refuelling stop betwixt shopping and a night out at the theatre. (Closed Sundays.)

FEATURES: HANDY FOR: British Museum

Blue Posts

RATING:

22 Berwick Street
W1F 0QA
020 7437 5008

A lively pub at the top end of Berwick Street market. The surrounding area with the market and shops is still a bit of old London (although changing fast) and this pub is just what most pubs in the area used to be like. There are a couple of real ales on the hand pumps and the rest is what you'd expect from a proper boozer. Most of the clientele are regulars, supplemented by the usual Friday- and Saturday-nighters. Enjoy it while it lasts.

Bradley's Spanish Bar

RATING:

42–44 Hanway Street
W1T 1UP
020 7636 0359

This is quite a unique venue. Bang in the West End, it appears (to the non-Hispanophile) to be every bit as authentically Spanish as its name might suggest, perhaps with the principal exception that no tapas is served. There are two bars: a tiny one at ground level, where there is a vinyl jukebox with a grand selection of (Anglophone) tunes from the fifties to the nineties and a (slightly) larger, cavern-like bar downstairs. There are a lot of Iberian knick-knacks all around, Spanish magazines available and a wide range of lagers from that country. It is a bit expensive, and at times rather too crowded for comfort, largely because of its minuscule scale. Nonetheless, it's charming enough, and there's a mixed range of regulars both Spanish- and English-speaking; given its location – highly visible from the scummy end of Oxford Street – other passers-by and tourists are liable to drop in too. We heard a slightly inebriated chap enter and announce loudly to all around that he was 'going out on the pull tonight'. We've no idea how successful he was, or if he was welcomed here, but it's not a bad place, and an institution of a kind.

FEATURES:

Carlisle Arms

RATING:

2 Bateman Street
W1D 4AE
020 7479 7951

A pretty straightforward little pub with no surprises. Popular at lunchtimes and evenings with the people who work nearby. It's pretty quiet, in fact so quiet it often appears to be overlooked in favour of some of the more strident premises around, which may be a good thing if you're looking for a quiet pint after a hard day's shopping.

FEATURES:

Dog & Duck

RATING:

18 Bateman Street
W1D 3AJ
020 7494 0697

A tiny pub with a very well-preserved Victorian interior and well worth a visit at quiet times to have a shufty. For years, whenever we were in Soho, we'd usually pop in here, but as time goes on we find ourselves doing this less and less. It still does a decent pint of Guinness and the other beer's pretty good – with Pride, Landlord etc. on the hand pumps, but the atmosphere is not what it used to be. The whole area has changed and has become far more touristy – Soho is not the dodgy area it once was – and the crowds thronging the pavement around it in summer bear witness to this. Now at the Dog & Duck there's more emphasis on the traditional fish and chips and less on the beers and a picture of Gladstone has been replaced with one of Henry VIII. Is this a good thing?

The George

RATING:

1 D'Arblay Street
W1F 8DN
020 7439 1911

Splendid late-Victorian pub in a reasonable state of preservation. Decent beers and pleasant and efficient bar staff. Full at the times you'd expect – lunchtimes, early evenings and most of Friday. Clientele are a typical mix for the area, and, even considering where it's situated, it's pretty pricey.

FEATURES:

Museum Tavern

RATING:

49 Great Russell Street
WC1B 3BA
020 7242 8987

This lovely pub has maintained its standards over the years and, despite having a regular clientele of tourists, still manages to be a decent place – a rare occurrence in our opinion. There's usually a guest beer or two on and the quality is good. It can get busy at lunchtimes, but that's no surprise, as it serves reasonably priced food during the day. There are also a fair few after-workers, so, If you want it quieter, give it a go later in the evening.

FEATURES: HANDY FOR: British Museum

The Plough

RATING:

27 Museum Street
WC1A 1LH
020 7636 7964

Quite a handsome Victorian pub (particularly after a recent lick of paint) that's in an area overrun with tourists going to the British Museum. The results are what you would expect – no matter how hard the management try (and they do pretty well, considering), it will always be a tourist pub, but it's worth a pint or two if you can get it when's it's quiet. A nice little earner, though.

FEATURES: HANDY FOR: British Museum

The Ship

RATING:

116 Wardour Street
W1F 0TT
020 7437 8446

Apart from the odd lick of paint here and there, this pub has not changed much over the years. No bad thing in this area, where you only have to turn round for ten seconds and yet another style bar has opened up to cater for the media luvvies. It's a good, solid pub. The beer's excellent, and with the eclectic music on the PA (a bit on the heavy side for some tastes, but we like it), and a good atmosphere any time of the day, definitely a pub to seek out.

The Tottenham

RATING:

6 Oxford Street
W1D 1AR
020 7636 7201

Like most of the Nicholson's pubs in the West End, this one's gleaming after a polish and general tidy-up. It's doing its best to stand out from the general madness of this part of town. Unfortunately, it's still all you'd expect from the only pub on London's busiest shopping street. It serves an ever-changing throng of shoppers, tourists and chancers, and quickly fills up. The Victorian décor hints at past glories, but, unless you enjoy hopping over shopping bags and then a scrum at the bar before you get served, head downstairs for a slightly more peaceful drinking environment.

FEATURES:

The Toucan

RATING:

19 Carlisle Street
W1D 3BX
020 7437 4123

A tiny Irish pub, with quite a good atmosphere, good Guinness (of course), but way too easily overcrowded. When you can get in, it's OK; otherwise, you're standing on the street with the rest of the media types.

FEATURES:

Wheatsheaf

RATING:

25 Rathbone Place
W1T 1DG
020 7580 1585

When beer was 6d (2½p) a pint in the 1930s, George Orwell, Dylan Thomas and other assorted bohemians drank here. These days, the beer has gone up in price and the pub always seems oddly, and pleasantly, quiet. A couple of real ales and a lunchtime menu are on offer. There's some nice stained glass here, too. If you have a soft spot for atmospheric old boozers, give it a try.

FEATURES:

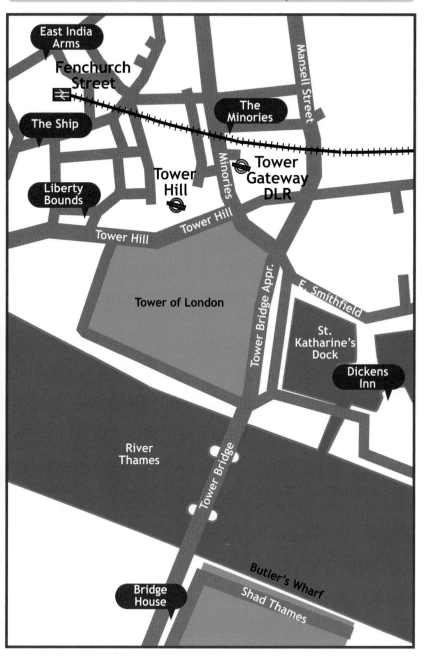

The Bridge House

RATING:

218 Tower Bridge Road
SE1 2UP
020 7407 5818

If the phrase real ale style bar sounds like an oxymoron, give this one a look as it's probably the best way to describe this Adnams house on the south end of Tower Bridge. Excellently kept Adnams and guest ales in an interior in keeping with the converted warehouse flats of the area. So, you can enjoy a decent pint and ponder laying down a deposit on one of the displayed works of art ...hmm. Somehow it works: it helps that the food's very good and the Irish landlord is a friendly soul. Even if the racked magazines seem a bit Toni & Guy, the fayre on offer is impressive making their 4 pinter status inevitable. A good spot whilst walking along the Thames, visiting the Tower or an inspection of the GLA space oddity.

FEATURES: HANDY FOR: Tower Bridge, Tower of London

Dickens Inn

RATING:

St Katharine's Way
E1W 1UH
020 7488 2208

This pub, situated in St Katharine's Dock, is next to one of the biggest tourist attractions in London and, consequently, has a huge number of visitors. As a result, we hardly ever venture near the place. It has two restaurants (one specialising in fish), a large terrace (not as big as it used to be since the residents complained) that closes at 9.45 (for the same reason). The building itself was once the structure of a brewery, which was then incorporated into a spice warehouse and subsequently restyled as a coaching inn, when it reopened as a pub in the 1970s. The location is great, picturesque and historic, and everyone else seems to think so too – this pub is just too crowded for our tastes.

FEATURES: HANDY FOR: Tower Bridge, Tower of London

East India Arms

67 Fenchurch Street

EC3M 4BR

020 7265 5121

A rather handsome but, unfortunately, smallish pub in the heart of the City, en route to Fenchurch Street station. Unsurprisingly, this pub's clientele is mostly the lunchtime and commuter crowd and, accordingly, is thronged at these times. It's not a bad place at all outside these times. The beer is pretty decent, with plenty of real ales on the hand pumps, and the service is good – when you can get to the bar.

FEATURES: HANDY FOR: Tower of London

Liberty Bounds

15 Trinity Square

EC3N 4AA

020 7481 0513

Another Edwardian commercial property gets converted into a Wetherspoon pub, hardly a newsworthy item nowadays, an almost everyday occurrence in the City, it sometimes seems. As ever, there's the range of well-priced, well-kept, hand-pumped beer and the cheap food to accompany it. And, as ever, the place is packed with people throwing cheap drink down their necks as if they were going to get their throats cut very soon. All predictable stuff, but at least it gives tourists in the area a chance to sample something approaching the British pub experience without having to sell their offspring into slavery in order to pay for it.

FEATURES:

The Minories

RATING:

64–73 The Minories
EC3N 1JL
020 7702 1658

Largish pub catering to local City workers. It comes into its own on Thursdays and Fridays when a 'party atmosphere' descends. Cheesy as hell, often with a DJ (who probably does weddings as well) proffering big shouts out to the homies in Accounts (with fine tunes from Kenny Loggins and Bruce Springsteen). Not the place you come for a quiet drink; but, if you're in the right mood (i.e. plastered), there's entertainment to be had. If the thought of a pub based on an office party appeals, come on down.

FEATURES:    HANDY FOR: Tower of London

The Ship

RATING:

3 Hart Street
EC3R 7NB
020 7481 1871

A pleasant little pub run by people who know how to pour a Guinness and with some real ales on the hand pumps, too. The décor, especially the beams, looks a bit contrived (we guess aiming to mimic a ship), but this doesn't detract from the general conviviality of the place. Just off the beaten track enough for it to miss most of the commuters heading back to Fenchurch Street station, but it can get quite full at times, owing to its small floor area.

FEATURES:

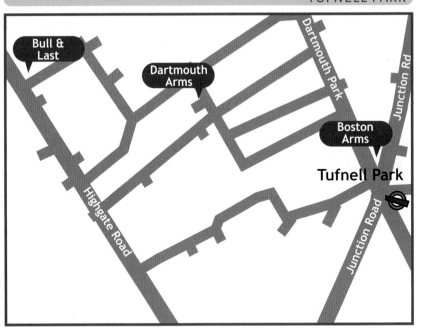

Bull & Last

Dartmouth Arms

Boston Arms

Tufnell Park

Dartmouth Park

Junction Rd

Highgate Road

Junction Road

Junction Road

Boston Arms

RATING:

178 Junction Road
N19 5QQ
020 7272 8153

What with the stately exterior and the renowned Dirty Water Club next door, we've been keen to have a look at the Boston Arms for a while. Unfortunately, we were somewhat disappointed when we finally got there. Perhaps that tower on the outside promised too much, but we thought there would be an inkling of that grandeur inside. Alas, much of the décor seems to have been stripped away, leaving an interior not unlike that of a large social club – the cry of the bingo caller never seems too far away. Still, the punters seem happy enough with the entertainment on offer: giant TV screens fill the perspective but there's a pool table, and there are also two tucked-away dartboards, suggesting a pub that takes its games seriously (and one look at the packed trophy cabinet proves it). An adequate range of drink behind the bar but with cheap and filling food really hits the spot.

FEATURES:

TUFNELL PARK

Bull & Last

RATING:

168 Highgate Road
NW5 1QS
020 7267 3641

The Bull & Last is very much in keeping with its quietly prosperous location, but, judging from our visit, plays host to a range of punters, whether they be locals or parched walkers in need of quenching their thirst after a stroll across Parliament Hill. Down the road in Kentish Town, there's been a spate of pubs going gastro. This one, though, had placed an emphasis on food for a good few years and, despite the stripped-out interior, there's still a pub feel to proceedings (especially with the upstairs dining room taking care of the food part of the equation). The London Pride tasted fine on our last visit and a lengthy wine list is worthy of investigation. Where this one also scored over similar pubs was in the approachability of its staff and the variety of music aired over the CD player. Simple stuff, but done well. Just like this pub.

FEATURES:

Dartmouth Arms

RATING:

35 York Rise
NW5 1SP
020 7485 3267

Set in a quiet backstreet this is a bustling, lively and (more often than not) full pub. With a foot in both the traditional and gastro camps, it manages to keep its punters happy, whether they're here for the food or the drink. There's also a book-lending scheme (makes a change from chain pubs and their bulk buys from antique shops). This pub offers a good medium between the full-on gastro of the Lord Palmerston and the more hardcore boozers of Junction Road. This is arguably the best pub in the neighbourhood. That said, the number of toddlers running about on our last visit wasn't necessarily a point in its favour.

FEATURES:

378

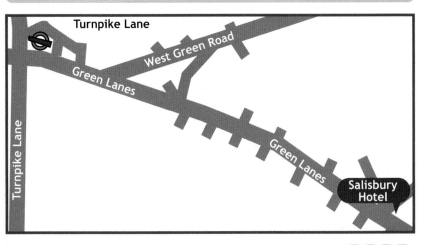

Turnpike Lane
West Green Road
Green Lanes
Turnpike Lane
Green Lanes
Salisbury Hotel

The Salisbury Hotel

RATING:

1 Grand Parade, Green Lanes
N4 1JX
020 8800 9617

Once a no-go, care-in-the-community pub, this one's been transformed into as good a recreation of a grand Victorian pub as you're likely to see in London. It's a truly stunning achievement on the décor front but, if you stop yourself gawping at the scenery, you'll find it works as a practical pub as well. Behind the rebirth is the Remarkable Restaurants group, owners of a number of pubs in north and east London that can be identified by their esoteric jukeboxes (including here Charlie Parker, Led Zeppelin and the Stanley Brothers), stylish food and decent beer. Unlike the case with your Wetherspoon makeovers, the budget hasn't been blown just on the furnishings – there's a little left over for some entertainment for the punters. There's a pub quiz on Mondays and DJs plying their trade later in the week. They've even had a string quartet in. A downside? Well, if you're being picky, the pub may take a bit of effort to get to (it's midway between Manor House and Turnpike Lane tubes) but if any pub is worth travelling to it's this one. This place is one of the best in north London for a Sunday roast, but make sure you pitch up early to get a seat near the fireside.

FEATURES:

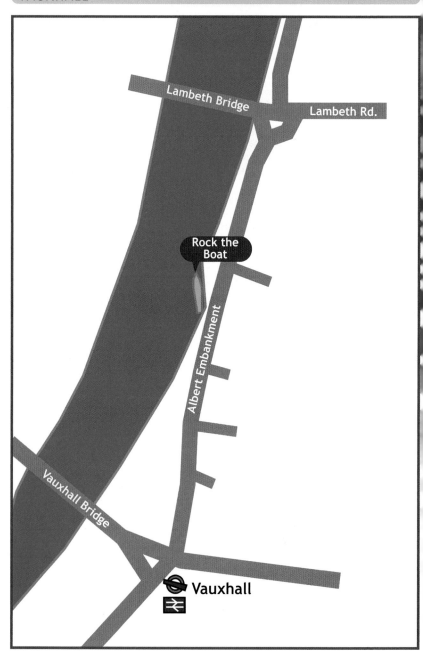

Rock the Boat

Anna G, Albert Embankment
SE1 7TP
020 7582 1006

A boat moored on the Thames between Lambeth and Vauxhall Bridges, this place disappeared for a while, but came back with new management and a new moniker (it was formerly the English Maid). Having had a bit of a refurbishment, the top deck is still a little basic, but it has plenty of seating and wonderful views towards the Houses of Parliament, and is certainly a decent place to while away a few hours over a drink on summer afternoons. The beer is pretty standard, really, with John Smith's the only bitter on tap and Guinness, Kronenbourg, Strongbow and Foster's providing the other pints. There's also bottled beer and a selection of wines. The interior is on two levels, with the top one being more, but not exclusively, for eating. The bottom level is larger and has much more seating. With wooden floors and tables and a large leather sofa in one corner, this is a relaxed place to catch up with friends, even in the winter. A jukebox provides the soundtrack, something not enough places have these days in our opinion. The food is of the jacket-potatoes-and-sandwiches variety and it's all very reasonably priced. The owners are friendly, it's licensed until 1 a.m. and you can hire it if you fancy a bit of exclusivity.

FEATURES:

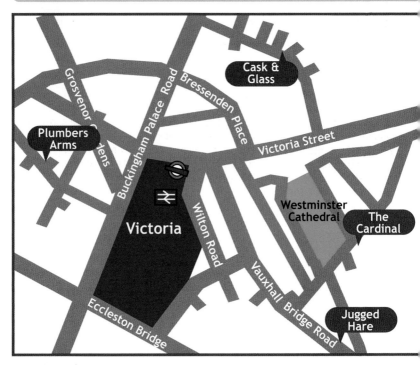

The Cardinal

23 Francis Street
SW1P 1DN
020 7834 7260

RATING:

We like this place – a comfortable Sam Smith's pub next to Westminster Cathedral. Its proximity to the cathedral means that the walls are covered in portraits of popes, cardinals and other papist 'royalty'. As is usual for Sam Smith's, there is little or nothing else on offer other than their own beers – if you want something else, you're stuffed. It has an extensive menu, with good inexpensive food, and a lovely Victorian interior. Worth a look if you're in the area, and it is open at weekends too.

FEATURES: **HANDY FOR:** Westminster Cathedral, Tate Britain

Cask & Glass

RATING:

39–41 Palace Street
SW1E 5HN
020 7834 7630

The Cask & Glass is a cosy, friendly little pub that is just far enough away from the main drag to avoid the hordes of local office workers. It seems to be a particular favourite of Home Office employees who linger for a pint or two before going home (usually a few more than that towards the weekend). The beer is Shepherd Neame and is everything we've come to expect of the brand.

FEATURES: HANDY FOR: Buckingham Palace, Westminster Cathedral

The Jugged Hare

RATING:

172 Vauxhall Bridge Road
SW1V 1DX
020 7828 1543

Fuller's started putting their Ale and Pie houses in former banks a few years ago, with some success, and this one's no exception. It's a lovely building with lots of interesting nooks and crannies to hide away in, and an upstairs balcony area for a bit of interest. It is a little bit further away from a lot of the attractions in the area, so tends not to attract many tourists. The pub can get busy with local civil servants and office workers, so we'd recommend arriving sometime after lunch and before home time.

FEATURES: HANDY FOR: Tate Britain

Plumbers Arms

14 Lower Belgrave Street
SW1W 0LN
020 7730 4067

A busy one-roomed affair that's near enough to Victoria station for in-the-know commuters, but just far enough away from the busloads of tourists. With a fair selection on tap, this one's a decent enough pub with a livelier atmosphere than you might expect from a Belgravia boozer. (Closed weekends.)

FEATURES:

WAPPING – *see Shadwell, pg 331*

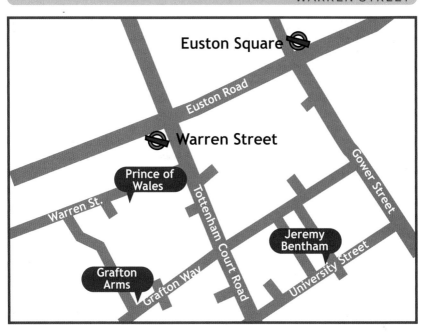

Grafton Arms

RATING:

72 Grafton Way
W1T 5DS
020 7387 7923

The takeover of this pub by Greene King has certainly raised the standards, particularly in Fitzrovia, as you're spoiled for choice when it comes to pubs. The refurb has made a lot of difference, as the downstairs pub is more welcoming than it used to be, and friendly staff make all the difference. It does have an upstairs bar, which doubles as the private function room, so is frequently closed. And topping it all off is a handy roof garden. The walls may be too high to get a view, but it's still a welcome relief in summer. It does get busy at lunch and commuter times, but it's ideal for a quiet drink in the afternoon should you be in the area.

FEATURES:

The Jeremy Bentham

RATING:

31 University St
WC1E 6JL
020 7387 3033

This pub's proximity to UCH means it can often be crowded with students and medicos, but don't let that put you off. This pub has a pretty impressive range of guest ales supported by the T & J B range of pub grub, which is adequate, but unlikely to win Michelin stars. If you've been pounding the streets of London, looking for that elusive (electronic, round here) bargain, you might find this pub a welcome respite.

FEATURES:

Prince of Wales Feathers

RATING:

8 Warren Street
W1T 5LG
020 7255 9911

The exterior of this one's recently popped up in a period drama, but the interior is definitely in the vein of that modern-pub style: wood floors, some overstuffed furniture and a couple of plasma screens to edge things into the twenty-first century. It's one of those solid and unspectacular pubs that might not have you crossing London to visit; but, given its proximity to Warren Street, this one is never going to be short on punters at commuting times. It does the job, then, as a handy meeting spot, certainly as a starting (or finishing) spot for a Fitzrovia pub crawl.

FEATURES:

WARWICK AVENUE – *see Maida Vale, pg 249*

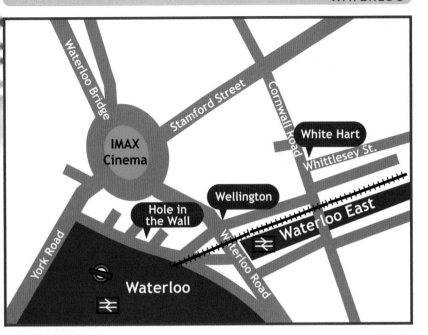

Hole in the Wall

RATING:

5 Mepham Street

SE1 8SQ

020 7928 6196

Pretty much an institution in these parts, this pub is actually quite a large hole in a wall, being situated in railway arches in front of Waterloo Station. It has been a watering hole of choice for commuters for many a year. It's never a place one would ever describe as spick and span and, with conversation drowned out by the trains rumbling overhead every few minutes, the appeal of the place is not easy to identify. But, when you consider its proximity to the station and the excellent range of beers on the hand pumps, the penny drops. Not a great place for a romantic tête-à-tête, but a handy one to put right the evils of another day in the office.

FEATURES:

HANDY FOR: National Theatre, London Eye, London Imax Cinema

The Wellington at Waterloo

RATING:

81 Waterloo Road
SE1 8UD
020 7928 6083

There are few pubs near railway stations that we would recommend and this, unfortunately, isn't one of them. If you like the idea of drinking in a bright, barn-sized place, this is the one for you. It is a giant pub – about the equivalent of four normal pubs – with pretty average fare and illuminated in that extra-bright way that makes you feel as if you are drunk before you've even started. If you're desperate for a pint and time is short before the train departs, then it's handy.

FEATURES:

White Hart

RATING:

Cornwall Road
SE1 8TJ
020 7401 7151

The formula's becoming more and more familiar as M&B convert more pubs to this winning format, but that doesn't mean we're getting tired of it. And why should we, when you are offered excellent hand-pumped beers, a very extensive range of Continental beers (with all kinds of exotic stuff such as Fruli), a decent wine list and decent food? Add to this a comfortable, friendly environment and decent service and you don't mind that bit extra on the price for the extra you get in return. If it does have a downside, that's the fact that this pub is even more popular than it used to be. But, if you get in early and snaffle a settee or corner table, you're going to be happy here.

FEATURES: HANDY FOR: National Theatre, National Film Theatre

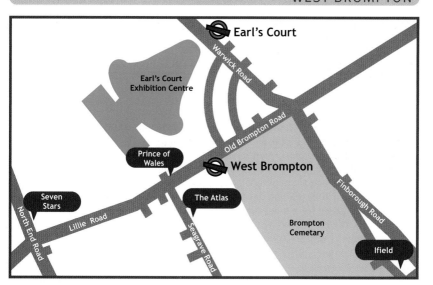

The Atlas

RATING:

16 Seagrave Road
SW6 1RX
020 7385 9129

A fairly sensitive gastropub conversion. The mix-'n'-match wooden tables and chairs are *de rigueur*, and, even though more thought appears to have gone into the wine selection than the beer choice, this one's still a pub first and foremost. Fairly standard beers on tap with London Pride and Adnams Broadside, but it was nice to see Deuchars IPA on when we were in last. The excellent food is reasonably priced, if a bit gastro, and a proper coffee contraption takes up one end of the bar. There's a nice suntrap at the side too, for the occasional pleasant evening drink. It's also got a function room that's available to hire, with a large telly in it, but they show big games only on terrestrial, because there's not enough demand for the pub to fork out for Sky. It's close to Earl's Court for a pre-concert/post-exhibition drink, so gets accordingly busy. It is popular in the evenings – the outside has an awning, which the pub uses at nights to double its space. Definitely worth a visit. The only complaint we've heard is that they don't do bubbly by the glass – well, if you're that tight ...

FEATURES:    HANDY FOR: Earl's Court

389

The Ifield

RATING:

59 Ifield Road
SW10 9AU
020 7351 4900

An old pub that's been redecorated in the trendy, seedy bar style that's a reaction to the clinical All BarSlugPitcherHeeltap style. It's decorated to look as if it *hadn't* been decorated – windows painted out, most surfaces painted 'Ifield blue', chairs, tables, settees etc. all kind of thrown together. The young things who crowd the place seem oblivious of this and really are there only for the buzz. Food and drink seemed decent enough, but nothing remarkable is on offer. Not the place for a quiet drink and a gentle perusal of the Sundays. You'll be here to kick off the evening's proceedings with your mates. Many of the pubs and bars in this area come and go, but the Ifield is one of the more established venues.

Prince of Wales

RATING:

14 Lillie Road
SW6 1TU
020 7385 7441

In the shadow of Earl's Court, this is a great place to go when the weather is agreeable, as it has a large garden in the back and a substantial terrace on the front. Not surprisingly, it gets heaving if there's a gig on next door, but the staff (usually) do a good job dealing with the crowds.

FEATURES: HANDY FOR: Earl's Court

Seven Stars

253 North End Road

W14 9NS

020 7385 3571

A fine, pretty large 1930s pub with lots of original wood panelling, giving it a clubby/parlour sort of atmosphere – challenged only by the decks and the disco lights. This place sets out to look after, entertain and perhaps even stimulate the local inhabitants. There's a DJ on Friday, karaoke on Sundays, and on Wednesdays there's chess! The beer is Fuller's finest and the service is fast and friendly. If any of the entertainment on offer is your pint of ESB, then you'll be happy.

FEATURES:

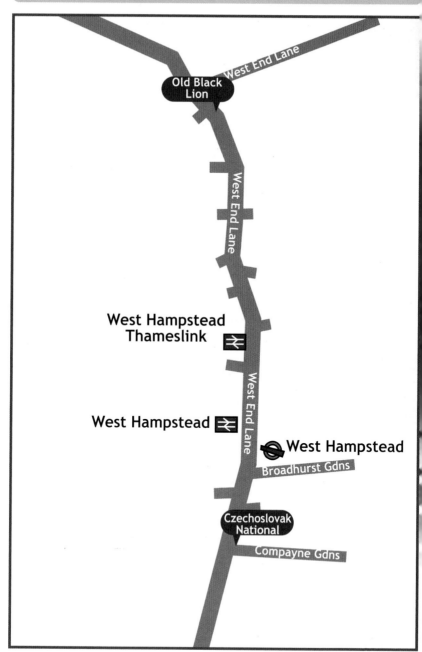

Czechoslovak National House

RATING:

74 West End Lane

NW6 2LX

020 7328 0131

The bar is just one part of this club for exiles from Czechoslovakia (as was), and has been going since the late 1940s, apparently. There's also a restaurant open to all comers. But for our purposes the most important thing is beer. Czech beer. Which is why we go here. And, of course, it's excellent stuff. There are bar snacks too, such as herring and bread, in case you feel peckish. The expats still predominate but there are plenty of other visitors. During one visit, instead of meeting, say, a group of gorgeous young ladies with impossibly long legs, we encountered a group from Glasgow and Belfast exchanging Republican and Unionist slogans. This sums up our lives too perfectly to dwell on further. Instead, we should warn readers that, apparently, they won't serve halves because (in true Eastern bloc spirit) 'if I gave you one, then I'd have to give everyone one'. They do spirits, but, if you come here, just drink pints, hey?

FEATURES:

The Old Black Lion

RATING:

295 West End Lane

NW6 1RD

020 7435 4389Address

On a street lined with many cafés, the occasional trendy bar, restaurants of varying qualities and, arguably, the finest fish-and-chip shop in the land (NB: not the one adjacent to this boozer), the Old Black Lion is a rare pub. There is an emphasis on sport – even the lion on the pub sign is carrying a football – while the outside boasts the establishment is 'passionate about sport' - and there are many screens to watch it on. That's not all: there is a moderately splendid beer garden on several levels, with shelters and heaters to make it viable all year round, and a small seating area outside at the front, too. Sometimes a bit raucous, the pub has a lively atmosphere, and attracts a diverse crowd. We watched a Czech-vs-Greece football game in here a while ago alongside members of the local Czech and Greek communities; despite the fact many Czechs were intermittently cheering for Turkey, all went swimmingly.

FEATURES:

WEST INDIA QUAY – *see Canary Wharf, pg 74*

WEST KENSINGTON – *see Barons Court, pg 33*

WESTBOURNE PARK

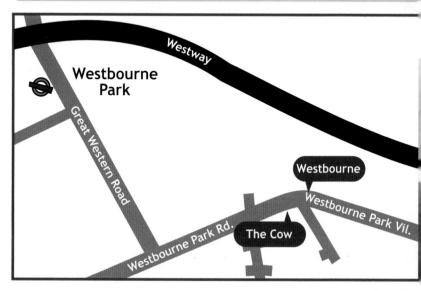

The Cow

RATING:

89 Westbourne Park Road
W2 5QH
020 7221 0021

Still a trendy little pub with a restaurant upstairs. It is pretty small and it's always crowded with beautiful (at least they think they are) people. The food and drink are pretty good, if phenomenally expensive, but the overbearing clientele usually make the novelty wear off before too long.

FEATURES:

The Westbourne

101 Westbourne Park Villas

W2 5ED

020 7221 1332

A large Victorian pub that's been gutted to turn it into a trendy bar. Very popular with the young locals, who like what the Westbourne offers, which is not really a pub experience. Fine if you want to spend your time spotting celebs, but we feel there's a more pleasant drinking experience to be had in the bars and pubs north or east of here.

FEATURES:

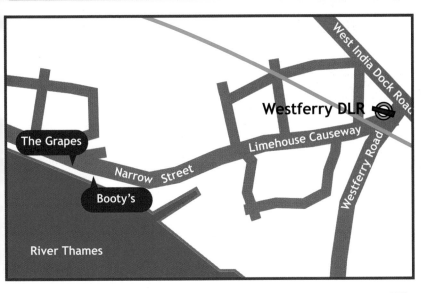

Booty's Riverside Bar

RATING:

92a Narrow Street
E14 8BP
020 7987 8343

Like its famous neighbour the Grapes, this pub enjoys a splendid location on the Thames. It has a fair history, too, being originally a barge builder's premises and later an inn called the Waterman's Arms. There are lots of interesting old photos on display, and, although there is no river terrace, a couple of the window tables overlook the river. When we visited, the service was excellent, and the homemade food tasty and reasonably priced. While there's no great beer on offer, a decent wine list is available. Booty's has a late licence until midnight throughout the week and cheap booze all night on a Monday.

FEATURES:

The Grapes

RATING:

76 Narrow Street
E14 8BP
020 7987 4396

We like this place – it's a quaint, narrow, little pub in a very old terrace on the north bank of the river at Limehouse. There's a tiny terrace at the back that you can squeeze on to, if you're lucky, and enjoy views of Limehouse Reach and Rotherhithe. The beer's pretty good and the décor old and genuine. But there's more to it: there's a sort of timeless traditional atmosphere about the place, and in an area where property booms and yuppiedom have wreaked their worst. The restaurant upstairs specialises in fish and is pretty good too. If you do go, try to book the table that looks out over the river (you need to book, anyway, since it's pretty popular). The food is traditional seafood and is entirely dependent on what is good at the market that day. It's well presented, but can be a little pricey. The service is friendly and prompt, and, with the fare on offer, what more could you want? It just looks, acts and feels like a proper English pub. It's just perfect for the area.

FEATURES: *Reviewers' Award Winner 2004*

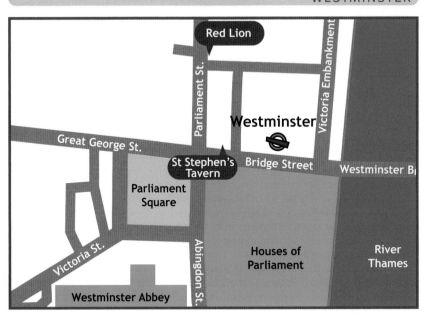

Red Lion

48 Parliament Street
SW1A 2NH
020 7930 5826

Often cited as having the most popular pub name in the UK, the most famous Red Lion of them all is probably this one in Westminster. This isn't for its attractive turn-of-the-century features, etched glass or surfeit of mahogany, but because its the nearest pub to Downing Street. So often is it frequented by MPs and various politicos that its televisions show the BBC Parliament channel, instead of sport. Apparently, it even rings a division bell to alert the more right honourable customers of an upcoming vote. In usual media attention-grabbing style, it was also the place where Culture Secretary Tessa Jowell happily announced an end to UK's antiquated licensing laws (even if ironically the Red Lion was refused a late licence itself). The pub's small size and quantity of besuited regulars mean it's often very busy, even if a cellar bar and upstairs dining room help alleviate the pressure. Still, it's worth a look out of peak times and you never know when some titbit of political gossip might be overheard.

FEATURES:

397

St Stephen's Tavern

RATING:

10 Bridge Street
SW1A 2JR
020 7925 2286

This Grade II listed pub was one we didn't think would ever open again. Having been closed for the best part of fifteen years, it quietly reopened its doors just before Christmas 2003. From our research, it appears that this 125-year-old watering hole has been frequented by many notables, including prime ministers such as Baldwin, Churchill and Macmillan. The results of the refurbishment are fantastic – they should be, after a multimillion-pound restoration done with the help of English Heritage (or interference, depending on whom you talk to). Apparently, many of the fittings are from the original pub, having been stored since the pub closed. Thankfully, the couple of years' wear and tear since it opened have started to take off that 'brand-new' patina, and it's mellowing nicely into a distinguished pub. One thing to note: the chairs chosen have curved backs, making the small rooms feel more crowded than they actually are – sometimes ending up feeling rather cramped. It is very popular straight after work, with political hangers-on and civil servants standing around and braying, shoulder-to-shoulder, until around eightish, when things start to quieten down. There's a good range of well-kept beers on the hand pumps – Tanglefoot and Badger's Best among them. Outside of crush times, this is a fine place and well worth a visit if you're in the area.

FEATURES: **HANDY FOR:** Houses of Parliament, Westminster Abbey, London Eye

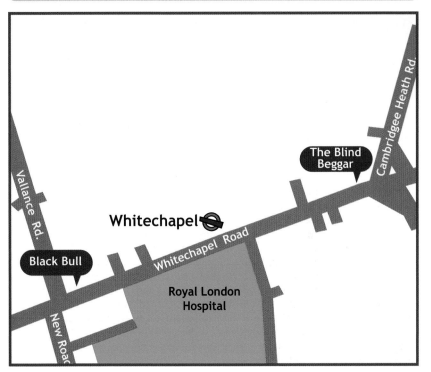

Black Bull

199 Whitechapel Road
E1 1DE
020 7247 6707

This is a well-run, well-looked-after and, thankfully, ordinary local, which is a bit of a relief after the grimness and/or forced 'trendiness' of some of the other boozers around here. It's a good pub for watching the big match, and, if there's nothing notable on air, the screen is used for music videos. For such an ordinary pub (and we do mean that in the nicest possible way), the booze is a bit of a surprise, being almost all Nethergate Brewery's offerings on the four hand pumps, including the excellent Priory Mild. The clientele is mixed but mostly blokes, especially on a Saturday afternoon.

FEATURES:

fancyapint?

WHITECHAPEL

The Blind Beggar

RATING:

337 Whitechapel Road
E1 1BU
020 7247 6195

Most people have heard of this pub, thanks to an infamous gangland murder that happened here in 1966, and some even make a trip to see it just for that reason. When they get here, they will find a decent, ordinary boozer that serves the locals well, but nothing out of the ordinary and certainly no bloodstains – or stains of any kind, for that matter. The fare on offer is pretty unremarkable – OK, but nothing special – and the accommodation offers a little bit of something for everybody: you can choose from beer garden, conservatory, comfy chairs, bar stools and more. Popular with locals. Pop in if you're in the area, but it's not worth a special effort to get here.

FEATURES:

Index

INDEX

Fancyapint? on your mobile

When you're out and about and you've forgotten your Fancyapint? book, get Fancyapint? information sent to your mobile.

Text "pint" to **83248*** and the mobile network will work out your current location and we'll send a text message back to your mobile with the names, ratings and addresses of our three nearest pubs, based on your location – all for only **£1**.

And if you text "pint map" to **83248** we'll send you a map of where you are, via WAP – again only for **£1**.

If it is not possible to retrieve your location from the network, the system will send back a message telling you this and you won't be charged for the message. People can usually be located to within a few hundred metres in built up areas although if you're out in the sticks, where there are few mobile network masts, it's not quite as accurate.

If your mobile phone is web-enabled you can also see the text only version of Fancyapint.com at http://mobile.fancyapint.com. This service is free from us and will only cost you the data charges from your mobile service provider.

*by using this service the network will do a lookup of where you are.

Notes

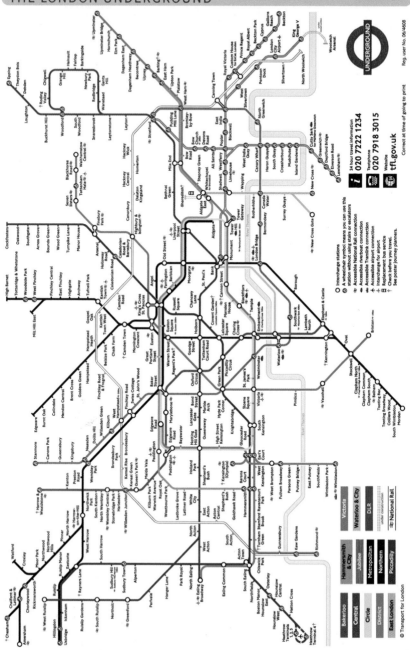